A World Beyond Difference

TO BO

A World Beyond Difference

Cultural Identity in the Age of Globalization

Ronald Niezen ──────────────────

Blackwell
Publishing

BLACKWELL PUBLISHING
350 Main Street, Malden, MA 02148-5020, USA
108 Cowley Road, Oxford OX4 1JF, UK
550 Swanston Street, Carlton, Victoria 3053, Australia

The right of Ronald Niezen to be identified as the Author of this Work has been
asserted in accordance with the UK Copyright, Designs, and Patents Act 1988.

First published 2004 by Blackwell Publishing Ltd

Library of Congress Cataloging-in-Publication Data

Niezen, Ronald.
  A world beyond difference : cultural identity in the age of globalization / Ronald
Niezen.
    p. cm.
  Includes bibliographical references and index.
  ISBN 1-4051-2737-6 (hardback : alk. paper)—ISBN 1-4051-2690-6
(pbk.: alk. paper)
  1. Civilization. 2. Globalization 3. Group identity. 4. Ethnicity. 5. pluralism
(Social sciences). 6. Human rights. I. Title.

  HM626.N54 2005
  306—dc22

                                                                    2004008956

A catalog record for this title is available from the British Library.

Set in 10/13pt Meridien
by SNP Best-set Typesetter Ltd., Hong Kong
Printed and bound in the United Kingdom
by T.J. International, Padstow, Cornwall

The publisher's policy is to use permanent paper from mills that operate a sustainable
forestry policy, and which has been manufactured from pulp processed using acid-free
and elementary chlorine-free practices. Furthermore, the publisher ensures that the
text paper and cover board used have met acceptable environmental accreditation
standards.

For further information on
Blackwell Publishing, visit our website:
www.blackwellpublishing.com

Let us take hold of the fact that there are two communities – the one, which is great and truly common, embracing gods and men, in which we look neither to this corner nor to that, but measure the boundaries of our state by the sun; the other, the one to which we have been assigned by the accident of our birth.

Seneca, *On Leisure*

Contents

Preface

This book is inspired by a recently heightened interest in cosmopolitan culture, much of it centered on the term *globalization*. One of the things that this concept has done is to swing a wrecking ball through some long-established disciplinary walls, making it more acceptable and feasible to pause on the rubble and take in a wider intellectual landscape. Sociological meta-theory has made a comeback on a scale not seen since the stimulus provided by the concept *evolution* in the nineteenth century.

Past experience, however, should tell us that this is a risky venture. One of the consistent errors of grand social theory is a failure to correctly portray the scope and dynamics of social differences on a global scale. Marxism assumed all societies to be moving irrevocably and immediately toward the capitalist mode of production, toward a common fate of misery and exploitation. Socio-evolutionism assumed societies to be rank ordered on an elegantly simple social hierarchy, with European civilization occupying the summit of human achievement and all others to be either "uplifted" or to suffer ignominious defeat and dissolution, left behind by the march of progress. This was an idea that inspired all sorts of philanthropic efforts with the goal of collectively saving and improving the stragglers of history, efforts that Herbert Spencer dismissed as counterproductive interference in the competitive foundations of progress. Everyone was soon to be alike in terms of core values, technologies, and institutions.

The tendency to leap onto unwarranted generalizations in grand social theory even extends toward criticism of such generalization-plagued paradigms of history. The Enlightenment, its postmodern or postcolonialist critics often say, was little more than an intellectual apology for bourgeois life and values, inextricably bound up with colonialist expansion, capitalist domination, notions of cultural and racial supremacy, and other less direct (but no less constraining of human creativity) forms of hegemony. The way we interpret the world, it seems, is increasingly divided between absolutes and absolute rejection of them.

My starting point in setting out to navigate this intellectual terrain has been a struggle in which various forms of relativism (usually falling into the rubrics postmodernism or postcolonialism), which reject the scientific/scholarly search for truth and suspect its adherents of complicity with elite power interests, are pitted against those who still want to believe that rigorous, dispassionate research can lead to lasting insight and occasionally improve public policy, the administration of justice and, ultimately, human lives. Having been witness to the internecine struggle between postmodernists and Enlightenment-inspired rationalists in anthropology and (in more muted form) history virtually throughout my career, I felt as I set out to write this book that some of the ideas that are emerging about globalization and world culture were familiar and called for exposition and clarification. But globalization is a topic in which this dualism transcends academic enclaves. So I began by abandoning specific, discipline-bound terminology and looked instead at a wide range of ideas about global culture – not a world in which differences no longer exist, but a world in which differences are inconsequential, a world *beyond* difference, a human world made whole by imagination and effort.

I wrote this book mainly for those who recognize the importance of ideas in shaping civilizations or even in changing the world itself, but who are experiencing difficulty arriving at an overall sense of the major ideas currently being contested and above all the kind of society that these ideas aspire to bring about. Part of the problem faced by many students and scholars in the social sciences and humanities, even those advanced in their studies, is that much of the literature on global culture relies on a rejection of clarity, seeing direct exposition as a source of hegemonic deceit. But stripped of philosophical free-association, allusions to fashionably obscure sources, and other efforts to display superior learning and detachment from convention, the ideas ultimately being presented and contested are usually not very difficult, and at the very least can certainly be made more accessible.

I am prepared to admit that my decision to cover this multi-disciplinary topic in a relatively short space leads me to oversimplify some ideas in favor of the effort to briefly present a wide range of thought. But I, like many others, sense that something new, on a grand scale, is happening in the world that requires understanding, which can only be approached by sacrificing some fine-grained analysis in favor of a wider scope and a more ambitious conceptual structure. I am also willing to agree that this is very much a personal exploration and that no two people who undertake to better understand the world by looking at the way it is understood will choose the same material for examination. This is not inconsistent with my main purpose, which is neither to create a "master-narrative" nor a postmodernist master rejection of such narratives, but rather the more limited goal of inform-ing debate, of re-opening, in response to new global circumstances, a controversy that produces influential sociological cosmologies.

I am grateful to the Institute for Human rights at Åbo Akademi University for inviting me to teach a course on the human rights of indigenous peoples in the spring semester of 2001, an experience that I have found to be a lasting source of inspiration (especially evident here in chapters 4 and 5), and for providing me with a titular affilia-tion long afterwards. While based in Åbo, I benefited from seminars that I was invited to conduct in the Thule Institute at the University of Oulu and the Norwegian Institute of Human Rights at the University of Oslo. In the last phase of my work on this book, the Institut für Europäische Ethnologie at Humboldt-Universität zu Berlin welcomed me as a research affiliate and provided a cosmopolitan atmosphere for fine-tuning my ideas on cosmopolitanism. I also owe thanks to those individuals who, at various stages, looked over my shoulder with helpful intent: David Harvey and Charles Tilly vetted an early proposal in a way that could not have been more encouraging; John Hall took an early draft in hand and made remarks that led me to reassess the way I had framed some of the central themes; three anonymous readers made very useful comments once the manuscript had taken shape; and Greg Nielsen and Richard Terdiman made insightful observations on the penultimate draft. To D and B, I owe the inestimable contribution of a place to work.

Although I have included only a few ethnographic sketches in Chapter 4, the influence of the experiences behind this exposition is more significant than might appear. I therefore feel compelled to thank once again the indigenous representatives whom I met in various international meetings, the Grand Council of the Crees for sponsoring my attendance at several of these meetings, the members of the Sami Council and the Sami Parliament of Finland who introduced me to their political experiences and concerns, and the people of Gao (in the Republic of Mali) and its surrounding villages, who surprised me with their trust in circumstances that encouraged suspicion and over-whelmed me with their generosity in a time of need.

Gig Harbor
July, 2004

1

Introduction

This book is about the contest between two intellectual currents attempting to define a global identity, one sometimes referred to as cultural universalism and the other cultural particularism; but unlike most accounts of stark dualisms, it is also about the paradoxes that lead each to occasionally overlap or draw inspiration from the other. One is mainly an outgrowth of the rationalist Enlightenment, approaching the challenges of world integration with the tools of science, commerce, and bureaucracy. On the surface, it is pedestrian and instrumental, but at a deeper level tends to be inspired by an ideal of universal peace, democracy, and prosperity. The other current looks to an absence of frontiers as a possibility for unrestricted cultural freedom and creativity. It begins with a relativist negation of social progress and the search for knowledge, proceeds to a valuation of indefinite, changing, unknowable identities, and arrives, sometimes without intending to, at an ideal, borderless world of tolerance, cultural playfulness, and a form of absolutism that paradoxically reposes on a rejection of all absolutes.

The burgeoning literature on globalization now represents a conceptual microcosm in which this major intellectual struggle – one that for the past several decades has divided numerous academic disciplines – has been refined to its essence. Seneca tells us (in so many words) in the epigraph of this book, that the utopian imagination tends to move in opposite directions, toward either a universal commonwealth or to restored, autonomous communities; but the story that he does not, and in his time could not, tell is that each ideal tends to feed off its contrary, and that efforts to combine or accommodate them then tend to fall into irresolvable dilemmas. One of the consequences of globalization that has not been adequately discussed is the paradoxical stimulus of social convergence on the rearticulation of distinct cultures. The act of rallying against the almost identical cultural pressures occurring in many parts of the world, using supranational legal mechanisms and lobbying strategies, has produced global or quasi-global political entities – such as "indigenous peoples," "ethnic minorities," "Subalterns" and the anti-imperialist nations of the "South" – all directed toward cultural survival.

This would seem to provide a stimulus to the relativist ideas of the cultural contingency of truth and moral standards and the importance of protecting discrete societies as the best source of nurture, growth, and guidance for individuals. But the most recent trend in cultural studies is to take this one step further, to go beyond all boundaries, to emphasize cultural movement, migration, diaspora, and dissolution; and above all to negate the value of research-driven description. This makes it possible to arrive at dreams of perfect cosmopolitanism from the direction of cultural irrationalism. A world lacking all secure boundaries and sources of identity becomes, almost by definition, free of nationalist closure and ethnic rivalry, a haven of perfect peace and freedom.

More than ever before, the opposition between universalism and particularism reaches those societies that are on the margins of nation-states, societies that are attempting to preserve their cultural distinctiveness, either as minority participants in national and international political culture or through efforts to become, to the maximum extent possible, self-determining isolationists. Complete insulation from competing civilizations, ideas, and political currents, however, has become a near impossibility. The mere effort to impose and protect total community autonomy takes on some of the qualities of sectarian fanaticism. The real choice for those being forced into uncomfortable proximity with the forces of globalizing modernity is not a stark one between exercising autonomy or falling into assimilation. The self-determination of distinct peoples largely depends on the ideas and institutions of outside "others." It is often applied by choosing among various ideas, institutional models, and strategies, originating from dominant societies and global institutions, which hold out the possibility of protecting a distinct community's ability to make such choices in the future. Universal ideas of liberation are growing in importance and are introducing a central paradox to the universalist/ contextualist divide: it has become universally necessary to draw upon universal ideas for the protection of social distinctiveness. The very process of trying to hold social integration at bay is a force of social integration.

This refusal of the major trends to stay within a tidy dualism makes the task of piecing together the intellectual puzzle of global convergence that much more difficult. I have therefore decided to begin (in chapter two) with an introductory outline of the utopian antecedents of the globalization concept; then, (in chapter three) I discuss the most familiar, widely identified global processes: cultural globalization and the corner-piece of the puzzle, free-trade globalization. The latter is a version of the idea that every nation and people in the world can be competitively enhanced with a good, solid dose of systematic technical know-how. Societies that make creative use of science and technology have shown themselves to be capable of accomplishing ever-greater feats of engineering, environmental control, and social harmony, all of which are fueled by the engines of world capitalism. Advocates of free trade argue that commerce mediates the expansion of technological resources now at the disposal of local groups and interests and that if only this process were allowed to proceed globally without interference from international institutions, nation-states, and nongovernmental organizations, it would result in a new era of prosperous world integration.

Globalization cannot be adequately understood without considering efforts being made by defenders of communities to resist or control it, especially if one wishes to argue (as I do) that such efforts often lead paradoxically to more complete community integration with transnational forces. Thus, another way to try to create a world in which human differences are inconsequential is through the assertions of communities, local cultures, or micro-nations, through the creation of microcosms shored up against the intrusions of global integration. This strategy tries to resolve the uncomfortable inconsistencies of modernity by excluding the influences of other (especially dominant, "civilizational") ways of life. It relies on a moral filter to exclude those technologies and social arrangements that are seen as dangerous innovations, while only admitting the useful and wholesome. A new source of local power and authority can be found in the role of gatekeeper, the intermediary between chaos and certainty. Under the sway of such moral truth-defenders, the world beyond difference becomes a microcosm of reinvented tradition and/or world-rejecting faith, a community of the elect that acts to nullify the influences and consequences of cultural intrusions and Diasporas. It builds an adamantine barrier of faith, birth, or culture around "Us" and "Them," around those who belong and those who cannot.

I illustrate this in chapter 4 by temporarily setting to one side my central concern with social theory and its utopian imaginings of a global community and turning instead to ethnographic examples of community reassertion that I encountered in several separate research projects, one provided by the activities and ambitions of a Muslim reform movement in West Africa and another by the more global process of indigenous identity-formation, particularly the identity inscribed in sophisticated information and communication technology, as adopted by the Crees of northern Canada and the Samis of northern Europe. Although reformist Islam might appear to be turning toward a universalist faith as an answer to the onslaughts of modernity, it does so in a way that rejects not only the inroads of the West but also the tolerance observed by the vast majority of Muslims. By contrast, those who participate in the international movement of indigenous peoples sit more firmly astride the organizations and technologies commonly associated with western liberalism and globalization in order to redefine and reassert community values and integrity.

The influence of such boundaried communities is reflected in intellectual expressions of utopian longing. In particular, the idealization of communities that resist global forces has become an active ingredient of the sociological imagination, based primarily on an idea that tries to shrink cosmopolitan prophecy down to manageable size. It finds inspiration in the conception of a closed, culturally self-defining community – or in a world populated by them, a "heterotopia."[1] But this ideal cannot be maintained for long under the influence of direct, careful, thoughtful examination. Actual experiments in closed identities, no matter how picturesquely rebellious and critically inspiring, often rely on despotic forms of power and grossly repressive techniques for maintaining them. The utopian sociological imagination therefore blurs the image of closed, self-defining communities to the point at which such blemishes are no longer visible. This permissive cosmopolitanism revels in hopeful abstractions and retreats into vague "descriptions" of counter-modernity in which the "tribes" or "local cultures" naturally offset the alienation of a globalizing world, or it combines an argument for the virtues of the oppressed with the assertion that looking too closely into actual conditions of peoples' misery and marginalization is itself an act of oppression.

Community-affirming cosmopolitan idealism takes a variety of forms. The human rights movement (the topic of chapter five) is a source of rationalist world identity, which constitutes a system of universal morality that has become the world's most popularly accepted system of law. At one level, it derives its appeal from its opposition to the worst state-sponsored practices of tyranny, torture, and genocide. At the same time, however, it approaches the overwhelming problems within its purview with the assumption that law changes social orders progressively through its inherent superiority over the inflexibility and irrationalism of tradition. In a way, this rights-oriented perception of necessary change in community-based identity is just an extension of the expected emergence of a unified global community. But there is also a strong collective-rights orientation in the human rights movement, and with it an infusion of relativist pluralism that runs counter to the individualist orientation of human rights, and more widely the statist orientation of the United Nations. In the aftermath of World War II, and even more after the political decolonization struggles of the 1960s, a concern in the human rights movement with the liberation and self-determination of distinct peoples took shape. This was an entirely non-universalist stimulus to social reform. So the human rights movement is now divided between the desire to preserve distinct societies through collective rights and the need to change them through individual rights and the leveling mechanisms of law and bureaucracy. Human rights therefore have the potential to be both socially liberating and a powerful force of cultural homogenization and global integration.

The relativist elevation of cultural self-definition is another pathway to permissive cosmopolitanism, through "grassroots globalization" or "globalization from below." I deal with this phenomenon in three closely connected chapters (six, seven, and eight), covering postmodernism, neo-Marxism, and postcolonialism. We should use the labels that apply to these sociological/philosophical systems with caution, in part because they are (to some degree purposively) difficult to define, defying strict categorization by avoiding the unambiguous use of categories, and in part because they merge into one another. Without recognizing the interconnectedness of these approaches to social critique and sublimated radical hope, the cultural contests of globalization cannot be adequately understood.

The postmodern movement (introduced in chapter six), ironically did everything it could to excoriate all varieties of universalism from intellectual life – starting, naturally enough, with almost the entire gamut of political and intellectual "isms" (Marxism, communism, liberalism, pragmatism, etc., but, unaccountably, stopping short of postmodernism itself), then moving on to disengagement from the public sphere and rejection of all forms of instrumental reason. Yet its very sweeping condemnation of these things itself took on the quality of a universal; and, what is more, some wayward postmodern souls were unable to cope with the movement's nihilistic implications and began looking for a way to express their bent toward sociological optimism, toward the possibilities inherent in postmodern society – a utopian mass society that rejects universals. The dualism between universalism and particularism is not as stark as it might at first seem. Reality-bending radical hope in one form or another proved to be inescapable.

Some postmodernists (as I illustrate in chapter seven) are shifting away from the nihilistic implications of their early ideas, responding to their diminishing popularity by finding inspiration in the intellectual rehabilitation of neo-Marxism, occasionally expressed quietly as a "certain spirit of Marx" or a Marx-inspired rejection of a wide range of social injustices and inequalities. Freed by postmodernist methodological looseness, Marx is now being used to advance the idea of a global post-revolutionary society of infinite and indefinite cultural possibilities. Until quite recently it was generally supposed that the legitimacy of Marxism and the revolutionary ideals that stem from it took a last step into oblivion with the "fall of the wall" and the subsequent breakup of the Soviet empire. "The end of history," approach to the global supremacy of American values, while provoking much interesting controversy, nevertheless reflected and popularized the erroneous view that the legitimacy of Marxism lay almost entirely in the fortunes of Soviet expansionism, that the post-1989 fragmentation definitively vindicated American-led capitalism as the sole remaining ideological and economic force of the new world order.[2] But the combined influences of world events and intellectual fashion have produced two alternative forms of Marxism. One, inspired largely by postmodernism, takes the shape of a Marx-inspired celebration of alternatives in which Marx's abiding concern with world history has been largely replaced with speculation about the contours of post-revolutionary society, a society that Marx never really bothered himself about, at least not far beyond a concern with how it was to emerge from world capitalism. Another approach to neo-Marxism sheds almost all speculation about revolutionary transition and draws instead from the ideas of human rights and the Enlightenment tradition of reason-based social reform as guiding principles of radical politics.

The rejection of universalism, while retaining a core of postmodernism's critique of instrumental thought and institution building as well as Marxism's egalitarian values, is expressed more overtly by those who, in practical ways, want to reverse globalizing trends by protecting or returning to community-based existence. Such political aspirations have received support and affirmation from the intellectual movement known as postcolonialism (discussed in chapter eight), one of the recent avatars of relativism. Postcolonialism approaches the most overt actions and symbols of colonial domination as metaphors for more subtle and insidious forms of domination. Subjection of the Other can begin with intellectual constructions, or even with the refusal to acknowledge the impenetrability of identities and belief systems. Cultures are, at a fundamental level, incommensurable. Such postcolonial concepts as cultural diaspora and hybridity are in this sense an extremely appealing alternative to the once-prevalent colonial-era practice of forced assimilation. Now no one need be subjected to the traumas of a policy-driven cultural erasure and indoctrination, once thought necessary to bring about the breakdown of local cultural barriers. The inexorable forces of modernity and technology are doing this on their own. Out of this new condition of cultural detachment and uncertainty there must be, according to one trend in postcolonialism, a greater possibility for – or even imminent certainty of – the emergence of a truly shared humanity.

If we usually fail to recognize the intellectual antecedents of the current perceptions of cultural globalization, it is mainly because earlier theorists of social integration, many inspired directly or indirectly by the universal ambitions of the French Revolution and the unprecedented powers of industrialization, used an entirely different terminology. They were centrally concerned with the growth of the state, the expansion of empires, the progress of civilization or some particular extension of civilization manifested in such things as family patterns or law. These were phenomena that entailed profoundly important processes of power accumulation and social uniformity, sometimes with a view to a terminus of history, the centralization of governments, and an end to all significant human differences; but because the term globalization is missing from their exertions, our attention tends to be drawn elsewhere, closer to the present.

Another reason for our lack of recognition is that until recently it was unfashionable to express hopes of universal human liberation, still less to construct designs for it. Even the world religions, especially Judaism, Christianity, and Islam, seem to have solidified the commitments of their believers by upping the tempo of intolerance, as evident in the protracted hatreds of the Middle East, Northern Ireland, and (notwithstanding recent glimmerings of peace) Kashmir, rather than dedicating themselves fully to the universal harvest of souls. The optimistic campaigns of proselytization that marked the expansionist centuries of Christianity and Islam and the Christian conquest of newly-encountered people during the Age of Discovery – people seen as ignorant, benighted, and ripe for conversion – seem, since the collapse of the Ottoman Empire in the East and the rise of secularism in the West, to have settled into relatively fixed boundaries between believer and infidel and a renunciation of the idea of an earthly paradise to be formed by uniting an entire humanity of co-religionists. The human obstacles to fulfilling the dream of a pure faith for all of humanity have become insurmountable, aside, of course, from the idea, beloved of fanatics, of apocalyptic judgment.

Christian ecumenicalism, oriented toward a sort of compromising spiritual unity, was central to the development of world-utopian aspirations, perceived by many as a way of transcending the intractable hatreds and clear moral bankruptcy of the crusader mentality. According to the most extreme form of ecumenicalism, God does not favor those who harbor their spirit in a particular race, homeland, or nationality; and divine grace can even fall upon those of other faiths, or of no faith at all. Human souls can only be judged according to each person's willingness to dim or fan into flames the same inner spark that is given to all. And if all individuals are the same in this most basic sense, then the most spiritually meaningful community can and should be a heavenly city on earth, built on the bedrock of a common humanity. Christian ecumenicalism, from the early Enlightenment onwards, was usually less theologically grounded and more often a supplement to scientifically-based conceptions of the way the world should be, providing an element of spiritual prophecy, varying greatly in their inventiveness or orthodoxy, to the otherwise diverse imaginings of such visionaries as Francis Bacon, Henri Comte de Saint-Simon, and Herbert Spencer.

After World War II, however, things appear to have taken a different turn. Several of the most astute analysts of late modernity have noted that even as technological achievements and supranational politics contributed to and reflected the accelerated pace of "global shrinking," the popularity of overtly utopian ideas has gone into decline.[3] Habermas contends that the projects of social democracy and the welfare state removed much of the vitality of the utopian imagination, not so much by supplanting utopian ideals with unambiguous conditions of prosperity and security as by creating an ambiguous politico-economic order that forbids any recognizable alternative, or at least inhibits radical designs for a better future.[4] The renunciation of overt social idealism is unquestionably also related to the spectacular failure in the twentieth century of all forms of overt political imperialism: the defeat of fascism, the arrangements of independent statehood for the overseas colonies of Western European powers, and the relatively peaceful dismantling of the Soviet empire. There is intensifying debate over whether or not the United States constitutes an empire and, if so, in what way it does; but the idea of a chosen people, of conquest motivated by faith in the superiority of civilization, or what Nazi ethnologists called "high-cultural existence" (*hochvolklichen Dasein*), was, for a while at least, thoroughly discredited.[5]

I do not want to argue, however, that world-historical idealism has come to an end, but rather that utopian or radically liberative imaginings are being expressed differently. The decline of overt utopianism has been a recent and, as I will show in this book, a temporary phenomenon. The roots of universal hope run deep. It can even be, as in postmodernism, hidden by outward rejection of universals. The human propensity for radical hope seems inexhaustible. For the most fervent of freedom-seekers, nationalist aspirations are often not enough; the ultimate goal must be something higher: a network-based identity, a global community of the liberated, a "New International," some conception of a universal *we* without an adversarial *they*. Under accelerating conditions of human integration, universal paradigms of liberation have become increasingly "good to think" and capable of being acted on. Almost everywhere, the accepted limits of political constraint are being lowered, the expectations of freedom raised, and the extent of the hoped for community-of-the-liberated expanded.

So what was, until recently, a near-universal consensus on the supreme importance of avoiding a political empire of the kind imagined at various points in the western utopian tradition, is now breaking apart. Even postcolonialism and postmodernism, the theoretical paradigms that reject such concepts as "mankind," "civilization," "progress," and any notion of the inherent superiority of western philosophy and literature in favor (when they do express positive conviction) of giving voice to colonial subjects and "subalterns" or privileging the anti-imperialism of boundaryless, hybrid, mobile social formations, have failed to move from theoretical critique to social reform, and occasionally themselves lapse into musings about a new, emergent humanity. The sublimation of hopes for world liberation is attenuating. These hopes seem to be, sometimes in a confused, chaotic, and oblique way, coming closer to the surface. Dreams of a global empire, or a world state, or a perfect global community of free-floating individuals have once again emerged as stimuli to political action. In the western imagination, these dreams are recurrent. A tradition of aspirations toward earthly perfection informs our thinking in ways that seem hardly to be noticed in our efforts to understand the forces of global transformation.

2

The Tradition of Rational Utopianism

A Durable Ideal

Those who harbor an active hope or fear of an impending world order, an order lacking meaningful cultural, ethnic, or national boundaries, usually do so without full regard for the long, rich, and varied history of ideas associated with the longing for a fully integrated global society. The small number of cross-sections or profiles from western intellectual history that I present in this chapter should serve to illustrate this complexity. I have not chosen these at random, but with a view to outlining some of the basic ideas about global culture that continue to be drawn upon today. One of the temptations one is faced with in undertaking this kind of exercise is to use the long history of the idea of integrated world culture to argue that globalization is a useless or meaningless concept, but I have come to feel that even the ancient Greeks would have liked the term, close as it is to their own conception of the *cosmopolis*, the universal city. And since it now seems beyond question that both world governance and local cultures are changing with exponential speed, it seems reasonable to look into a few of the ways that world integration has already been imagined.

My sense is that this exercise is important because such conceptions are not just a reflection of cultural dissolution and exchange; they are an impetus behind them. Postcolonial literary critics have described western ideas of cultural superiority as a condition of intellectual malaise associated with imperial domination, and if we step into this point of view (as we do more fully in chapter eight) for a moment it becomes possible to see the idea of world utopia as a basic original stimulus to projects of domination.

Such ideas, however, are not the exclusive domain or burden of the West. There are, for example, a number of expressions of the same original, radical hope from modern (and modernizing) China, including the utopian vision of Kang Youwei, who, in *The Great Unity* predicts the inevitable demise of the "inferior" races, such as the "fierce and ugly" races of India, soon to be overcome by epidemics and hence unable to prevail against the British, and the Negroes, who will be unable to lower racial barriers against them and to socially progress because their bodies "smell badly." For Kang, the evolutionary principle favors the white and yellow races, which are to join in a new world order of love and equality.[1] Kang's adoption of evolutionism's most blatant, unfeeling prejudices is not merely an adoption of western ideas but is related to the moral quest and activism of several schools of Confucianism and Buddhism.[2]

Notwithstanding such Confucian and Buddhist influence, the western tradition remains the most important source of utopian ideas of global transition. This tradition is not unbroken, cohesive, coherent, or internally uncontested. But it does, as I intend to show in this chapter, tend to cluster around the question of human differences – how to overcome or preserve through the course of inevitable global changes the different, puzzling, and sometimes awkward or dangerously oppositional, ways of being in the world.

Early Imaginings

The tension between world culture and human differences is evident from the first imaginings of a temporal, universal city of peace and prosperity – the ancient Stoic ideal of perfect social order and the grand utopias of the early Enlightenment. The Stoics were not the only school of ancient philosophy to imagine a united world culture. What we know of Epicurean social thought points to a comprehensive, hopeful view of the world, as in the writings of Diogenes of Oenoanda, inscribed on stone in a public colonnade in central Turkey in the second century A.D.: "In relation to each segment of the earth, different people have different native lands. But in relation to the whole circuit of this world, the entire earth is a single native land for every-one, and the world a single home."[3] But the Stoics did this one better, with the imaginary construction of an ideal world, a world without war, famine, oppression, or insecurity.

Zeno of Citium, who founded the Stoic school during the waning years of ancient Greece, was probably the first to conceive of a program of utopian world citizenship, a perfect society with a timeless existence to which all of humanity would belong.[4] His "Politeia" was a society in which state control and institutions were unnecessary. There was to be no money, no law courts, no public buildings (including temples), and no domination of the ruled by the powerful. Competition, an unwhole-some source of division among men, was to be banished. Even the master/pupil relationship of wrestling schools was to have no place in this new world. Instead, friendship, in small circles and large associa-tions, was to be a natural guarantee of coherence. It was probably Zeno, and not his follower Chryssipus, who introduced the justifications for incest and cannibalism that were to embarrass later Stoics, but his con-temporaries were probably not much less scandalized by his proposals to extend citizenship to women, to introduce unisex clothing, and to make the sex drive a foundation for social solidarity. Virtue alone was to define the worth of individuals. Humanity possessed the inherent capacity to live in perfect peace, equality, and contentment. It was to be a society so encompassing in scope, and so great and good in the reality it created, that it could never be matched by anything else, and hence never harbor dissent or challenge.[5]

But neither Zeno nor his followers seem to have said anything about how this harmonious existence was to be realized. This left the door open for later adherents of Stoicism to develop the ideal of a peace-able empire of the known world. When Plutarch extolled Alexander the Great as the accomplisher of the Stoic ideal, one who brought together many ways of life and distinct nations into a single empire of brotherhood, he could not have better expressed the practical dilemma of an idealized world.[6] And when Marcus Aurelius wrote his Stoically-inspired *Meditations* during the Roman campaign to suppress the bar-barians in the Danube region he was apparently displaying more than a tension between his natural sensitivity and his professional obliga-tions as a ruler and warrior. "A little flesh, a little breath, and a Reason to rule all – that is myself," he reflected, leaving it ambiguous as to whether the primacy of reason applies to his human faculties or to humankind.[7] The fortunes of empire were somehow consistent with a yearning for human perfection growing out of a conflict between inner loneliness and the possibility of a universal community based on reason or, to begin with at least, a peaceable empire based on victory in war.

The ideal of a just, rationally ordered, universal society that promotes the accumulation and application of knowledge is not taken up again until the European discovery of the New World and the first halting developments in modern scientific method of the seventeenth century. The vision that developed in early modern Europe of an ideal society based upon the accumulation of knowledge is without question a far-reaching innovation that has in many ways influenced subsequent conceptions of a unified, harmonious world order.

The utopian imaginings from this period were a radical departure from the Judeo-Christian apocalyptic tradition, in which the coming of a messiah was expected to bring about the cataclysmic reordering of the universe, banishing death and sickness, allowing the blind to see the day, opening the ears of the deaf, making the deserts blossom. Nor do they resemble the hopeful portrayals of other, "primitive" forms of life, such as Montaigne's description, written between 1578 and 1580, of Brazilian "savages" who embody a simplistic opposite of European vices and morally compromising strengths, a nation with "no occupations but leisure ones, no care for any but common kinship, no clothes, no agriculture, no metal, no use of wine or wheat. The very words that signify lying, treachery, dissimulation, avarice, envy, belittling, pardon – unheard of."[8] Even cannibalism finds a place in Montaigne's pluralism, with the observation that the Inquisition displays more cruelty in roasting men still alive or torturing them on the rack with their bodies still full of feeling, than in merely roasting and eating people after they are dead. The age of exploration, discovery, and encounter produced a literature of indirect social criticism based on supposedly direct accounts of "noble savages."

This age, however, also developed a literature of hope that subsequently became more influential, one that was to inspire an approach to universal morality and liberation that cut itself loose from its Christian moorings, based on the radical idea that the perfect society could be a product of willed human agency. Francis Bacon's *New Atlantis* is an example from the early Enlightenment of what was to become a genre of sociopolitical imaginings inspired by the inherent promise of science and exploration. Not content with advancing the nascent scientific method of the Elizabethan age of exploration, Bacon expressed an ambitious program for applying new powers of thought and systematic accumulation of knowledge to the improvement of society. This was still expressed within a largely Christian framework, but the utopian vision of Bacon's *New Atlantis* was rife with ideas that point to a new way of improving the human condition.

His imaginary ideal society, Bensalem, had the good fortune of inheriting some of the discoveries and institutions of the apocryphal lost civilization of Atlantis, including its ability to amass knowledge in a methodical manner and to travel with the goal of uncovering the valuable secrets of the world's great societies.[9] Bacon's ideal society began as a typical perfect-island utopia, but developed into a grand vision for humanity. Its lessons were conveyed not so much through a single, isolated example of perfection as through a new method of social construction: a concrete synthesis of the world's genius amassed by globetrotting observers, later advanced by his fictional Bensalemites through systematic experimentation. But there was something strange and vaguely sinister about this imaginary world. It possessed a central, secret, semi-autonomous center of power, given the biblically allegorical name "Solomon's house," the purpose of which appears to have been coordinating expeditions of information gathering and, in general, advancing the connections between scientific knowledge and political power. Science, from the very beginnings of the Enlightenment, was seen not only as a power that can unlock the secrets of the universe, but also as a source of political virtue, a new foundation for empire building that somehow avoids the competitive realities of real-world sovereignty.

Only those dreamers who restricted the scope of their ideal society to utopian city-states were sometimes able to avoid the idealization of scientifically inspired empire building. Thomas More's playfully rendered *Utopia* circumvented the problems of expansionism and confrontation with the sovereignty of others through a limited and local totalitarianism. His Utopia was required to deal only with the internal problems of crime and dissent, which in More's ambivalent, multi-layered imaginary social world were handled with greater legal consistency and more humanely (bonded labor for criminals, who were to be identified by the excision of the tip of one ear, and a limited scope for the death penalty) than the actual practices followed in Renaissance England (involving the profligate use of torture and execution).[10]

Bacon was more serious and outwardly ambitious than More. He imagined a benevolent political application of knowledge, a source of virtue and social good, a way to overcome humanity's burden of suffering, vanquish poverty, universalize prosperity, and improve human welfare in all places, for all time to come. His vision of an ideal world culture embodies scientific virtues that have since found many imitators, though rarely expressing the same naïve simplicity or the same trust in the purveyors of secret knowledge intended for social welfare.

Scientific Discovery and Universal Rights

Scientific paradigms also had a more autonomous influence on the idea of universal rights. Newtonian physics, and to a lesser extent Darwinian natural science, probably influenced political and legal imaginings more than we normally realize, by providing overwhelming evidence of order in the universe while tacitly justifying efforts to establish a corresponding precision and regularity in human affairs. Unlike Bacon, Newton did not have to elaborate a plan for a new social order intended to reflect the advances of his science in order to promote the idea of a universal morality and system of law. The pervasive influence of his science did this on its own. If the order of the universe can by revealed by systematic observation, measure, and experimentation, then why should humanity continue to be subject to unreasonable inequalities, arbitrary rule, and injustice? Surely a way can be found to bring a similar order to the moral universe, to protect individuals above all from the inconsistent and illogical uses of political power.

This spirit of hope was undaunted by the grim realities of the industrial revolution. If anything, the social misery brought about by the factory system was a stimulus to rational imaginings of a better world. Much as we are accustomed to the view that science in the hands of a political elite is a recipe for the grossest form of tyranny, this was not altogether absent from nineteenth-century utopianism. Henri Comte de Saint-Simon, for example, looked at industrialization (a term he coined) in a much more favorable light than many prophetic socialists of the nineteenth century, basing his conception of the ideal society almost entirely on the contributions of uncontrolled science and industry. Application of the powers of science for the benefit of society would, he thought, eliminate war, poverty, and injustice. His conception of this ideal world was highly detailed, though unevenly and sporadically expressed in torrents of writing in which he laid out plans for the organization of industry, labor unions, welfare programs, financial institutions, and even the design of cities. And, despite (or perhaps because of) his intellectual eclecticism and eccentricity, he seems to have predicted, probably in greater detail than any of his contemporaries (including Marx), the emergence of the institutional environment that we live in today.[11] But he did not anticipate the persistent attachment of moderns to individual rights and freedoms. The new industrial/political order, he thought, would not be able to fulfilll its destiny without a firm collective will. Individual freedoms would have to be sacrificed to allow the unhampered functioning of a technological, cultural, political, and cultural elite.

Auguste Comte, in his *Course de Philosophie Positive*, applied some of Saint-Simon's ideas to the study of society by offering a social-Darwinist perspective on human history in which three stages of human cognitive development – theological or fictitious; metaphysical or abstract; and evolutionary or scientific – end in just such a technocratic social order. To us this is a nightmarish order in which the empirical sciences are the sole adequate source of knowledge and, what is more, the only true source of political perfection, with an elite placed in power through ability rather than democratic procedure, using scientific methods to relieve suffering and to create conditions designed to bring about human happiness.

The human rights movement is a more recent expression of universal rational idealism. Political revolution was the context in which the language of universal human rights, expressed and acted upon as the ultimate source of a just, well ordered society, achieved its first direct expression. The Virginia Bill of Rights, drafted by George Mason in 1776, was the most influential of the state-sponsored bills of rights to emerge from the rebellious American colonies, proclaiming in its opening article "That all men are by nature equally free and independent, and have certain inherent rights . . ." These words were a direct challenge to the legitimacy of both monarchy and colonial rule, and provided inspiration for revolutionary law making on both sides of the Atlantic. The Declaration of Independence of July 4, 1776 heralding the American Revolution[12] reveals in its few opening sentences the same sweeping affirmation of equality as the Virginia Bill of Rights and the combined influence on Thomas Jefferson's thinking of Christianity, natural law theory, and other ideas from the Enlightenment political philosophy in which he was steeped, resulting in a document that goes further than throwing off the yoke of British domination and exploitation, that offers the notion that every legitimate government should be based upon equality, expressed in divinely endowed unalienable rights, acted upon through democratic principles, and realized and renewed, if necessary, by revolution.

In terms of the revolutionary implementation of a rational, rights-based political order this was only the beginning. Rationalism in the service of a planned society intended for export to humanity achieved its fullest expression a few years later in the French Revolution. And among those intellectuals who strove to bring Enlightenment to the politics of revolution, Condorcet is a leading figure, in part because his direct involvement with the Jacobin cause gave his vision of human perfectibility a sense of realism that tempered his tendency toward extravagant optimism. It was while in hiding, shortly before he was to die at the hands of those very political forces that he had, as a member of the Legislative Assembly, helped bring to power, that he wrote his most important work, *Esquisse d'un tableau historique des progrès de l'esprit humain* (Historical sketch of the progress of the human spirit). He was proscribed during the Reign of Terror of 1793 and, probably expecting execution, committed suicide in his cell. Despite these awful circumstances, the writing that he completed while in hiding is full of hope in the future of humanity. Condorcet's faith in human perfectibility, which he expressed in such conditions of political and personal misfortune, is sometimes taken as an example of touching and tragic irony; but there is more to his outlook than misplaced optimism. His outline of human history through nine stages, beginning with the unification of groups of families into protective communities, through the inventions and discoveries of pastoralism, agriculture, and science, the retreats of the Dark Ages, the resumptions of the Renaissance, the use of mechanical printing, up to the genius of Descartes and the establishment (of course) of the French Republic, contains no shortage of examples of ignorance, greed, tyranny, and misplaced attachment to oppressive traditions. Such examples provide one of the central points of his historical exercise: although improvements in knowledge and the wider benefits to humanity of its application lead to inevitable progress, history shows us that Enlightenment must nevertheless unceasingly struggle against the fanaticism and corruption of priests and kings.[13]

It is in his tenth stage, the future progress of humanity, however, that Condorcet gives full vent to his remarkable capacity for hope. Through a new approach to morality and the social good, tempered and guided by science, humankind is capable of bringing about progressive improvements in health, subsistence, and general prosperity. Science is not only instrumental in making useful discoveries; it begins with a moral influence. Law and science are therefore interdependent. The foundations of collective morality, expressed in law, cannot be properly understood without the scientific uncovering of social interests; and the work of science cannot be protected from immoral interference without equality under the law, without the shelter of individuals provided by universal human rights. In a passage reminiscent of Plato's *Republic*, Condorcet points to the cardinal place of knowledge in overcoming the passions and guiding behavior:

> Men cannot enlighten themselves on the nature and development of their moral sentiments, on the principles of morality, on the natural motivations that make these principles conform to their actions, or on their interests both as individuals and as members of a society, without also applying them to the not less real, practical morality of progress that belongs to science. Is not interest, poorly understood, the most frequent cause of actions contrary to the general good? Is not the violence of the passions often the effect of habits one does not abandon only because of a false reckoning or ignorance of the means to resist their first stirrings, to quiet them, to divert them, to control their action?[14]

From here, all other benefits of science follow. In time to come humanity will transcend the limitations of ignorance, superstition, and blind religious faith, and will be set free from the arbitrary rule of tyrants. The powers that will lead to this many-sided victory are the rights of man and the unfettered pursuit of knowledge. The principles of equality – equality of wealth, control over means of subsistence, and education – are already reaching the far corners of Europe. Enlightened men, Condorcet supposes, are already too widely distributed and too well placed for the reactionary efforts of oppressors to keep the message of liberty from penetrating as far as the shanties of their slaves. The principles of the French constitution will awaken in the souls of the oppressed a need for freedom and justice, intensified by indignation at their present conditions of humiliation and fear. All the enemies of progress are soon to fall. The friends of humanity who led the revolution at home will soon take upon themselves the task of bringing its guiding principles to the unenlightened everywhere.

Condorcet amplifies these themes in *Fragments sur l'Atlantide* (Fragments on Atlantis), in which he is directly inspired by Francis Bacon's utopian vision of a society based upon a restless search for knowledge. Condorcet does not suppose his expectation of a new world guided by men of genius to be fanciful; it is built into the very nature of scientific discovery, an almost inevitable outcome of the upper hand possessed by the Enlightenment in its universal struggle against tyranny and ignorance. This possible society that inspires his revolutionary fervor is a "general assembly of the scholars of the world in a universal republic of the sciences,"[15] in which "a strong and pure reason will have determined laws and combined institutions."[16] None of this would be possible, however, without an approach to the law in which the natural rights of the individual are protected, in which nothing is prohibited beyond those actions that infringe upon the rights of others, and in which rights and duties apply equally to all. These underpinnings of universal rights are inseparable from scientific discovery; they comprise the most important conditions necessary for the freedom of scholars and fulfilllment of the social promise of science.

These rational principles led Condorcet toward the most thoroughgoing approach toward rights of his time. In 1781 he published an anonymous pamphlet denouncing the slave trade, not just on the grounds that it was cruel and degrading and could not be condoned for reasons of economic necessity, but above all because it deprived slaves of their rights and violated the basic principles of "inflexible justice." To this he added, for good measure, condemnation of judicial torture, of the persecution of Protestants, and of the harshness of laws against hunting (reflecting unjust noble privilege).[17] In other writing, he objected to the burning of "sodomites" and any other legal inequality affixed to homosexuals on the grounds that, when not associated with violence, homosexuality violates no one else's rights.[18] He swam against the tide with his affirmation of equal rights for women, arguing that rights must be the same for all sentient beings endowed with moral ideas and the faculty of reason. And although he believed that the female sex did not as a whole possess the same strengths as men, they were undoubtedly possessed of reason and moral judgment. While they could not hope to reach the lofty heights of Voltaire, women could at least hope to equal such thinkers as Pascal or Rousseau (both of whom he passionately disliked). Any inherent differences between men and women were insignificant and could not be used to justify inequality of rights.

This is the kind of symmetric justice envisioned in the opening article of the Declaration of the Rights of Man and Citizen drawn up by the deputies of the French National Assembly in 1789 as a prelude to drafting a constitution: "Men are born and remain free and equal in rights."[19] (This line was later built into article 1 of the Universal Declaration of Human Rights of 1948: "All human beings are born free and equal in dignity and rights.") These few words capture the essence of the rights-based society ushered in by the American and French Revolutions; they point to the implementation of rights as a new source of political legitimacy, a radical departure from the divine right of kings and monopolization of power by a nobility; and they suggest universality, making this (more than the Declaration of Independence which invokes God as a source of natural rights) the first fully *secular* version of the idea that fundamental moral truths exist (perhaps yet to be discovered) that apply to all people in all times and places.

Such an ambitious starting point to nationhood inevitably faces, at least to some degree, a loss of original vision, even ultimate failure. And fail it did, in a spectacular, appalling way when the Reign of Terror took away civil liberties, including the right to life, as a way of bringing about "equality" and when a solution to the need to restore order was found in a series of dictatorships. But the struggles that followed the ambitious program of the French Revolution were not just political; they were in a more lasting way legal, following from the ideal, expressed by Condorcet in advance of others, of a universal empire of equality.

Although we are accustomed to thinking of human rights as embedded in secular idealism or the extension of Enlightenment rationalism to an international moral order, one of the most important philosophical strands that made up the post-World War II universal rights regime was strongly opposed to the idea that rights could be based on a worldly, non-theistic approach to human nature. Its main premise was that the essential truth of the earliest natural law theory – beginning with the legacies of Antigone and Sophocles, the great moralists of antiquity, through to the universal moral reflections of St. Thomas Aquinas – all of which emphasized a divine origin in human nature and the ethical principles that follow from it, had been corrupted by the secular tradition in natural law founded by Hugo Grotius, followed, each in their own error-laden way, by the luminaries of modern political philosophy: Locke, Hobbes, Rousseau, and Kant. According to this theistic approach to natural law, the intellectual revolution begun by Grotius in the early seventeenth century erred in its search for an intrinsic morality outside of God's will, which considers things to be good or bad from their own nature, prior to the commandments or unseen will of God; in particular, it was misguided in considering things associated with the natural, social character of humanity to be intrinsically good.[20]

Modern conceptions of rights would not have taken their current form (or perhaps any form) without the West's long exposure to Christian universalism. This was not necessarily to be expected, given the Catholic Church's understanding of a chronology of errors, which included pantheism, naturalism, rationalism, and "contemporary liberalism."[21] But in the aftermath of World War II such reservations – about rationalism and liberalism at least – were shed to make room for a secular approach to human rights and the venture of world unity. In human rights circles this compromise was matched by a tacit repudiation of the Enlightenment's – in particular the French Revolution's – legacy of atheism and anticlericalism.

One consequence of this mutual openness of rationalism and theism was the infusion of Christian ideas into the postwar human rights project. Against the secular idea that humans are by their nature disposed to build communities and preserve social peace, for example, the theistic approach to natural law emphasized a natural human conscience, a moral essence hard wired into the species, a necessary virtue ultimately originating in God's will. For Jacques Maritain, the most influential exponent of this approach to natural law and one of the most active members of the influential 1947 UNESCO-sponsored Committee on the Theoretical Bases of Human Rights, such moral knowledge is a kind of unsystematic ethical musicality, a form of "vital knowledge by connaturality or congeniality, in which the intellect, in order to bear judgment, listens to the inner melody that the vibrating strings of abiding tendencies make present in the subject."[22] Biblical teachings were, for Maritain, a source of transcendent truth with its ultimate source in human nature, truth that arises "from the simple fact that man is man, nothing else being taken into account."[23]

There are strong overtones of utopia in Maritain's idea of human rights as reposing on common elements of faith, on acceptance of all believers, Christian and non-Christian alike, in the good society, or "a brotherly city wherein the human being will be freed from servitude and misery."[24] (The use here of the word "city" to describe this society is metaphorical, incorporating the important quality of close civic-mindedness required of a polity that was to be more than "decoratively Christian.") The unity of the faithful in this society arises, "from the moment [its members] recognize, each in his own way, the human values of which the Gospel has made us aware, the dignity and the rights of the person, the character of moral obligation inherent in authority, the law of brotherly love and the sanctity of natural law." From this starting point all would "be drawn into the dynamism of such a society and would be able to cooperate for its common good."[25]

The formulation of a new human rights instrument of global applicability following World War II was an ideal way to begin the effort toward what Maritain called "practical convergence," toward world unification through a pragmatic assemblage of moral principles (not theories, which are inherently dissent-ridden) that could ultimately "claim to establish in actual fact universal ascendancy over men's minds."[26] In other words, drafting a new human rights instrument was in large measure a global ecumenical exercise. Theology was intended by some to give the Universal Declaration a truly unifying character, a moral authority that could not be provided by mere legal or philosophical reflection.[27] The participation of Christian churches (especially the Catholic Church) in the reinterpretation of human rights was intended to make available a tool to uncover the geology of the conscience and provide a source of universal legitimacy that could not be claimed by liberal individualism, the dominant creed of western lawmakers. This was to be a truly universal approach, wherein perceptions of the spiritual sources of human dignity and ethics were solicited not only from a variety of Christian authorities but also from those knowledgeable about other major religions: Islam, Hinduism, Buddhism, and Confucianism. The ultimate source of this broad search for a religious foundation to human rights, however, was the idea of a "common religious creed" expressed by Christian theologians.

There are practical reasons for the emphasis placed by the Universal Declaration's drafting committee on the ideas of major religions (but not, as we will see, reaching as far as oral traditions). For a nonwestern philosophy to make a worthwhile contribution to human rights it has to begin with a global conception of humanity. The major philosophies of religion used as resources for arriving at universal rights were each based upon their own version of universal truth, universal in the sense of applying to all rational beings. It was Mahatma Gandhi's observation that "the very right to live accrues to us only when we do the duty of citizenship of the world,"[28] that was seen to be a noteworthy contribution, rather than the caste exclusivism of Hinduism.

The push for consensus among the major civilizations was in the long term undeterred by such points of difference. Behind the superficial divergences of faith, there must be a foundation for universal brotherhood. After all, even if Islam draws a sharp boundary between believer and infidel, it begins with the conception of a common humanity, endowed with reason and free will. Muslim governments could point to the important practice of almsgiving (*zakat*), for example, as a simplified and popular equivalent of the social security provisions of the Universal Declaration. And certainly no believer would publicly condone racial discrimination against fellow Muslims, each of whom is capable of devotion, piety, and finding favor in the afterlife.

The emphasis on religio-civilizational ethical consensus in the drafting of human rights instruments also influenced the subsequent debate on human rights universalism. Much of the intellectual legitimacy of human rights has come to rest on demonstrations of the consistency between the ethical perspectives of the world's "high cultures" and the Universal Declaration of Human Rights of 1948. Hence the Confucian preference for the moral restraint of rites over laws may lead to some weakness when it comes to curbing the excesses of autocratic power, but this does not mean that in essence it does not similarly value justice, good government, and respect of the person through community relationships – establishing a basic consistency with human rights that puts the lie to any promotion of distinct "Asian values" as a justification for authoritarianism.[29]

Such was the influence of religious ideas in the establishment of a new regime of human rights after World War II that one of the central points of contention in meetings of the General Assembly on the final drafting and approval of the Universal Declaration centered upon proposals to include a reference to God. The Brazilian delegate proposed the following wording for Article 1, to be linked to the affirmation that all human beings are born free and equal in dignity and rights: "Created in the image and likeness of God, they are endowed with reason and conscience, and should act towards one another in a spirit of brotherhood."[30] In the ensuing debate, in which Brazil was supported by Venezuela, Argentina, Columbia, Bolivia, and the Netherlands, the reference to God was expunged, largely because of objections by the Soviet delegation that theological passages were fundamentally unacceptable to "some states." A second, slightly more circuitous effort to include religious language in the Universal Declaration was made by the Netherlands in a proposal for wording in the preamble: "whereas recognition of the inherent dignity and of the equal and inalienable rights of all members of the human family based on man's divine origin and immortal destiny is the foundation of freedom, justice and peace in the world."[31] This was similarly withdrawn after extensive debate. The Dutch proposal did not reach the consensus it needed largely because of objections by several delegations (not just those representing communist governments) that the United Nations was a secular institution that needed no religious legitimation.

It would seem that a vision of human rights as a product of rationalism in the spirit of the Enlightenment *philosophes* and the French Revolution had prevailed over a neo-Thomistic, theological, divine-spark approach to natural law. But the absence of religious language from human rights instruments does not mean that the lofty idealism of someone like Jacques Maritain finds no outlet. The Universal Declaration of 1948 was the first human rights instrument to accommodate a multiplicity of ideals, religious and secular, to the extent that it is built on both the highest aspirations of the "Age of Reason" revolutionary tradition and on Christian ecumenical utopianism. It is a secular codification of basic moral principles that goes further than the separation of church and state in liberal constitutions – the Universal Declaration aspires toward a separation of all rights and all "isms." Its consensus orientation was intended to even out the influence of dominant ideologies and exclude expression, in rights form, of particular political or religious aspirations. At the same time it has proven to be a carefully polished mirror for all sorts of idealists, who find in it their own vision of a better world, despite the absence of direct references to faith or divinity.

Socio-evolutionism

From roughly the mid-nineteenth to mid-twentieth centuries socio-evolutionism was the dominant way of conceptualizing human progress and Herbert Spencer its most influential exponent. Spencer looked forward to the emergence, from the universal principles of competition and adaptation, of a "perfect society," a society of autonomous individuals living in the greatest possible freedom, unhampered by restrictions imposed by the state.[32] The work in which Spencer developed an organic analogy for human progress, or "natural adaptation," *Social Statics: The Conditions Essential to Human Happiness Specified, and the First of them Developed,* was first published in 1850, some nine years before Darwin's *The Origin of Species*. The timing of the first appearance of the two works is important because Spencer's vision of human development, at the height of it notoriety, came to be associated with the scientific outlook of natural science, even to the point of garnering the label "social Darwinism."

Spencer's starting point was an extreme reserve, even antipathy, toward state authority and a model of world historical progress that situated particular societies on a scale of development, with great value placed on a society's ability to accommodate individual freedom. From this point of departure, however, Spencer arrived at a position that celebrated social competition and the global supremacy of market forces, even, in his youthful work, to the point of anticipating a universal utopia. The emergence of this perfect state required but one condition: the absence of government interference in natural conditions of liberty, in particular interferences in the natural course of trade. This was not the trade of early industrial manufacture, the pin makers and woolen manufacturers that populate Adam Smith's classic statement in favor of free trade liberalism, *The Wealth of Nations*. Nor was it the kind of free trade advocated by Ricardo, which combined politics and economics in a way that emphasized democratic citizenship as a precondition for economic growth.[33] It was the free trade of a mature form of globalizing capitalism that largely transcended the constraints of representative democracy.

In *The Man versus The State*, first published in 1884, Spencer objected vehemently to the "interferences" and "coercive rule" inherent in what he saw as the misguided legislation that restricted the activity (he would say "freedom") of capitalist enterprises. Among these inappropriate laws were those that "meddled" in the labor of children, such as an act of 1860 which made it illegal for mining enterprises to employ boys under twelve who were not attending school, a Bakehouses Regulation Act of 1863 which regulated a minimum age of employees, and the Agricultural Children's Act of 1872 which made it illegal for farmers to employ children without a certificate of elementary education. Spencer objected to the "tinkering" manifested in successive Factories Acts, which regulated the hours and conditions of labor. Such things extended the reach of government too far. The State, he felt, was also wrongly taking on the burden of education for the poor, and its involvement with public health and working conditions in factories was sentimentally-inspired, ruinous nonsense. All such "restrictions" and "coercion" increased the state's levels of taxation, and this, he argued, resulted in an unconscionable restriction of the freedom of the citizen. "[E]ither directly or indirectly, and in most cases both at once, the citizen is at each further stage in the growth of this compulsory legislation, deprived of some liberty which he previously had."[34] In keeping with these ideas, Spencer later established himself as mentor to the Liberty and Property Defence League, formed in 1882 as a mouthpiece of extreme laissez-faire and source of opposition to a wide range of capital-restricting parliamentary initiatives.

He underpinned his advocacy of laissez-faire with a muscular form of socio-evolutionism, characterized by an unshakable faith in the global supremacy of civilization. This cultural model relied on a kind of trickle down effect of civilization, a celebration of its expansion and domination on those who do not yet share in its riches. Spencer's great guarantor of social justice was ideally nothing more or less than the universal principle of organic and social progress that he made famous (and infamous) – the "survival of the fittest" – a principle that rendered all state efforts to secure the welfare of its citizens not only superfluous, but above all backward, postponing the beneficial outcome of competition.

Consistent with this conception of virtuous competition is the idea that the ultimate destination of civilization is the perfect freedom of the individual. For competition to work, individuals must be free to compete, unhampered by any unnecessary, arbitrary constraint. "To be that which he naturally is – to do just what he would spontaneously do – is essential to the full happiness of each, and therefore to the greatest happiness of all. Hence, in virtue of the law of adaptation our advance must be toward a state in which this entire satisfaction of every desire, of perfect fulfilllment in individual life becomes possible."[35] Under so-called primitive governments the repression of individuals is at its greatest, while it decreases through the advance of humanity toward civilization. All forms of despotism, whether political or religious, and whether discriminating on the basis of sex, caste, or custom, are limitations of individuality. These are limitations that civilization, by its very nature, acts to remove. There are, of course, intermediate stages in the advance of civilization. Aristocracy and democracy can in various ways combine to create governments that are, unlike the coercive rule of earlier ages, only a little despotic. Monarchy can itself undergo changes in which it sets fewer limits on the freedom of individuals. Human advancement is not marked by social harmony and cooperation, but by competition and struggle, of which the activities of commercial ventures are a perfect example.

Spencer does not resolve the apparent contradiction between his ideal of perfect freedom and his advocacy of unrestricted capitalism, which included a blatant and sordid advocacy of child labor. In his view, the freedom of the individual and advance of civilization were still best expressed by the unrestricted activities of free market capitalism. Only through ingenuity, adaptation, and consistent dedication to improvement could an enterprise come out ahead of its competitors.

Other forms of social competition were also beneficial. Even religious schisms were for him a sign of progress, for as sects divide into ever-smaller groups there will emerge, through continual subdivision into numberless, unclassifiable congregations, a pure Christian faith and a society of "general similarity, with infinitesimal differences."[36]

He therefore popularized a surprisingly durable solution to the problems posed by human differences. Spencer was not squeamish about the need to displace and supplant those whom he saw as inferior creatures, dedicated for their survival to hunting and warfare, and in the process inclined to be cunning, treacherous, and unsentimentally ruthless. "Human beings are cruel to one another in proportion as their habits are predatory," he asserted.[37] And for a civilized being to "multiply in a world already tenanted by inferior creatures – creatures that must be dispossessed to make room – is a manifest impossibility."[38] Yet civilized people are by nature sympathetic toward others, as evidenced by the great number of charitable works and organizations active in Spencer's time. Such sympathy is part of the order of things. So, if civilized people cannot be convinced of the need to destroy uncivilized others directly and expeditiously, they must use their natural philanthropy as a tool of civilization. And when civilized beings have succeeded in "molding" those who lack the virtues of philanthropy and charity, virtues that emerge from a heightened feeling for one's fellows – at that point all selfishness in unjust laws, all savagery, barbarous customs, murders, robberies, enslavings, and dishonest dealings, will fall away from human experience, bringing about a new world society of perfect peace and freedom.

His conception of human progress therefore implicitly enjoined the destruction and assimilation of so-called uncivilized, non-competitive societies. The game of survival has its winners and its losers. Savagery and treachery must make room for those with civilized constitutions. Harm comes from interfering in social competition, giving weak individuals, social practices, or societies an unnatural advantage, thereby corrupting the soundness of civilization as a whole. Prominent among such interferences are arrangements that alter the natural course of trade or commerce: "mercantile bribes," or, more commonly and banefully, "tyranny in commercial laws."[39]

One of the hallmarks of Spencerist socio-evolutionism was a blind faith in the power and benefits of the "survival of the fittest" and an equally blind negligence of the suffering and grievance this would cause, especially in the colonial context. From a nineteenth-century perspective, who could have predicted the extent of resistance to benevolent governments striving to bring the benefits of civilization to those left behind by progress? Were not their lives more secure, their rulers less brutal and tyrannical, under colonial government than in a state of savagery? Had they not been shown a way out of wretched-ness and thralldom? And could they not plainly see the increase in their prosperity brought about by decisions made in overseas capitals? As I demonstrate in the next chapter, such questions, based on dangerous assumptions of the need for all to quickly conform to the virtues of civilization, continue to hold sway over some of the most influential ideas of global development and prosperity.

World History and World Revolution

More than any champion of global culture considered so far, Karl Marx has been outwardly the most politically influential. He was greatly inspired by Enlightenment conceptions of unilinear history (including Spencer's evolutionism), the patterns of which he felt could be revealed by rational method, but he situated the conditions for human emancipation in history itself rather than in a clearly imagined ideal society. It is principally to Marx that we owe the popularization of the idea that history can be understood as a world-historical process leading to human liberation. The perfect society does not need to be described because it is both unknowable and inevitable; its emergence is built into the misery and contradictions of capitalism. His approach to history can be characterized as a kind of fatalistic anti-pluralism. Every society is soon to be absorbed and transformed by the productive activities, institutions, and social relations of capitalism; and this process would eventually (he thought imminently) create catastrophic, global conditions for a Great Revolution that will usher in a world of social harmony and individual fulfilllment.

For Marx, capitalism is to be the last economic formation built upon domination and exploitation. There is no place for societies to exist outside of this history, beyond the reach of capitalism. In *The Communist Manifesto*, Marx and Engels even go so far as to describe global social integration as an already-accomplished fact: "The bourgeoisie has through its exploitation of the world-market given a cosmopolitan character to production and consumption in every country. . . . In place of the old local and national seclusion and self-sufficiency, we have intercourse in every direction, universal inter-dependence of nations."[40] World history is not understood by Marx as a reflection of social progress, but rather of the progressive immiseration of workers.

There can be no pluralism of social formations when the conditions for revolution are conceived in world-historical terms. It is through the full realization of capitalist forces of production and class antagonisms everywhere in the world that a unified proletariat will be formed and that the right conditions will be reached for world revolution. The rise of global capitalism is part of an unavoidable design; a burgeoning, desperate proletariat dominated by a numerically declining bourgeoisie is the essence of capitalism. The revolutionary transformation of this world order is therefore built into the logic of history. The more capitalism refines its science and technology, extends its reach, and marginalizes workers, the more the world becomes the same, and thus predictable and susceptible to revolutionary change. The global uniformity of social relations that produce exploitation, displacement, and wretchedness make it possible for liberation to be a once-only event. Misery and conditions of liberation advance simultaneously.

In his longing for change, Marx was confronted with a tension between the idea that historical transformation is inevitable and irreversible and his desire to get involved, mix things up, and get the workers going toward their liberation. He partly resolved this by describing revolutionary praxis as a kind of historical midwifery, hastening and possibly easing transformations that, one way or another, had to be faced by everyone. Much of his unpublished writing is directly connected with this task of political midwifery, with moving the workers' parties toward coordinated effort and banishing from workers' programs any sort of political compromise that might dilute their commitment to the permanent revolution. In Marx's and Engels' 1850 Address to the Communist League, for example, the desire to revolutionize every aspect of society for the revolutionary proletariat was, they thought, being thwarted by piecemeal reforms promoted by the democratic petty bourgeois; this non-revolutionary class was actively counteracting the dominion and rapid spread of capital by such measures as restricting rights of inheritance, increasing workers' wages, undertaking charity measures, and in general seeking to achieve a more secure, tolerable, and comfortable existence for workers through democratic reform.[41] Committed communists could have none of this. According to Marx and Engels, the revolutionary potency of the proletariat was being compromised by what amounts to superficial alms giving; the workers' parties must counteract such reformist efforts by demanding, without compromise, measures that would bankrupt capital and that the owners of capital must inevitably refuse, ensuring the failure of democratic reform, deepening of misery, sharpening of class antagonisms, and thereby restoring the promise of imminent world revolution.

Another problem that caused Marx a certain amount of difficulty was the prevalence of rural folk who were stubbornly persistent in securing their smallholdings, maintaining the integrity of communities, interpreting the world with superstitions, acting and thinking in every conceivable way contrary to class consciousness and revolutionary mobilization. He was convinced that the European peasantry was unprepared for revolution, not just organizationally but organically, in the very essence of its being, because each community was a world unto itself, unable to communicate and cooperate with an international movement. He famously characterized the peasantry as being "formed by simple addition of homologous magnitudes, much as potatoes in a sack form a sack of potatoes,"[42] a quality that made it generally unfit for the coordinated efforts of revolutionary mobilization. Conservative peasants, Marx asserted, cannot articulate their own class interest and, if they do act politically, are susceptible to influence by authoritarian pretenders who reassure them that by lending support to just one uprising their lives can go on undisrupted. They can be bribed by the simple promise of being left alone. But insofar as capitalism extends its reach into the countryside, and displaces some of the peasantry into cities, the peasants can be shaken from their stupefied seclusion, led from below rather than dominated from above, can form alliances with workers, and develop a desire to overthrow the old order with new energy.

Europe, however, was not the only, nor the primary source of narrow, conservative rural communities. Marx was also concerned with the "backward," "stagnant" state of Asian societies, in which there was little immediate possibility of capitalist displacement and hence little incentive for peasants to strike out beyond their small social existence. His remarks on India and the Asiatic Mode of Production have spawned an entire corpus of secondary literature, including the observation by Edward Said that, despite his fellow feeling for the poor of Asia, Marx somehow succumbed to the Orientalist fantasy of European colonial mastery. A fragment of Marx's work, unpublished in his lifetime, reveals this sinister side to his vision of Asia: "England has to fulfill a double mission in India: one destructive, the other regenerating – the annihilation of the Asiatic society and the laying of the material foundations of Western society in Asia."[43]

There is no need, however, to connect Marx to the prejudices of nineteenth-century Orientalist scholarship to explain his juxtaposition of human sympathy with such a blatant disregard for India's sovereignty; it is enough to consider his utopian vision, his cataclysmic optimism, his understanding of the conditions necessary for the once-in-world-history end of exploitation and conditions of misery. To Marx, it was necessary for India to westernize and capitalize for the same reason that the European peasantry had to be transformed by capital. All societies had to fit within a single paradigm of world history for the world to be liberated. India, like all other stagnant societies, would need to be colonized because this was the only definitive way to proceed through history: into and out of colonial domination.

A great, final revolution, for Marx, was inevitable, built into the class antagonisms of capitalism. But nobody wants to (or is able to) wait centuries for the moment of liberation. If a proletarian world revolution were soon to occur, the world would have to quickly proletarianize. If the revolutionary vanguard was to be composed of none other than indigent wage earners, and if starkly oppressive, revolution-ripe capitalism was the only possible source of progressive global transformation, then stagnant pre-capitalist forms of production would just have to step up and be immiserated the same as everyone else.

My main goal in this chapter has been to make a single point: the term *globalization* that has found its way into fashion is only the most recent way of conceptualizing an idea that has been around for a very long time – essentially since humans have put pen to paper, and perhaps even before: the possibility of applying human energy to the creation of a world that transcends human differences. This makes it possible to argue that globalization is merely the most recent way of conceptualizing the longstanding process of social integration, that there is no cause for enthusiasm or disquiet over the most recent indications that cultures are disappearing, that civilizations are clashing, and that the many ways of being in the world, including the languages expressing them, are converging. But even if we accept the argument that different societies have intersected and transformed one another for a long time, and that these transformations have long moved in a direction of global integration, there is still something unique about global-ization, something that even goes beyond the pace of change: more than ever before, efforts to resist the forces of social transformation are paradoxically contributing to them. We find this as much in the pro-duction of ideas as in the trenches of political protest and reform. In the next two chapters and in much of what follows I will demonstrate that globalization can in part be defined by a central paradox: the ten-dency for societies to integrate through the very forces that are used to struggle against integration.

3

The Cultural Contradictions of Globalization

Cultural Globalization

The term *globalization* has come to signify so many things that it has become largely devoid of meaning, except perhaps for one thing: it is meaningful for this very variety of expressions and superabundance of content. Most of the ways that globalization is imagined begin with the impacts of science and technology: the speed of communication through satellite transmission, the explosive increase in computer speed, capacity, and availability to consumers and the corresponding increase in content of the Internet archive – these are the things from which globalization is often said to begin. Communication and information technology is what makes international electronic finance possible. It also expands the reach of an American-led cultural revolution, bringing to remote corners of the earth the consumer products and messages of pop-culture: Coca-Cola, McDonald's, MTV, CNN, Microsoft.

Beyond the immediate impacts of the new communication and information technology, the term globalization has come to mean almost any process in which distinct peoples, who possess unique languages and ways of life, are being assimilated into a wider humanity. This process is virtually boundless in its capacity to represent the changing possibilities of social autonomy and individual self-expression. In this sense globalization is very much like the culture concept, a potpourri of intangibles that constitute identity and way of life. Besides applying to the integrating powers of technology, globalization has come to mean the creation of a tradition- and nation-transcending, cosmopolitan way of life. Globalization is a concept that represents the contested visions of a universal identity.

The term globalization is therefore used to represent several distinct things, without any outward distinction being made between them. In the narrowest possible sense (which I discuss further in the next section), it applies to a very recent, electronically unbounded version of free-market economics. And in the widest sense it includes everything associated with the causes and consequences of global "shrinking."

This latter meaning points to a converging shift in the tectonic plates of civilizations, some say toward one basic form of human life. American-led consumer capitalism certainly seems to have a culturally homogenizing power, but this is only part of a much wider process. For some, the rapid pace of change attributed to globalization is a source of almost millenarian hope, an expectation of an end of history, the glittering prize of an integrated, unified, peaceful, and prosperous world order. For others it is alarming, out of control – as captured by the term "runaway world."[1] It builds traditions around a permanent state of uncertainty. This is upper-case Globalization, signifying a force of cultural convergence beyond human control. It is almost a secular source of spiritual awe that rules human fate beyond the reach of petition or salvation.

If we use the integration of formerly closed human worlds as the major criterion for defining and determining the process of globalization, it then becomes impossible to say when the whole process began. A quick overview of European exploration during the few decades that spanned the fifteenth and sixteenth centuries, for example, points clearly to this kind of global integration. When Martin Behaim invented the first globe in 1490 (consisting mostly of terra incognita) he was widely ridiculed, but the basic validity of his construction was soon confirmed: Columbus first traveled to the Caribbean in 1492; Cabot sailed to Labrador (and hence "discovered" the mainland of North America) in 1497, the same year in which Vasco da Gama sailed from Zanzibar to Calcutta, opening a sea route to India; in 1500 Cabral discovered Brazil; and from 1519 to 1522 Magellan performed what some consider the crowning achievement of European exploration – the first circumnavigation of the globe, from Spain to Spain. The first tangible byproducts of these explorations were the things that attracted curious onlookers to the docks of Europe, not only familiar trade items but previously unseen specimens of birds, animals, and humans.[2]

This was by no means the only age that experienced sudden world-shrinking encounters. The task of finding the earliest indications of this development would require us to venture far into prehistory, possibly as far as the first settlement of the globe by our humanoid ancestors. Any new technology of transportation or communication, any political alliance or expansion, becomes a step toward integration. The world has therefore seen major shifts toward (punctuated by retreats from) global integration during at least the last 100 thousand years as societies expanded the scale of their commerce, alliances, and coercion.[3]

Not only have the forces of human integration been pressing forward for a very long time, intellectual reflection on the process has long been part of our world. One strand of this approach to history, of course, was the ideal shared by Christianity and Islam of universal conquest by the one, True Faith; but there have also arisen many secular and not necessarily optimistic versions of the view that humanity is converging upon a point of sameness, that forces beyond the control of individuals, communities, or states are overcoming the variety of human worlds.

A central premise of social thought at least since the early Enlightenment has therefore been the inevitability of humanity merging into a single self. Usually this lifeworld-absorbing power is seen to come from the inherent superiority of European culture or civilization, which will then become a force for the liberation of humanity. Religion and savagery may be well and good, some have said, but *we* have logic, or science, or evolution, or liberty, or psycho-analysis on our side and it will carry us to the terminus of history. It possesses a power greater than all of us. There is no stopping it or modifying its course. Every society that refuses to conform will nevertheless be changed; all peoples will soon resemble each other, whether they like it or not.

If revolutions in the technologies of travel and communication have occurred on occasion since ancient times, if political imperialism forced distinct peoples into closer proximity even before recorded history, and if the related idea of a cosmopolitan global order has a similarly deep pedigree, then what, if anything, is there in current conceptualizations of globalization that makes *this* moment in history different from everything that went before it? This question is occasionally addressed, directly or indirectly, with some permutation of the concept of *de-localization*, encapsulating the idea that a dramatic increase in mobility is transforming the ways that people imagine their place in the world, their spatial and temporal location, their sense of belonging to a home or territory.[4] Although people have always traded, battled, and married with outside others, the accelerated pace and increased distance of interaction through the global reach of modernity is making abstract many of the commonly imported objects and ideas. One way of looking at de-localization stresses the invasion of local space with distant social forces and processes. The volume, pace, and reach of decontextualized culture is cutting people from their familiar moorings. The relationships between cultures and localities have become abstract, "unnatural." People almost everywhere are subjected to intangibles, objects and ideas that lack a definite place or provenance. Public spaces have been transformed to reflect or accommodate boundaryless commerce. The shopping mall and multiplex cinema are quintessential gathering points of global forces.

Another pattern of de-localization occurs more literally: societies are more than ever before being uprooted by economic intrusions and opportunities that lead to migration.[5] Extractive industries have never had a longer reach, either technologically or politically, and are more easily able to displace those who have inconvenient attachments to resource rich territories. There are also strong elements of voluntarism and opportunism involved in migrant labor. Whatever inconveniences nation-states might impose on migrant workers, the perils of travel in search of opportunity are much less today than they were when ruthless warlords and bandits were almost certain to be encountered at some point on an extended journey. Today, the main difficulty facing the would-be migrant, itinerant trader, or pilgrim lies in working and saving for the plane or bus fare. The opening of continents to seasonal or permanent migration has made it possible for the most ambitious and the least privileged alike to pursue opportunity wherever it might be found, usually in far away cities, often across national boundaries. The rapid growth of urbanization, industrialization, and mass communication is bringing tradition and modernity into a forced coexistence and dissolving sharp distinctions between urban and rural culture.[6] Migration is a clear example of de-localization approached as a literal expression of displacement.

The experiences of displacement, indistinction, or "in-betweeness" associated with the migrant experience often lead people to a search for more secure cultural footing by intermingling or self-consciously combining cultural elements to create new systems of meaning and forms of life. This process is sometimes referred to as *hybridization*. The displacements of globalization and the increased proximity of peoples and cultures can result in their combination into a new "hybrid" form, sometimes celebrated as a creative, spontaneous mélange of de-localized cultural ideas, objects, and practices, at other times as a form of "creolized," or "mestizo" identity, a superior type of "peoplehood" derived by grafting discrete cultures into new forms, a process often portrayed as a defiant, hopeful answer to the hegemony of the West.[7] Unfortunately, this approach reposes upon a distasteful, albeit indirect, use of biological metaphor (though one that is given a positive spin) and with it an implicit idea of original cultural purity, with new cultural forms derived from the undistorted genetic codes of their combined sources. If further reason were needed for rejecting such ideas, it can be found in Jean-Loup Amselle's *Mestizo Logics*, which argues – mainly from examples of the ways that African philosophers have used European ethnographic literature to render intelligible the mysteries of their own cultures – that syncretism and indistinctness have always been the essence of human identity.[8] And if there is no such thing as an original, pure culture, then there cannot be a process of hybridization that is uncomplicated by centuries or millennia of cultural exchange, penetration, and flux.

Another approach to hybridity, in my view a more realistic one, emphasizes the discontents of marginalization and the ambiguities of acculturation. Shorn of familiar anchorages, the experience of border life is uncomfortable, resulting in only partial forms of identification, producing ambiguous relationships with space and time in which, as Homi Bhabha writes, "there is a sense of disorientation, a disturbance of direction, in the 'beyond': an exploratory restless movement . . . hither and thither, back and forth," estranged from "any immediate access to an originary identity or a 'received' tradition."[9] Even if all identities are in some ways syncretic and even if there has never been a pure state of cultural being, there *is* a widespread sense of malaise that results from *rejection* of cherished identities (they become cherished largely through such rejection), from efforts to impose ideas, values, and technologies on those seen to be lacking the essential virtues of "civilization." Cultural *métissage* produces a heightened sense of vulnerability among those *subjected to* transition, those who are most likely to invoke strident forms of collective reawakening.

A corollary of de-localization, therefore, is reaction against it, manifested in efforts to rediscover and reestablish lost cultures, to "re-localize" identities in a supposedly original, pure form. Globalization entails not only diasporas and combinations, but an opposite tendency toward the erection of cultural boundaries, to the reclamation and protection of distinct territories and ways of life, sometimes underpinned by distinct rights. A particularly insidious way that people are shaped by distant social forces is through the ideas and strategies they resort to in efforts to protect themselves from external, alien social forces. The ever-closer proximity of peoples and cultures can also be found in strategies of community re-localization that draw upon global institutions and universal ideas of liberation.

The surest way to encourage renewed identity attachments is to disparage or try to suppress them; yet there is no indication that misguided philanthropy, directed toward the flawed cultural attachments of others, has entirely fallen from fashion. The temptation is almost overwhelming among liberals, for example, to see *every* society without formal democracy, without free choice in marriage, without gender equality, or without a system of unbiased justice backed up by punitive incarceration, as somehow a menace to freedom, a blight on modernity to be transformed or excoriated. Never mind that chiefs or councils of elders in most traditional societies cannot do entirely as they please but have informal obligations of "just rule" to their communities,[10] expressed, for example, in the Basotho maxim, "A chief is a chief by the people"[11] and the doctrine of "community consensus" (*ijmā'*) found in some Muslim societies;[12] never mind that this local form of accountability, applied to the state, has acted as a check on state abuses of arbitrary power;[13] and never mind that there are lessons to be learned when societies in transition borrow and adapt, on their own terms, western institutions, health services, and models of social security. Despite such possibilities, the tendency among some human rights activists and development workers (some of whom represent states) is to see human rights as the *only* source of political wisdom or guidance for social action. Everything else is a violation. Societies that consistently violate human rights must change or be changed. Such interventionism has at its disposal a strong justification: in a world of increasing social proximity, the illiberalism and intolerance of one society, no matter how small and seemingly powerless, affects the rights of everyone.

But in a roundabout way, narrow liberal individualism encourages zero-sum conflict in state/minority relations. Those who are oppressed for their failure to integrate feel their distinctiveness all the more sharply; they lobby for recognition; they assert their rights to self-determination and other collective rights equal to or against those of states. And when this leads them nowhere, when their claims are consistently denied, they in turn can become filled with hate and driven further toward an all-consuming collective will.

The liberal emphases on individualism and equality ironically reinforce the urge of nation-states toward cultural and constitutional homogeneity. This serves to justify attempts by states to assimilate or expulse, by force if necessary, those who are distinct and excluded, above all to erase all constitutional exceptions, all special rights protections, all treaties between states and parties *within* the state, all differences enshrined by law. If the goal of rights is to make all citizens equal, distinct rights are anathema. Troublesome identity attachments must be gotten rid of. If legal protections have their ultimate origin in cultural differences, then those clamorous cultures must assimilate, either on their own, in the absence of legal protections, or with the help of "friends." There is often a constitutional, not just philanthropic or spiritual, conviction behind the efforts by states and private missionary organizations to "educate," "uplift," or "develop" those seen to be floundering in darkness.

As we have just seen, nineteenth-century socio-evolutionism was a prominent and in some ways catastrophic version of this kind of convergence hypothesis. It proved a fertile justification for the establishment of overseas colonies, and was vindicated at every turn by the "backwardness" and "depravity" of any society considered to have been left behind by evolutionary progress. Those living in the reign of nature were residual, somehow remaining stagnant, benighted, incomplete, or Asiatic, but soon to be enlightened, uplifted, and absorbed. In North America, Australia, New Zealand, and elsewhere, evolutionism formed unlikely alliances with Christianity in a variety of efforts to assimilate aboriginal societies, vanquished already, it was widely supposed, by the inevitable advance of civilization.

Others from the colonial era took a more culturally self-critical approach. In a career that spanned the late nineteenth to early twentieth centuries, for example, the German sociologist Max Weber saw with great clarity the dark side to guiding forces of modernity. Weber's was the twentieth century's most powerful vision of human social convergence, the idea that something in the very nature of modern society irrevocably changes the way people live and diminishes the contrasts, diversity, and possibilities of social life.[14] The current incarnation of this approach, stripped largely of Eurocentrism, is the idea that the integration and homogenization of social worlds have accelerated dramatically and are leading humanity toward a single type of society with similar uses of technology and bureaucracy, similar family patterns and political arrangements. All that will remain to differentiate people and provide anchorages for identity will be languages and a few reinvented vestiges of cultural ceremony and symbolism. For those who fear collective immersion in the melting pot of history, the only answer is to make their identity indissoluble. But this effort is fraught with contradictions. Even those who want nothing more than a return to community, to the values of small economies, kinship, and personal recognition, are drawn by visions of universal identity.[15] The pull of world culture is not only strong, it is also almost impossible to resist without at the same time giving it more strength.

Weber failed to see (it was impossible from his vantage point before the twentieth century's extensions and explosions of nationalist fervor) the extent to which colonized societies would redefine themselves and occasionally prepare for a fight to the death against the encroachments of modernity. Of course, this had already happened many times over, before and during Weber's time, in largely futile resistance against colonial annexations. What he and those who adhered to his model *really* did not expect, however, was traditional societies' use of the tools of modernity (including, on occasion, its weapons) to effectively defend themselves, to bring together all like-encultured peoples set on maintaining or returning to a "pure" integration of spirituality and the social order in efforts to resist the desecrations of modernity. As an overwhelmingly rational thinker, Weber could not anticipate an anti-rationalist use of rationalism to defend what he saw as non-rational.

The implications of this fact of modernity are only beginning to be felt. One of the historically resonant characteristics of the twentieth century was the widespread discovery by oppressed peoples that imperialism is best shed through use of the entire gamut of powers introduced by the imperialist power. Technology could be accepted piecemeal, while the market forces and mass culture with which it is commonly associated were categorically rejected.

The most obvious and menacing form this kind of revolt against modernity has taken is terrorism – the use of computers, modern methods of organization (members of the al-Qaida network, for example, referred to their organization as "the company" and its leadership as "the general management," terms that invoke multinational corporations), and the most lethal forms of industrial societies' means of destruction that can be deployed. All of this is single-mindedly directed toward bringing down those societies that are the sources of the terrorists' power and bringing about a return to the one True and Pure form of life, simplified by scripture and tradition. The perils of tribal or religiously fanatical ignorance are often seen to stem from the very openness of liberal democracies to diversity and the influx of people from impoverished, war-torn countries around the globe. The loneliness of the migrant experience can lead people toward the cultivation of hatred and a zealous attachment to one choice among cultural possibilities – sometimes taking the form of zealously intolerant religious convictions coupled with radical anti-democracy. Yet the more nation-states respond to domestic anti-westernism (of which terrorism is only the most extreme example) by resorting to restricting immigration and extending the legal limits of surveillance and other police powers, to limiting freedom for the sake of security, the more they give up on the universal rights and freedoms they have sworn to defend, the more they nurture the wounded pride of marginalized communities. Terrorism is a sickness that uses its host's own immune system against it.

But there are many others who have made the commitment to exclude weapons and warfare from the menu of liberation. This does not mean that their desire to preserve distinct ways of life are any less meaningful to them or that they are any less likely to challenge the premises of free market liberalism. Through the strategic limitation of nonviolence, the new traditionalism takes more commonly peaceful, less dramatic, and therefore less noticed forms: through the mechanisms of lobbying and law. When indigenous peoples or tribal minorities make use of state courts and legislative assemblies; human rights instruments, compliance mechanisms, and standard setting procedures; and sophisticated techniques of political lobbying and information campaigning, they are not doing it to forsake their traditional identities but to reinforce them.

This strategy leads inevitably to a number of dilemmas. It is not just that traditional societies are making good use, for their own purposes, of legal formalism; the law itself can be legitimated through irrational hopes; it can repose upon fervent nationalist aspirations of self-actualization, inspired by utopian hopes for a world order brought about through shared values, peace-instilling moral common denominators, the uncorrupted kernels of universal tolerance and love. But these global goals of human rights lead to the convergence of human societies. Human rights are inspired by hopes that far exceed the voices and powers of international treaties. And the specific contents of laws derived from these hopes are forces of global integration every bit as powerful as the autonomous effects of bureaucracy and legal rationality. The integrity of distinct societies is therefore being enthusiastically and innovatively defended using legal mechanisms and standards that act to reduce cultural possibilities.

The cultural contradictions of globalization come out even more clearly when we consider the growing importance of e-democracy in the international dynamics of grievance, resistance, and redress. Direct or indirect access to computers and computer literacy is without question becoming one of the prerequisites for the success of a wide array of resistance campaigns, including those mounted by peasant and hunting-gathering societies. In the first United Nations-sponsored meeting of indigenous peoples that I attended in 1994, laptop computers were a rarity among the indigenous delegations, but in the most recent one that I went to in 2000 they were much more noticeable, and put to good use in printing speeches, press releases, and protest signs on short notice. The success of information campaigns and even street demonstrations has come to depend on the organizational and publicity-enhancing powers of e-mail and the Internet.

But who in village societies has access to this technology and the ability to use it? Despite all that we have heard about the ways that information technology is turning everything upside-down, most of the world's people still go about their daily business without it. Most countries, especially those outside of Western Europe and North America, do not make wide use of information technology. In Mongolia (which I have chosen as an example because it is synonymous with isolation, but is nevertheless not atypical of the so-called developing countries) there are only 0.1 Internet hosts per 1000 people, compared to an average of 158.5 in Europe's Nordic countries, the world's most computer-resourced region.[16] In the remote corners of countries like Mongolia a computer with Internet access is probably something only heard about in pastoral camps, occasionally described by visiting city-dwelling youth over campfires to a bemused audience. And it is this youth living between vastly different environments of nurture and livelihood that is at the forefront of e-democracy among the world's most remote, marginalized, and politically unrepresented peoples. This is a source of great possibilities. It creates new avenues for making community-threatening injustices known to a wide audience, and thereby occasionally becoming *causes célèbres* through the informal politics of shame. Those who understand and make use of this process are often leaders in every sense of the word; but they are not elders in the sense usually understood in their natal communities. The growing importance of e-democracy elevates the status of a formally educated elite. Members of this elite may grow old, and may even acquire local power, but they will not grow to be elders, or if they do, the knowledge that they transmit to succeeding generations will be vastly different from that given to them by their parents and grandparents. The foundations of local identity, transmission of knowledge, and political authority have been changed by the need of nearly every subsistence-oriented people to acquire access to the technological powers of dominant societies. Without these powers, isolated communities more easily fall prey to the depredations of states and international industry. But even with them, distinct societies are fundamentally and irrevocably altered by being brought into closer proximity with both the menace and sympathy of an expanded outside world.

So the forces of social convergence are the same as those of reconstituted, distinct identities. The essence of modernity is not captured by the insidious progress of bureaucratic legitimacy as much as by the increasingly common experience of diaspora, of living in an unfriendly, uncomfortable social world, brought about by migration or the encroachments of "others" into one's own unprotected realm, and by the growing (or increasingly felt) need to protect oneself from these encroachments with the technology and knowledge of the encroachers. Defending against the unwelcome intrusions of industries, peoples, and cultures calls especially for a reinforcement of social boundaries and a reconstitution (or invention) of the warmth, color, and comfort of the old order. Convergence stimulates and empowers a contrary movement toward cultural neo-conservativism; and the architects of tradition make creative use of the sympathies, technologies, and ideas of those to whom they are drawn into closer proximity.

Free Trade Globalization

There is another, more specific conception of globalization, which often sees it as powerful and dangerous but not quite as multifaceted and invulnerable as the upper-case form. *Free trade globalization* is the view of world integration that begins with the growth of capitalism, the extended reach and power of corporations and their international support institutions. In the ideal global culture of free trade there are no nations or peoples. The world, as described with great prescience by Paddy Chayefsky through the voice of a fictional CEO in the screenplay for the 1976 film *Network*, "is a college of corporations, inexorably determined by the immutable laws of business . . . one vast and ecumenical holding company for which all men will work to serve a common profit, in which all men will hold a share of the stock, all necessities provided, all anxieties tranquilized, all boredom amused."[17] In the form it sometimes takes in non-fictional advocacy, free trade is presented as the ultimate answer to the major ills created by nation-states: poverty, tyranny, and bloodshed. By creating prosperity and a thriving middle class that depends for its affluence on international commerce, it creates at the same time the social conditions for resistance to narrow, nationalist authoritarianism. It is considered, in other words, a politically and technically achievable source of prosperity, democracy, and peace – but only if the barriers to it erected by lobbies pursuing narrow environmental and social agendas can be lowered.

This has become the globalization of pundits and protesters, the intellectual turf of the so-called Seattle generation with its rejection of a world order fueled by a hegemonic alignment of capitalism and politics (national and international) that fails to address basic problems of security and social justice. Those who perceive and oppose this form of globalization include, sometimes in uneasy alliances, environmentalists, trade unionists, and human rights activists, as well as a sprinkling of uncontrolled independents who simply take pleasure in mayhem. Travel and communication have made it possible for youth to see, often first hand, the backwaters of human misery, and to receive the calling of compassion. They are also to some degree motivated by the conviction that globalization is not inevitable; its worst aspects can at the very least be brought under control. If globalization is little more than a regime of corporate excess and unholy alliances, it can perhaps be vanquished. There is a way back to community and a way forward to prosperity.

For Pierre Bourdieu, those who unquestioningly accept the use of the term "globalization" in the context of deregulated markets are being subtly deceived. Globalization is a myth, an idea with social force used to ratify and glorify a radical, unfettered capitalism "with no other law than that of maximum profit."[18] It is part of a broad campaign of misinformation, a "symbolic drip-feed," expressed through compliant or complicit journalism aimed at strengthening the idea that there is no reasonable alternative to neo-liberal free market capitalism and its erosion of the European welfare state. David Harvey, arguing along the same lines, finds that the term "globalization" originated quite simply in efforts to legitimate the deregulation of financial markets. The term was possibly first used in an American Express advertising campaign in the mid-1970s, then spread widely and was applied to the purpose of liberating markets from state control, becoming "a central concept . . . associated with the brave new world of globalizing neoliberalism."[19] Free trade, however, is not a spontaneous outgrowth of global convergence. It requires careful cultivation by nation-states and transnational organizations. The aura of inevitability associated with the global convergence hypothesis is being applied to a set of economic and cultural policies that are far from inevitable, or that become so only through political intervention or inaction. Thus, "globalization" implies a conspiracy of teleological inevitability that thwarts or channels the energies of resistance to capitalism, smothering the critical meaning inherent in words like "Colonialism," "Imperialism," and "Empire" with a bland, corrupting value-neutrality.

Bourdieu and Harvey fail to note, however, that the neutrality of the term globalization, far from dampening protest against neoliberal excess, appears to have encouraged it by establishing a broadly accepted terrain of debate. Those who have rallied a resistance movement around the term clearly do not accept it as a representation of inevitability. The international structure of trade liberalization is just that – a *structure* that can be traced to the post World War II planning at Bretton Woods, which led to the creation of the World Bank and the International Monetary Fund (IMF). If globally deregulated markets were inevitable, they would not require justification or boardroom planning; they would simply be a fact of modernity. Free trade is made possible by globalization, but it is not globalization itself. It is refutable and opposable.

There is another side to this conceptual appropriation, one that centers on the term *antiglobalization*. If free trade globalization is somehow associated with the wider, upper-case Globalization, with the march of time and historical inevitability, if it is in fact the remote, inaccessible *deus absconditus* of unstoppable modernity, then those who oppose it must be out of step with the rest of the world. They must be conservative in the sense of being inflexibly attached to things as they are and unwilling to accept inevitable change. This view is reflected in the term occasionally used in the conservative Spanish-language press: *globalfóbicos*. The "antiglobalization" protesters are therefore implicitly seen as actively resistant to everything that contributes to a new and (if not for them) inevitable global reality.

None of the many groups and interests that have participated in the so-called antiglobalization protests, however, have consistently shown themselves to be resistant to globalization in this broad sense. The term "antiglobalization" is a misnomer. There is nothing to indicate that they are against all manner and method of global integration. In point of fact, most are every bit as much products of global networking and integration as the IMF, the World Bank, or the World Trade Organization (WTO). The most effective international nongovernmental organizations (NGOs) have a strong international flavor and could not exist, or at least not function effectively, were it not for their frontierless networking and representation of interests. No interest group in the world today is unambiguously opposed to globalization (in the broad sense) or unambiguously in support of it. Insofar as the contests over globalization are more than semantic distortions, they are about how the new powers of a rapidly integrating world are to be defined, used, and controlled, and by whom. So it is not quite true that those who protest the workings of global capitalism reject globalization. They are often rejecting only a specific version of globalization. The contest is more about the conditions, or the form of life, to be created by world integration than whether or not integration is to occur.

Those demonstrating at the police barricades of international summits seem to be largely motivated by a longing to see greater democracy in the highest reaches of international and supranational power. According to a recent account of the grievances expressed in the streets of Genoa, "this new order has no democratic institutional mechanisms for representation, as nation-states do; no elections, no public forums for debate."[20] Global institutions have, according to this view, far overextended their legitimate reach, making global governance an extension of the interests and actions of states and multinational corporations, even, according to some, making up an unprecedented global empire, unresponsive to the influence of democracy. And it is not only apologists for the "antiglobalization" movement who have called for greater effectiveness and transparency in the structures of global capitalism. George Soros, a prominent international financier, has questioned the inequities and injustices inherent in international commerce, taken issue with blind faith in market forces, and called for open regulation of market forces;[21] and Joseph Stiglitz, a Nobel Prize-winning economist and former chief economist of the World Bank, similarly argues for well chosen government interventions in international commerce and has sharply criticized the IMF for misguided, uninformed engagement with inadequate markets and unworkable institutions, narrow belief in the efficiency of free markets, and abandonment of its original Keynesian goal of maintaining high levels of employment through the course of intervention in undeveloped national economies. Stiglitz concludes that, "we have come to take for granted the important role that an informed and free press has in reining in even our democratically elected governments. . . . Transparency is even more important in public institutions like the IMF, the World Bank, and the WTO, because their leaders are not elected directly. Though they are public, there is no *direct* accountability to the public. But while this should imply that these institutions be even more open, in fact, they are even less transparent."[22]

Since the grievance that many international NGOs share is their lack of access to the decision-making processes of the major institutions of global capitalism, therefore, they can perhaps be more accurately described as *global enfranchisement* activists. This terminology has several advantages. Because it focuses on the central point of contention surrounding economic globalization rather than implying a point of view that few might actually hold, it allows us to see the protest movement without needless distortion. At the same time, it exposes contradictions between specific positions taken by some enfranchisement activists and the theoretical approaches to oppression and liberation that they start with, in particular between their immediate goal of securing institutional representation and their adoption of philosophical positions that minimize the utility of piecemeal change and democratic process.

If the human rights abuses of states tend to cluster around the misuse of power and failures in the administration of justice, those of multinational corporations – products of intensified forms of competition and merger that former German chancellor Helmut Schmidt refers to as "predatory capitalism"[23] – tend toward indecent forms of labor exploitation and environmental conquest. The social-Darwinian struggle for economic survival in the new world economy has intensified through global integration, largely because of the ability of some corporations to tap new and cheaper labor markets, in which the lower barriers to exploiting children, imposing long work hours, and offering low wages, poor social benefits, or no benefits at all, provide a considerable edge over those who rely upon workers whose rights to decent conditions and remuneration are comparatively better respected.

The same accountability vacuum applies to environmental issues. Transnational corporations, implementing large scale projects usually sanctioned or initiated by states, hold no legally enforced international responsibility for the imposition of these projects on relatively powerless peoples and communities whose livelihood depends upon their own uses of their own lands. Extractive forestry, mining, oil and gas, and hydroelectric projects that encroach upon traditional uses of land are major sources of population displacement and collective trauma. This encroachment sometimes includes misappropriation of intellectual property, use of the medicines, plants, technology, and genetic material of distinct peoples – property holders – without providing them with compensation, revenue sharing, or other immediate benefits of commercial development.

The most significant challenge posed by multinational corporations is not that they occasionally commit abuses – one would expect that where there is a law, any law or any moral standard, there will be violations of it. The real challenge is that they are beyond reach through the usual channels of democratic reform and largely untouchable by effective sanction. That which often commands the attention of anti-globalization activists is the cavalier attitude that these "non-state actors" tend to take toward human rights and environmental standards in conjunction with the actual abuses some commit, justifying almost any of their actions as necessary for "development" and turning to ineffectual agencies as their sources of accountability. They are largely immune from the politics of embarrassment. Multinational corporations are mobile, almost by definition, so that even if embarrassment is caused by human rights activists or limits are set by states or U.N. agencies in one part of the world, they can relatively easily pull up stakes and go to where the grass is browner.

Serious defense of electronic neoliberalism from those who welcome world market deregulation and who see it as the only way to fully achieve the prizes of modernity has only recently come into full view. To the few who have taken on this challenge, the protestors are "kids" suffering the delusions and overzealousness of youth. For free trade advocates, globalization in the realm of multinational corporations is not the cause of misery in the backwaters of the world economy; it is the solution to it. The discontents of globalization are not a product of world integration, but of the fact that it is incomplete. To extend the benefits of commerce through the arm of capitalism, markets must be liberated, trade deregulated, the logic of classic free-trade economists (such as Adam Smith, David Ricardo, and Friedrich von Hayek) realized to the fullest extent possible. Antiglobalizationist activism from this perspective is therefore not just an error-laden inconvenience; it stands directly in the way of capitalism's ability to fulfill the dream of world progress and prosperity. It pressures governments and intergovernmental organizations to impose limits, vicariously encourages markets to close, throttles down development and, no doubt unintentionally, increases the world's burden of poverty.

Free trade liberalism outwardly takes a position of embracing globalization, characterizing it as historically and economically inevitable. But it is in fact every bit as hostile toward legal limits and control of its central values and activities by global institutions as the so-called anti-globalization movement. This hostility is largely hypothetical, mainly because free trade has advanced toward influencing the agendas of global institutions to a historically unprecedented degree. If global institutions were to create effective limitations on the activities of global corporate ventures, however, free trade advocates (if they were to argue consistently with their rejection of state interferences) would vehemently oppose them, no matter what form they took or what constituency they were intended to protect. Like Spencer, but facing a wider range of both possibilities and possible limitations, today's free trade movement is deeply hostile to effective control of global capitalism through global governance.

There is a fundamental reluctance among apologists of free trade to underpin market liberalization with national or international legislation intended to apply human rights or environmental standards to corporate entities. "No NGO or government," Jagdish Bhagwati declaims, "has the wisdom or the right to lay down what corporations must do."[24] Corporate ethics are best influenced informally, through moral suasion, through the very market forces that give capitalism life. In *Free Trade Today*, Bhagwati reiterates this argument, "[A] good tongue lashing, based on evaluations that are credible, impartial, and unbiased, can push a country into better policies through shame, guilt, and the activities of NGOs that act on such findings."[25] In his view, therefore, the NGOs, which he claims lack both the wisdom and the right to lay down the limits to corporate behavior, are expected to provide "tongue lashings" to influence the behavior of countries, which, as he argues elsewhere, have no place trying to influence corporate ethics.

This kind of inconsistency is also evident in debates over the parameters of global capitalism in the form of a tendency to assign responsibility for upholding the social and moral agendas of production and trade to agencies that, while overburdened with new responsibilities, are contemptuously delegitimated and under-resourced. The International Labour Organization is perhaps the clearest example of an agency that has received the burgeoning responsibilities associated with investigating and mediating labor practices worldwide, without the means or legitimacy to fulfill its mandate. At a 1996 ministerial meeting in Singapore, the WTO membership asserted that it lacked the institutional expertise and resources to deal with labor issues that were properly the concerns of the International Labour Organization (ILO).

(This was also the upshot of the North-South dispute in the 2002 World Trade Organization meeting in Dubai, United Arab Emirates – an indication that the issue had reached a point of stalemate.) Yet the ILO is widely recognized as being relatively powerless to check the abuses of large corporations. At the outset, its tripartite structure of State, Industry, and Labor puts the onus on labor organizations to initiate complaints; and those who are the victims of the worst labor abuses are not always in a position to organize themselves in an effective way. Although the ILO oversees more than 180 conventions covering a wide range of labor practices and rights, very few of them have been ratified by all or even most ILO members. The United States, consistent with its unilateralism on a wide range of human rights issues, has signed only 14 of them.[26] And even if the ILO were to secure wider ratification of its conventions, it lacks the mandate to impose meaningful sanctions on those who violate them. It relies instead on behind-the-scenes persuasion and mediation, processes invisible to those who seek concrete signs of progress achieved through a balancing of powers.

According to the "moral suasion" argument, no matter how much we may be moved by the plights of those who appear to be the victims of untrammeled capitalism, legislation against corporate behavior ultimately has an adverse effect on individual liberty; it limits economic growth, limits the earning and spending power of individuals, and therefore limits human freedom and prosperity. Just such an argument (reported on the Internet by a scandalized representative of the Center for Science in the Public Interest and later reported in *Le Monde Diplomatique*) was made in an address by the Brazilian foreign minister (of a government that has since suffered electoral defeat) to a March 2000 meeting at the Cordell Hull Institute in Washington, D.C., with its 50 participants consisting mainly of civil servants, ministers, ambassadors, and advisors to business. The minister, to general applause, defended child labor in Brazil; the children earning a few *reales* by hauling bags of coal from depot to steelworks, he argued, were providing their families with a supplementary income that helped them out of even worse poverty.[27] But if members of human rights NGOs were outraged by this unofficial Brazilian position on child labor, Bhagwati has gone further, openly applying the issue of child labor to his advocacy of free trade. The objections raised by "industrial" or "northern" nations against the practice of child labor in the "south" are, according to Bhagwati, merely "cynical exploitation of moral issues for de facto protectionism."[28] Trade sanctions only increase the immiseration of those families that require children to work, furthering the likelihood that they will resort to more desperate means, including prostitution, to secure income. He rightly points to the need for a broad strategy, one that ensures schooling for children and a minimum living standard for their families, but fails to explain how this sensible approach necessarily excludes a Marshall Plan style of intervention, or even sanctions. For Bhagwati, bad PR should be the only thing between children and the steel works, or more generally between the easily dominated and those forms of exploitation that resemble the abuses of an earlier age of unregulated capitalism, the glory days for which Herbert Spencer felt nostalgia.

In this context it is worth remembering that the United Nations Convention on the Rights of the Child, entered into force in 1990, is the most widely ratified treaty in the world, with one hundred and ninety states becoming parties to it by 1994. If the advocates of free trade express such unwillingness to comply with the most fundamental principles of the most widely ratified human rights treaty protecting children, the world's weakest and least represented people, what hope can there be that nation-states and their corporate partners will commit themselves to human rights in general, to other rights held by those who fall into other categories of the weak and marginalized?

Free trade liberals attempt to extend their carefully reasoned rejections of economic chauvinism, protective tariffs, and the global tangle of regional trade agreements to a more general rejection of all limitations on the activities of international capitalism. They confuse free trade with a more sweeping deregulation of large corporations. This evinces a skewed understanding of freedom, one that sees it as the absence of all effective restraint on the behavior of multinationals, a kind of corporate existentialism, beyond the petty reasoning and limitations of established morality. This goes to show that the macroeconomic transformations of production and trade can be measured with the precision of natural science, while entirely overlooking the implications of human attachments to spirituality, culture, and identity. A narrow focus on market dynamics leads to a disregard for the diversity of, and will toward, human self-development.[29]

Ideas that are broadly Spencerist in orientation are therefore flourishing in a new climate of capitalist deregulation. Just as Spencerism resolved the contestations of human differences – differences that were magnified and given wide importance by Victorian era colonial ventures – in favor of unalterable laws of evolution, modern free trade theory has no answer to the socio-cultural dislocations of economic globalization other than the need to submit to them. But free trade is not only about macroeconomics; it is also about the choices available for culture and group identity.[30] Clearly there are limits to the ability of indigenous and tribal societies, rural communities, participants in alternative lifestyles, or even old-fashioned cultural conservatives to shelter themselves from the reach of economic globalization.

The Spencerist resemblances to the current advocacy of free trade and capitalist deregulation illuminate the fervor of anti-globalization activists and widen the scope of those who could, especially in conditions of non-materializing or dwindling prosperity, join forces with them. Even in conditions of growth (and by strictly economic measures this would surely include periods of colonial expansion), social and moral agendas have a habit of placing greater value on immediate yearnings for dignity, freedom from servitude, and self-determination than the more remote, less inspiring hopes for market growth.

It could well be that there is no answer to the socio-cultural dislocations of modernity. It is plausible, if not entirely convincing, to argue that there is no escape from certain forces of social convergence. But this does not mean that the social transitions resulting from globalization are seamless, benign, and uneventful. It is either profoundly naïve or supremely irresponsible to take the Panglossian position that everything resulting from free trade is for the best, that the competitive individualism of free enterprise will effortlessly override the atavistic and authoritarian values of traditional societies, that all enlightened men and women will inevitably develop a commitment to deregulated capitalism as the path to their prosperity.

Such faith in the innocence of the social transformations of modernity is entirely misplaced. It is not the success of social and civil resistance to globalization that should be of concern to us, but its failure: an unreformed global economy that feeds an increase of misery and wounded pride and the reduction of strategic options to alleviate them.[31] Given the profound attachments of many peoples to ways of life that are in harm's way of capitalist ventures, and given the prevalence of systems of values that are fundamentally at odds with consumer culture, confidence in the possibility of a smooth and democratic transition to market deregulation appears unwarranted. It underestimates above all the zeal behind defenses of local or regional self-determination – sometimes taking the form of an irrational preference to be ruled by a familiar tyrant than by an unfamiliar, unreceptive, unpetitionable stranger who may act with a view to the greater good.

The two most common conceptualizations of globalization that I have just outlined – one that approaches it as a process of almost irrevocable cultural convergence and the other as a process and set of institutions that underpin a minimally regulated system of global capitalism – are of course not at all mutually exclusive. The social dislocations and obstructions that sometimes follow from free trade economics are a fundamental aspect of global cultural realignments. And a central flaw in the thinking behind many of the justifications and arrangements of free trade is a failure to go beyond purely economic concerns, to include considerations of identity and yearnings for a life of autonomous simplicity.

4

(Anti)Globalization from Below

The Dilemmas of Resistance

Globalization can refer to both powerful forces of social integration and to the internationalization of resistance to those forces. Correspondingly, there can be two distinct but complementary ethnographic approaches to the social and cultural forces of global convergence. One approach is to investigate those forces that produce victims of globalization, to concentrate on the dislocating or de-embedding consequences of loss of land and local subsistence through the aggressions of agribusiness and resource extraction, to simultaneously examine state-sponsored programs of cultural assimilation, and then to consider the resulting misery, migration, diaspora, and cultural hybridization of those who are the casualties of change.

The other approach – the one that I have chosen for this chapter – is to look more exclusively at the international opposition to these global forces: the avenues of transnational civil society, the creation of networks that connect lobby groups, the erection of globally similar social boundaries and patterns of exclusivism. On occasion we can see this kind of opposition take the form of lobbying in the United Nations and its satellite agencies, principally the International Labour Organization, the World Health Organization and the Organization of American States. Such open lobbying for cultural protection has been pursued mainly by nongovernmental organizations in efforts to make the plight of distinct societies more public, and ultimately to change the relationships between these societies and the states and industries that dominate them.

Even if we agree that the peoples and cultures of the world are being brought irrevocably into ever-closer proximity and that something that might be called a global culture is emerging, there is still no evidence that those distinct peoples that face the greatest dislocation through cultural convergence are willing to accept the choice of being uprooted or living on the margins of a state or civilization. Many of these marginalized people are the hunters, farmers, and pastoralists who, despite formidable obstacles, remain attached to remote territories and subsistence economies. States and industries often have designs for their land and strip them of their rights or frame their rights in such a way that they have no choice but to lose their way of life. Pressures on local economies increase the appeal of migration. Migrant labor, in turn, increases the distance, literally and figuratively, between family members, substituting the nuclear household of husband, wife, and children for extended networks of kinship and patronage.[1] Wage labor in formal economies is making inroads into autonomous subsistence and many distinct societies are losing the economic and social foundations of their distinctiveness, leaving only the symbolic husks of "invented traditions."

These economic and social pressures are the most visible indicators of globalization, but the inescapability of a deep level of cultural ambiguity also arises from a less apparent paradox of modernity: it has become nearly impossible to effectively assert community values without recourse to ideas with global reach, directed toward an international audience. To stand against the forces of convergence, distinct peoples must be "heard," the attractiveness of their way of life must be communicated to an audience of sympathizers, and their leaders must be prepared to make a case for cultural preservation, even if this involves a campaign that immerses their people further into dominant cultures and international orders. Within the constraints of this dilemma there are choices to be made. The assertion of distinctiveness can be made through channels that reject difference, exploit intolerance, and work against the interests of wider pluralism, or it can be made through compromise, cultural brokerage, forging wide-ranging alliances, and acting on a collective willingness to change through negotiated peace.

As with all contrasts of this kind, of course, there are shades of gray and colorful exceptions, but in this chapter I still want to briefly take a step back from my central concern with social theory, to describe several examples of counter-globalization activism, which illustrate the mobilization of international defenses for community values, and the liberal and illiberal forms this can take. In one example, I will draw upon experience I had some twenty years ago trying to understand and explain a radical Islamic reform movement in a village society in Mali, West Africa.[2] And by way of comparison, I will discuss the creative uses of democratic values and electronic media by those who sometimes refer to themselves as "indigenous peoples."

Defiant Islam

The greatest difficulties that followed from a decision that I made early in my career to try to understand a radical Islamic reform movement in Mali, West Africa had little to do with securing the cooperation of the movement's leadership, gaining access to the reformist communities, or overcoming the suspicions and hostilities of the movement's followers (although these hurdles were not negligible). They had more to do with confronting the wider prejudices against the reformers and against the project of understanding them. In the current climate of inter-civilizational tensions, these prejudices are more salient than ever. There are some readers of my work who, caught up in the War against Terror and the fervor of dismantling anti-western dictatorships in the Arab world, would dismiss out of hand any effort to sympathetically understand an Islamic movement. Others would be unreceptive to such a project for quite another reason: they might see it a part of a tradition of Orientalist scholarship that constructs hegemonic stereotypes in the interests of colonialist or imperialist domination. I am aware of the strong feelings that sometimes accompany such views. But, in this case at least, I would argue that the interests of peace are not served by willful ignorance.

My decision to pursue this project was prompted in part by a memorable visit in 1984 to the Songhay village of Dar al-Salam, located on the northeast portion of the Niger Bend in the Republic of Mali. (This proved to be the first of many visits I was to make with the Muslim reformers of Gao and its surrounding villages during the ten months that I spent in Mali.) Several weeks before my departure, I had made a written request in Arabic (making painstaking use of a dictionary) for a meeting with the central leadership of a reform movement called the Jama'a Ansar al-Sunna, the "community of helpers of the Sunna." As it happened, the movement's Imam, Abu Amra Saīd ibn Idrīs, or Seydu Idrissa as he was commonly known, was impressed with my ability to write in Arabic, especially my careful handwriting, which one of my teachers at Cambridge had compared to that of a meticulous Arab schoolgirl. Seydu Idrissa promptly sent me an invitation for a one-week visit Dar al-Salam, the "capital" of the Ansar community.

I was to travel by canoe across the Niger River, and was given a time and place of departure. The two men who met me at our rendezvous point on the shore wore similar clothing and trimmed their beards identically, in the style that has since become famous in depictions of the Taliban of Afghanistan (based on the same sources and interpretations of *hadīth*, the sayings of the Prophet Muhammad). As they poled and paddled our canoe, they sang praise songs to the Prophet, the only music allowed to them. The waters of the river were low and we walked the last half-mile to the village on hard-packed ground that in years of normal rain would have been fields of millet and sorghum. On our arrival in the village a crowd of boys gathered (girls and women were strictly secluded behind walled compounds), apparently outwardly curious about my appearance, touching my skin, hair, and clothing, until they were scolded and chased away. I was offered an apology by one of the men, with the explanation that the boys had never before seen an *anasara*, a European, and were understandably curious.

This last was a puzzling piece of information because the village was located on the shore of the Niger River only a few miles downstream from Gao, an administrative center with a population of more than 30,000. It was less than a mile from a busy cable ferry that serviced the only road to the southern cities. How could the children have avoided seeing at least a few of the many Europeans who traveled in and out of Gao, including a regular traffic of aid workers and, on occasion, a noisy, carnivalesque, dust-raising influx of competitors in the Paris–Dakar rally?

As I was later to learn, Dar al-Salam had been built some fifteen years previously and had ever since been largely closed off from the outside world. Its houses were the same kind of one-story, flat-roofed, adobe constructions common throughout sub-Saharan Africa, almost all of which were surrounded by high mud walls that provided compounds for secluded women. The mosque, a large, square building in the center of the village, was similarly flat-roofed and unornamented, with no minaret, only a set of stairs to the roof from whence the muezzin made his calls to prayer. The boys' madrasa, or religious school, was situated across a sandy thoroughfare not far from the main entrance of the mosque. It consisted of a long building divided into three small classrooms, each furnished with rough-hewn benches and tar blackboards. A long-delayed girls' madrasa on the opposite side of the mosque stood only in a low outline of unfinished mud-brick walls.

A catalyst for the development of Wahhabi-inspired reform in Gao had occurred in 1969, when the Busia government of Ghana deported over 200,000 migrants, establishing a trend in the direction of economic nationalization and xenophobia. The expulsions had brought about a sudden influx of returned migrants to the villages of the Gao region, some of whom had developed contacts with Middle Eastern centers of learning and built a movement of strict Islamic piety in the *zongos*, the immigrant neighborhoods of Accra and Abidjan.[3] It was at this time that Seydu Idrissa, who was to become the founder and leader of the Jama'a Ansar al-Sunna, shifted the focus of his preaching and proselytization from the cities of Ghana to the area surrounding his natal village of Kadji, five kilometers south of Gao. In the years immediately following the expulsion from the southern cities, Seydu Idrissa led an organized effort to base the religion of the villages on a scriptural model of Islam. This involved a rejection of the veneration of local clerics, the use of amulets containing verses of the Quran and other divinatory and protective practices using scriptures (so-called Islamic magic), propitiation of minor jinns and spirits, and spirit possession ceremonies.[4] The most conservative clerics of Saudi Arabia were to be the main source of inspiration for their restricted vision of the community of the faithful.[5]

Since the founding of Dar al-Salam, only adult men traveled regularly to Gao, and even then they never went alone. Solitary travel, even to distant fields, was forbidden. Failure to pray in a group for each of the five daily prayers was punishable, I was told, by confinement in a one-room "prison" on the outskirts of the village. The routines of village life never brought children into contact with a world that was seen to be corrupt, impure, and dangerous, especially to those who lacked the spiritual armature to withstand its temptations.

The reformers seemed to be spurning the influence of the West as much as they were building a spiritually pure community. They offered a rigid orthodoxy based on an Arab Wahhabi model that was intended to reinforce not just strict Islamic monotheism but also those community values that come under greatest pressure from mobility and uncensored ideas. This orthodoxy especially emphasized reliance on elders, which followed, in part, from the strict seclusion of women and the need for arranged marriages.

This is not to say that the village reformers refused all innovation or "progress." Their willingness to invite me, a curious non-Muslim, to their main village was indication enough of a readiness to take advantage of new opportunities. The same cautious adaptability was applied more broadly. They usually rejected cultural innovation, but gave technology careful consideration. In accordance with *ḥadīth*, photographs and representational art of any living beings were forbidden, and I was told in no uncertain terms to put away my camera when there were people around; but when it came to the prosperity of the villages, the reformers tended to be more accommodating. The Ansar communities were more experimental with crop selection, agricultural methods, and the organization of labor than their non-reformist neighbors. During the 1984–85 drought year, for example, they attempted (in vain as it turned out) larger rice crops than most other communities; they planted vegetables on a larger scale; and they even, in a radical departure from agricultural orthodoxy, planted an experimental potato crop, irrigated with a gas-powered pump, as an alternative staple to the failing rice and millet. The Ansar established a social network of cooperation, with Tuesdays set aside for community projects and collective labor. This was important in mitigating the marginal agricultural conditions of northern Mali, increasing the ability of member communities to survive environmental disaster. The willingness of the reformers to depart from Songhay tradition in efforts to improve conditions in the villages also went beyond agriculture, to acceptance of wider medical knowledge, even though this sometimes required overcoming the impediments of their commitment to female seclusion. When Médicins sans Frontières (Doctors Without Borders) conducted prenatal and childbirth classes in Gao, the women of the town were joined by two very diligent men from Dar al-Salam, who then returned to their village with detailed notes.

The main thrust of the reform movement, however, was toward isolation from the world, not just the strict seclusion and veiling of women, but withdrawal of entire communities or neighborhoods from the influence of the outside world and above all from rival neighbors. When Seydu Idrissa was at the peak of his missionary fervor in the early 1970s, he ordered Dar al-Salam (ironically meaning "dwelling of peace") to be built beside the original settlement at Kadji, with a space of about fifty yards between the two. Soon, about thirty villages along the eastern side of the Niger bend followed suit by almost literally drawing lines in the sand, establishing separate neighborhoods or communities that only the faithful were to enter. This fracturing of the villages, in fact, was not conducive to peace, as the name Dar al-Salam seemed to hopefully suggest, but created simmering resentment among the non-reformist villagers that occasionally erupted in violent (though not, to my knowledge, fatal) confrontations. The divisions were seen by the non-reformers as constituting an attack upon the beliefs and practices that were a foundation of their lives, a palpable rejection of all that they considered sacred and important, and a willful division of families between members who joined the ranks of the reform movement and those who stayed in the old villages.

This physical removal was understood by the reformers to be a *hijra* – a migration from the abode of the unfaithful to the abode of religion modeled on the prophet Muhammad's exodus from Mecca to Medina. Many who joined the Ansar completely cut themselves off from their families, even from aged parents who, in other circumstances, would be venerated as elders. In many families, even informal contact between family members of opposite camps became sporadic or ceased altogether. Rival kinsmen did not attend one another's funerals and the reformers established separate burial grounds so that the virtuous dead would lie only with the faithful while awaiting judgment.

Seydu Idrissa and other leaders of the reform group whom I talked to acknowledged the division of families and communities, and defended it as a necessary aspect of a correct observance of the faith. The religious primer *Mubādī al-Islām* (The manifest in Islam), many copies of which were left in the village by a delegation visiting from Saudi Arabia, summarized some of the teachings of the seventeenth-century reformer, Abd al-Wahhab, and became a source of the reformers' conviction that in abandoning their "unbelieving" family members, they were correctly observing the faith: "Whoever bears obedience to the Prophet and testifies to the unity of God," the *Mubādī* exhorted, "should not cherish those who deny God and his Messenger, even if they are his nearest kin."[6]

The drought year of 1984–85 was heavy with the frustration and suffering brought about by poor harvests, hunger, and the tensions provoked by religious dissention. Invective was one of the ways that this frustration found an outlet, as well as a way that the boundaries between factions were sharpened. For the reformers, the non-reformists were simply *kāfir*, "infidels," or *mushrik*, "polytheists," or *murtadd*, "apostates." There was nothing more to say, no more biting words to use. The non-reformist verbal arsenal was a bit more colorful. Initially, they called the reformers *"wahhabantye,"* the Songhay equivalent of "Wahhabi" or "followers of Wahhab," but this term lost its sting when many reformers began to consider it a more or less fitting summation of the main source of their religious allegiance. The most biting term of abuse used by non-reformers was *"alhawarintye,"* "those who follow their desires," a term that carried implications of promiscuity. "Those who follow their desires" were unable to control their sexual impulses and therefore needed to cloak their abnormal passion behind the veil of female seclusion, religious secrecy, and closed communities. The lighthearted scandalmongering among non-reformers often included stories of wife-swapping, adultery, and the licentiousness of "The Marabout" (Seydu Idrissa), whose appetite was said to be appeased only by his choice from among the village women who paraded naked before him after the Friday prayer. The significance of these stories, which circulated freely at least as far as Bamako, lies in the fact that they portrayed the reformers, and especially their leader, as hypocrites. Besides assuaging the pain of a major social rift, the stories exonerated non-reformist Muslims of accusations of improperly observing the faith.

For his part, Seydu Idrissa also offered a more practical form of invective. Summoned to Bamako in 1985 to attend a meeting arranged by the Malian government's Association Malien Pour l'Unité et le Progrès de l'Islam (AMUPI) in an effort to ease tensions in the Songhay villages, he insulted his hosts by refusing to eat food that was offered him, explaining that the meat it contained was slaughtered by infidels who only outwardly professed Islam, and therefore did not meet the requirements of his halal diet. He could not have found a better way to scuttle efforts at reconciliation.

Early in the development of the Ansar, this kind of defiance had brought the reform movement up against the limits of state tolerance. In 1974 Seydu Idrissa and about forty of his followers were arrested, publicly paraded, and flogged in the Place de l'Indépendance, a sandy terrain in the administrative district of Gao. They were given prison sentences of between six months and three years, to be served in Kidal prison, at a military outpost in the Sahara desert some 250 miles north of Gao, one of those terrible places that are virtually inescapable because of unforgiving surroundings. When I met him, Seydu Idrissa was still under a kind of house arrest in which he was not allowed to travel anywhere outside Dar al-Salam or Gao without permission from state authorities.

The Gao Wahhabis expressed their yearning for a better life – in this world and the next – through a rigorous approach to a universalizing faith; yet they did so in a way that emphasized exclusivity and separation from co-religionists. Above all, they rejected the tolerance of even minor variations within Islam, especially as institutionally encouraged by the government of Mali through the AMUPI. According to the leaders of the Ansar al-Sunna, Muslims who were forbearing toward different styles of the faith to the point of accepting practices that could not be traced back to Islam's origins had spiritually compromised themselves and no longer belonged to the community of the faithful. The House of Islam could only accommodate those with an unwavering orientation toward the practices and beliefs of Muhammad and his Companions, even if this involved intransigence in the face of opposition and acceptance as "brothers" and "sisters" of only those few who were willing to sacrifice their freedom for an elect community.

The isolationism of the reformist communities did not occur in the absence of the pressures and opportunities sometimes cumulatively referred to as globalization; it was an outcome of them. Above all, new opportunities for travel and study in the Middle East increased the profile of puritan Islam in the remote corners of West Africa. Other recent upheavals in history of the Gao region are also consistent with many ideas about the new forces of global shrinking: the economic necessity of migration, the opportunities and cultural displacements of (French language) state education, imposition of colonial governance and of post-colonial rule by strangers, and the partial introduction of a consumer-driven economy and international trade network, enough to create new wants and needs but not enough to satisfy them. Out of this new constellation of challenges and choices, the Ansar communities pursued a strategy of isolation through a rigorously interpreted scriptural faith. Strictly speaking they did not close themselves off from the world, but chose a form of trans-nationalism based on the scriptural piety and prestige of the conservative Saudi clerisy. The closure of the Ansar villages was connected to an international network of Islamic extremists. The reformers' revival of rural life received the sanction of a supra-state (and anti-nationalist) complex of co-religionists. At the same time, the Ansar movement seems to exemplify the truest form of "antiglobalization," a puritan village movement that has self-consciously removed itself from the world, or at least from unexpected encounters with human differences, competing values, rootless individualism, and the rapid pace of technological innovation.

International Indigenism

Another project provides an entirely different illustration of the ambiguities of community-based (anti)globalization. This project emerged unintentionally from my research in aboriginal communities in northern Canada and participation in international meetings in Geneva on the rights of indigenous peoples over the space of nearly a decade, starting in the early 1990s.[7] Many of the ideas that form the basis of indigenous peoples' claims have become part of common parlance; and only when I had been to several meetings did I begin to think seriously about indigenous activism as an "ism," as a social movement with a coherent network, a common world-view, and widely shared objectives.

One of the most compelling experiences I have had during international meetings of indigenous peoples has been simply being in a room with upwards of five hundred indigenous delegates who together outwardly seemed to represent the entire range of human genetic and sartorial diversity, but who at the same time professed to the fundamental commonality of being indigenous. The human diversity that is embraced by indigenous identity is probably greater than that of any shared conception of self. In *The Origins of Indigenism* I draw a contrast between two peoples with representatives who claim indigenous identity: the Tuaregs of West Africa, who are socially hierarchical pastoralists of the Sahara, and the Crees of northern Canada, whose traditional way of life centers on hunting, fishing, and gathering in the boreal forest. Were it not for those who lobby for their common identity as indigenous peoples, this comparison would make no sense whatsoever. But the fact is that they *do* share space in indigenous forums, together with thousands of others, many of whom express equally striking differences in their primary cultural attachments.

What is the basis of this shared identity as indigenous peoples? It is sometimes seen to be based on the experience of being the original inhabitants of a territory, of having attachments to a way of life that has existed "from time immemorial," and of being subject to the same patterns of marginalization, the same state-sponsored efforts at cultural assimilation, the same loss of land, way of life, and well-being through the predations of extractive industry. The main vehicle through which indigenous representatives express this common identity is international law.[8] Both their shared way of life and histories of oppression are expressed in the language of rights.

The global nature of the indigenous peoples' movement made itself most apparent to me during the World Health Organization's first International Consultation on the Health of Indigenous Peoples from 23–26 November 1999. This meeting revealed indigenous identity with particular clarity because it was centrally premised on an opportunity for indigenous peoples to collectively present themselves for the first time to a global administration. The World Health Organization had initiated an effort to address the particular health concerns of indigenous peoples worldwide and had reached a point at which indigenous people themselves were needed to provide information about their most important health issues, what they hoped to achieve from the WHO initiative, and, more generally, who they were as a global collectivity. The indigenous representatives approached this opportunity with alacrity. Their formal presentation of indigenous selfhood as it related to health began during the weekend before the WHO meeting in an informal panel that gathered at the headquarters of the World Council of Churches in Geneva. The goal of this panel was to hammer out a draft document intended to stand as the legal framework for the health aspirations of indigenous peoples. The resulting document came to be called the Geneva Declaration on the Health and Survival of Indigenous Peoples. From the point of view of a researcher interested in issues of identity formation and globalization, it was extremely informative to be present at a series of meetings attended by indigenous representatives from the Americas, northern Europe, Asia, Africa, Australia, and the South Pacific, who were assembled not only to formulate their most pressing health concerns but also to formally inscribe their common identity.

One of the most significant points of discussion during the framing of the Geneva Declaration turned upon the strategic value of stressing state affirmation of indigenous rights of self-determination as a necessary condition for the improvement of health conditions in indigenous communities. Some participants expressed the concern that an emphasis on self-determination would not sit well with state representatives and that politicizing health issues would complicate the development of new policies and the transfer of benefits. The more forceful majority view, however, was that self-determination is *the* indispensable precondition for the health and survival of indigenous peoples and that it was necessary to convince the leaders of the WHO of its centrality. Thus, we find in the first sentence of the preamble of the Geneva Declaration: "We, the representatives of indigenous communities, nations, peoples and organizations attending the International Consultation on the Health of Indigenous Peoples . . . reaffirm our right of self-determination . . ."[9]

Having established that indigenous peoples are a category of self-determining peoples, what other features do they share? The answer to this question, revealed by the Geneva Declaration and reiterated in every meeting of indigenous peoples I have attended, centers principally upon occupation of traditional territories "from time immemorial" and the loss of connection to those territories through histories of oppression and denial of collective being. The second paragraph accordingly expresses the most pressing concerns of the indigenous representatives: that, "the health of indigenous peoples in every region of the world is acknowledged to be in a poor state due to the negation of our way of life and world vision, the destruction of our habitat, the decrease of biodiversity, the imposition of sub-standard living and working conditions, the dispossession of traditional lands and the relocation and transfer of populations."[10] Aside from the usual target of indigenous activism – the nation-state – some of the most important culprits of this global pattern of negation, destruction, and oppression are the programs and activities of the World Bank, the International Monetary Fund and the World Trade Organization. The Geneva Declaration correspondingly exhorts the WHO to "take responsibility for engaging these institutions to rectify their policies and programs and [in particular] the imbalances and inequities in the World Trade Organization Treaties which have adverse health impacts."[11] Indigenous representatives reveal themselves to be members of a category of peoples oppressed in similar ways by the same global institutions. The overriding concerns of indigenous representatives in international forums thus center on the denial by those with power over them of their rights of self-determination. They accordingly emphasize their histories of oppression at the hands of colonial powers and states and the continuation of circumstances in which they are politically and economically disadvantaged. A delegate from Panama to the 2000 meeting on a Permanent Forum on Indigenous Issues once expressed to me the situation faced by indigenous people in just these terms: "we are impoverished and a slow death is looming over us."

But it is difficult to cement identities with exclusively negative forces. The magnetic powers of collective being require a positive polarity consisting of qualities that affirm a common way of life and conception of the universe. How, out of the tremendous diversity within the indigenous peoples' movement, is this affirmative dimension of common identity conceived? The Geneva Declaration provides less guidance concerning the positive common attributes of indigenous peoples, or the particular features of their "world vision." An effort in this direction is made with a few general observations, such as: "for Indigenous Peoples, health and survival is a dynamic equilibrium, encompassing interaction with life processes and the natural laws that govern the planet, all life forms, and spiritual understanding,"[12] but the Declaration offers little specific information to indicate the affirmative qualities that are universally shared by indigenous peoples. Gro Harlem Bruntland, Director-General of the WHO, provided a bit more of this dimension of indigenous identity in her opening address to the International Consultation:

"Indigenous peoples teach us about the values that have permitted humankind to live on this planet for many thousands of years without desecrating it. They teach us about holistic approaches to health that seek to strengthen the social networks of individuals and communities, while connecting them to the environment in which they live. And they teach us about the importance of a spiritual dimension to the healing process."[13]

Indigenous peoples thus collectively represent a corrective to the environmental and social abuses of modernity; and indigenous identity tells us as much about widely held concerns over the global impact of reckless industrialization as it does about the people and communities most directly endangered by it.

The international movement of indigenous peoples should therefore not be imagined merely as a global collectivity of those who claim indigenous rights and identity for themselves and their people. It derives much of its energy from a public that is sensitive to the uncertainties of a runaway world. It benefits materially and professionally from non-indigenous helpers motivated by their own visions of global social justice and environmental restoration. It represents an imaginary "world we have lost" (Peter Laslett's nostalgic expression) and the possibility of a return to, or at least protection of, the warmth and color of kinship-based communities. A public that is motivated by such concerns and sentiments is a major source of indigenous peoples' resources and leverage. Indigenous claims and grievances would have little effect on the behavior of nation-states if they were not also tied to a broad, international base of popular support. Indigenous leaders often present their people's way of life to the media as one of almost Rousseauian perfection, environmentally gentle, democratically consensual, and spiritually heightened. It matters little whether or not such qualities correspond with lived reality. What is important is that they have become part of an idiom of collective identity that circulates between a people and its popular audience. Indigenous identity is consumed and therefore at least to some extent outwardly shaped by the needs and inclinations of its consumers.

As an illustration of the reverse engineering (basing a design on specifications derived from an acquired product) that can take place in the indigenous politics of identity, let us briefly consider the key concept on which it is based. We have become used to the word indigenous as a term referring to human characteristics rather than, as was once more common, a botanical term referring to plant life native to a particular habitat. But use of the word indigenous in reference to a category of distinct peoples is in fact fairly recent, emerging in international law in the 1950s through efforts by the International Labour Organization to build new human rights standards with its Indigenous and Tribal Populations Convention and Recommendation of 1957. Since then, especially with the development of a United Nations Working Group on Indigenous Populations in 1982 and the establishment in 2001 of a Permanent United Nations Forum on Indigenous Issues, use of the term has flourished in international politics, in academia (especially cultural anthropology), and in creative uses of the politics of identity by indigenous peoples themselves. Although referring to some three hundred million original people worldwide who maintain attachments to ancestral traditions, wide recognition of the status of indigenous peoples is a product of the past several decades, originating in the terminology of international law and broadening out to become a new form of identity that has filtered down to a wider popular awareness of the world's social geography.[14]

The global nature of the indigenous peoples' movement can be gleaned from a small sample of its active nongovernmental organizations: the Sami Council, the Grand Council of the Crees, the Inuit Circumpolar Conference, the Russian Association of Indigenous Peoples of the North, the Native American Rights Fund, Indigenous Peoples in Latin America, the Asian Indigenous Peoples Pact, the New South Wales Aboriginal Land Council, and the National Aboriginal and Islander Legal Services Secretariat. The list could go on to include hundreds of NGOs dedicated to the defense of particular indigenous peoples, to organizing regional blocs of indigenous communities and organizations, or to disseminating information about indigenous peoples as a global entirety.

A specific illustration of indigenous activism that I would like to consider more closely is provided by technologically and bureaucratically sophisticated Samis of northern Europe. Recent assertions of Sami cultural distinctiveness, based on their traditional subsistence economy of reindeer herding, comprise one of the most compelling examples of the paradoxical uses of liberal institutions for the protection of closed societies. And as I will show later on, the Samis express the salient aspect of their culture, including their cultural boundary, in a way that is almost universally accessible: through computer networking.

Those who consider themselves Sami occupy a wide belt across the arctic region of northern Europe, extending from northern Scandinavia to northwestern Russia. Some 50,000 Samis live in

Norway; 20,000 in Sweden; 10,000 in Finland; and 4,000 in Russia, but they consider themselves to constitute a single people, represented by the Nordic Sami Council. Like many who identify themselves as indigenous, the Sami have faced the pressures of assimilative government education. In the late nineteenth and early twentieth centuries it was illegal for them to speak their language. Such were the pressures on their way of life that by 1900 they had officially ceased to exist in all four countries in which they lived.[15] More recently, having succeeded in garnering recognition as a distinct people from the Nordic countries and the European Union, they have been subject to unwanted hydroelectric projects, mining, and forestry – the common cultural and economic threats to distinct ways of life in the northern boreal forest.

The postwar development of indigenous identity and successful use of the "politics of shame" have given the Samis a new source of pride and assertiveness. They have taken a leading role in human rights standard setting, making their presence known in such international forums as the International Labour Organization, the Arctic Council, the World Health Organization and annual meetings of United Nations Working Group on Indigenous Populations; they have brought complaints against the government of Finland to the Human Rights Committee, which reports on State compliance with the International Covenant on Civil and Political Rights;[16] and they have been active in encouraging the European Union to frame an approach to multiculturalism that acknowledges and respects their status as a distinct indigenous people.

Rather than take a consistently antagonistic approach to the challenge posed by Sami activism, the Nordic states have accommodated many of their demands, especially those that relate to their identity and cultural autonomy. Competing uses of land remain a source of friction between the Samis and their host governments, with the Samis continuing to hold land in common, and with individual families having specific, inherited fishing and grazing rights and ownership of herds, while the governments of the Nordic countries and Russia and the corporate entities they support have other uses for the land, especially resource extraction. At the same time, the governments of Norway, Sweden, and Finland have each negotiated regimes of cultural autonomy with the Sami, which have been given institutional substance in Sami "parliaments." These parliaments are concerned principally with matters that relate to promotion of the Sami languages, cultural events, and the reindeer-herding economy. They do not have legislative powers, but are used to inscribe and protect Sami cultural autonomy.

The protective function of the Sami parliaments was especially noteworthy in Finland. Not long after its founding in 1973, the Finnish Sami parliament had to contend with the claims of rival "descendants of Lapps," reindeer herders who sought Sami status and the distinct political rights that went with it. In response to this potential influx of "outsiders," one of the first acts of the Finnish Sami parliament was the rejection of 1,128 applications by Lapps to the Electoral Board of the Sami parliament on the grounds that knowledge of the Sami language was the most important criterion for inclusion in the political community of Samis. In response, the aggrieved Lapps lodged more than 600 complaints in Finland's Supreme Administrative Court, which in its ruling upheld the Sami's language-based criterion for membership and rejected all but ten of the appeals.[17] The institutions of liberal states, as the outcome of this grievance illustrates, can sometimes act as defenders of distinct societies with closed cultural boundaries.

Those who are recognized (and recognize themselves) as indigenous are working within a diffuse, widely shared global paradigm of liberation to assert community values and distinct identities. They pose a challenge to nation-states by going further in their demand of state-sponsored multiculturalism than do most minorities, toward regimes of autonomy that sometimes amount to multi-constitutionalism. They assert not just distinct cultures, but distinct territories, ways of life, and political self-determination, without pursuing outright secession. Their overriding goal is the reassertion of community values and viability rather than the complex burden of independent statehood. For some, the nation-state represents a further imposition of colonial relationships, and their status as a subject society calls for broad legal, political, and social remedy. The ways that their grievances and identities are presented and pursued are principally through the concepts and institutions of their oppressors, through judicial mechanisms and international organizations largely controlled by nation-states. They have taken on the challenge of defending local cultures by striving to be recognized as distinct "peoples" and "nations" with rights of self-determination.

But there is a central ambiguity associated with this global strategy of mobilization, an ambiguity that can be more generally seen as a central feature of the current era of globalization: the defense of distinct societies relies on political forces that exert pressures of global conformity. The indigenous peoples' movement has made use of human rights and institutions of global governance in order to shelter their collective "traditional" ways of life. They attempt to protect their community existence, commonly based upon oral iteration and the authority of elders, through formal laws, legal process and bureaucratic organization. They are compelled to navigate bureaucracies and make use of nongovernmental organizations and transnational activism to protect ways of life based upon hunting, nomadism, or simple agriculture.

Collective self-identification as "indigenous" implies the acceptance and creative investment of a universally valid conceptual currency. More specifically, the use of human rights standards as way to protect indigenous societies implies a prerequisite of compliance with those standards, in other words, an end to the values of patriarchy, gerontocracy, and many other rigid, traditionally legitimated orthodoxies. Familiarity with the law implies formal education and a shift away from the values and perceptions of oral societies. At the very least, legally-based defenses of tradition require the formation of a new elite that meets two new criteria for leadership: skilled literacy and sophisticated familiarity with the workings of bureaucracy. In short, there is a trade-off between global strategies of cultural preservation and the strategic necessity of wearing a one-size-fits-all transnational identity.

Digital Identity

The Internet has become for many the leading source of borderless thinking, a medium in which ideas, sounds, and images can be made instantly available to a global audience, a communicative space in which there are few frontiers and little interference by the legal apparatuses of states. In this medium, the only limits to the construction and presentation of collective identities – even indentities that embody the primal values of technological simplicity and self-sufficiency – are access (directly or through intermediaries) to computer hardware, a telephone infrastructure, and a modicum of sophistication in their use. To anyone who has followed the activities of the so-called antiglobalization movement, it should be clear that simultaneous instant messaging to a large number of subscribers is a powerful tool of political activism, a tool now also serving the organizational purposes of a wide array of once marginalized communities. The global cognitive/political revolution following from the spread of alphabetic literacy to previously oral societies has therefore recently magnified its effects through information and communication technologies. And along with these technologies, a new stratum of computer literati is reshaping the status hierarchies, resistance strategies, and conceptions of collective self of many so-called traditional societies.

It should come as no surprise, then, that the wide currency of the term "indigenous peoples" and its concomitant elaboration of legal claims and human rights standards are revealed by a flourishing presence on the Internet. For example, on May 3, 2004, the search engine AlltheWeb.com produced 1,239,806 results for the word *indigenous*, while the more specific term *indigenous peoples* brought up 268,294 results. Such Web searches, of course, can produce varied results, both over time and between different search engines, but by any account the international movement of indigenous peoples is making very good use of digital self-expression and networking.

One of the growing uses of computer literacy by indigenous peoples and communities is traditional language preservation. The James Bay Crees, for example, have developed a cultural program that includes the promotion of indigenous language use on the Internet. In responding to the challenge of competing with the dominant English and French languages of Quebec, the Cree Regional Authority, the administrative umbrella of nine communities in northern Quebec, has for the past five years been developing a Cree Cultural Institute (referred to in Cree as the *Aanischaaukamikw*, the "bridge," or a bridge between generations), one of the main functions of which is language preservation.[18] Among the Cree Cultural Institute's initiatives has been the development of Cree computing resources, including a downloadable software package – "CreeKeys" – that facilitates computing using the Cree syllabic alphabet. CreeKeys automatically translates the Roman alphabet into Cree syllabics, a literal and figurative symbolic modification of the languages of dominant societies. It is now possible to conduct e-mail correspondence and Internet searches in Cree syllabics; and while the Cree language content on the Internet may still be limited (I was able to find only a scattering of material by doing a search of the word *acimowin*, "story"), the tool itself may provide a stimulus to the development of Web-based Cree literature.

A few indigenous societies have made even broader use of the possibilities of the Internet. Beyond their political engagement with nation-states and international forums, the Samis, for example, whom I have already introduced as one of the most generously supported and active participants in the indigenous peoples' movement, have developed a sophisticated infrastructure of information and communications technology – a surprising accomplishment given that they maintain firm attachments to a pastoralist subsistence economy. Besides hosting a number of radio and television stations, with their own coverage of local and international events, the Samis have developed SameNet (www.sapmi.net) described in its English language home page (also available in Sami, Swedish, and Finnish), as "a joint Nordic meeting place . . . founded on fundamental Sami values."[19] SameNet is a joint Internet/intranet system, with an open area for Web browsing and information-sharing with the outside world, and a closed area that is restricted to Samis (or non-Samis working in Sami institutions or state institutions concerned with Sami issues).

It is interesting to think of the login page as a digital manifestation of an us/them boundary. In this case, there is a sense in which the boundary promotes elements of both cultural vitality and democratic transparency. The closed network provides news, information, e-mail accounts, and offers courses in the Sami language, of which there are nine dialects. A complete "Internet school" for adult Samis is under development. More significantly, SameNet hosts discussions of the Sami democratic system, facilitates access to political candidates and incumbents, and provides information on voting procedures for elections of the Sami parliaments of Norway, Sweden, and Finland.[20] It is too soon to tell whether other indigenous peoples worldwide will make such creative use of electronic media, but if the Sami initiative is anything to go by, indications are that those whose identities are based on closed kinship networks and the simplest subsistence technologies can at the same time be at the forefront of cyberculture and e-democracy.

A significant paradox derives from the fact that the content of indigenous identity is usually oriented toward defending subsistence-based
economies and the local production of technology, while, at the same
time, advanced information and communication technologies now
have a prominent place in expressing and affirming this identity.
Indigenism is therefore inseparable from a global pattern of localism,
from sharpened boundaries of community identity and intensified pursuits of autonomy. Consequently, Web sites built around the term
"indigenous peoples" commonly make claims of representing living
peoples, of being expressions of their histories, cultures, and collective
aspirations. Although I do not have a date for the first Web posting by
an indigenous peoples' organization, it is safe to say that an animated
network of these organizations had developed by the late-1990s, some
time before the Internet could be considered a medium of mass communication. This simple observation indicates the rise of an elite with
the linguistic and technological skills to use the Internet as a tool of
global networking, lobbying, and self-expression, while being dedicated to applying these skills to the defense of ways of life that require
patience, stamina, simplicity, and close attention to the rhythms of the
natural world. This further implies that members of this elite occupy
an uncomfortable situation, a condition sometimes referred to as "bi-
culturalism," a state of "in-betweenness," or a condition of "diaspora,"
but with the added poignancy that arises from their reliance on forms
of knowledge that lie at the opposite poles of human experience.

A recent extension of the indigenous peoples concept makes the
Internet's powers of representation stand out more clearly. During the
last few years a surprising amount of interest has been built around
the idea of including the Palestinians as an indigenous people, manifested, for example, in 5,254 results for a Web search (on May 3, 2004)
that combined the words "indigenous peoples" and "Palestinian."

The connection between indigenous identity and Palestinian
nationalism is not something that would have arisen naturally through
face-to-face dialogue or through the epiphany of encounter at international meetings. High-ranking Palestinians and indigenous representatives simply do not mingle in the same circles. Spokesmen for
groups that engage in terrorism on behalf of Palestinians such as
Hamas or Islamic Jihad have not appeared (nor by U.N. rules are they
permitted to appear) at annual meetings of the Working Group on

Indigenous Populations or the Permanent Forum on Indigenous Issues. The inclusion of the Palestinians within the indigenous peoples' movement is mostly abstract and the principal venue for its expression is the Internet.

The Internet, then, is able to give shape and substance to political relationships that might otherwise be only fleeting, and even, in the case of the inclusion of Palestinians to the working definition of indigenous peoples, to define alliances that exist only as ideas rather than as personally negotiated realms of common experience and interest. This point can be taken further: Cultural boundaries are blurred in the unrepressed Web literature by the absence of limits on representation. Uncensored cultural representation makes possible the presentation of community ideals that originate in no recognizable community. More than ever before, it has become possible to express nostalgia for times that one has never experienced and pride toward peoples among which one has never belonged.

The very freedom that makes borderless thinking increasingly possible also contributes to the re-imagination and reinvigoration of micro-nations, local epistemologies, and languages of limited distribution. Commercial censorship no longer restricts the availability of print and visual media to large popular audiences communicating in homogenized languages of mass consumption. Among its many functions, the Internet is a bulletin board for small-scale collective self-perceptions and aspirations. There is an element of unbridled cultural democracy at work in the relationship between the Internet and identity attachments. The anchorages of identity can be at the same time informal and formal, local and global, making it seem possible, from a broader perspective, that we are approaching a time in which even those who want nothing more than a return to community, to the values of small economies, kinship, and personal recognition, are partly motivated by dreams of universal identity and, what is more, will often be required to appeal to the highest levels of global governance in order to realize them.

The collective sense of self, above all the sense of injustice and suffering based upon past wrongs, is not arrived at in isolation from behind closed cultural boundaries, but rather is inspired by and negotiated with others in personal, often professional, relationships and adjusted to the tastes of a universal public. Indigenous identity is part of a growing trend toward the use of lobbying – influencing political decisions through organized media campaigns – as a strategy of cultural survival. Cooperative relationships are an important part of the indigenous peoples' movement because of the complexity of the legal ideas underpinning self-determination and the difficulty one faces in bringing claims of distinct rights to a sympathetic audience. The essential features of a community's history and culture are now more than ever an outcome of global collaboration.

Not all individuals, communities, or peoples, however, have effective access to this tool of self-expression and liberation. The concept of the digital divide, the separation of those with access to information and communications technology and those without, can be applied to two contexts, local and global. First, it can be seen to occur at the community level, widening the distance between those with attachments to the inter-generational oral transmission of values and life skills and those who see important possibilities in reshaping and defending tradition through the tools of modernity. The computer literati are endowed with a unique ability to culturally represent their people, and in the process to redefine their people's values, opportunities, and even their criterion for group membership. The tools and strategies needed to lobby effectively for the protection of indigenous societies are at the same time instruments of the displacement of indigenous peoples' traditional authority.

The digital divide is more commonly recognized as having important implications for the communicative effectiveness of dissident peoples and communities, leaving those who are electronically disadvantaged in a condition of isolated powerlessness. The cultural survival of marginalized peoples may soon depend (if it doesn't already) on an ability and willingness among the otherwise defenseless to plug into – literally and figuratively – transnational lobby networks.

The dynamics of cultural activism through international lobbying could well become one of the few outlets for the expression of identity across cultural boundaries. Some effects of electronic activism seem to work in a direction of global cultural convergence, opposite to the reassertion of cultural boundaries exemplified by the Samis. The digital divide is in the process of becoming part of a wider phenomenon in which cases for protection of distinct societies can only be presented through globally uniform avenues, in other words, in which distinct societies are made essentially similar through their strategies of defense.

Two Approaches to (Anti)Globalization

One of the best ways to understand the scope and impact of the global forces of cultural convergence is to consider the strategies of resistance to them. The Muslim reformers of northeastern Mali sought to protect themselves from the influence of western culture and assimilation into the French language-based Malian state by interpreting their religious obligations to Islam in a way that no rival community could accept. Although they were ostensibly open to accepting "converts," drawn from among those who already considered themselves Muslim, their puritan approach to the faith effectively closed their communities and provided religious justifications for political autonomy and denial of the legitimacy of the state. Despite the fact that many of the Ansar's leaders were at one point brutally punished, it is a wonder that the movement survived the rule of several one-party dictatorships without being more harshly repressed. This is probably due to the political dangers inherent in suppressing Islamic extremism in a nation that is 85 percent Muslim. All the same, the Malian government seems to have come perilously close to violating the dictum that when yearnings for autonomy are ruthlessly stifled cultural boundaries do not necessarily disappear but can be reinforced with even greater militancy.

The boundaries of birth and heritage erected by indigenous peoples seem (notwithstanding the complexities that follow from the Palestinian appropriation of indigenous identity) more conducive to peaceful compromise and reconciliation with nation-states. The human rights regimes on which indigenous identity is largely based have been framed in such a way that it has been possible for indigenous claims of distinct rights to be made within the organizational bodies and systems of law of nation-states. More than this, indigenous peoples are defending closed communities with institutions and technologies that are commonly associated with globalization. The main difficulty with this strategy is the extent to which it requires (or furthers) literacy, bureaucratic procedure, formal education, and sophisticated use of information and communication technology – all features of fast-paced societies that are usually considered at a far remove from the essential qualities of indigenous cultures: oral iteration, the authority of elders, informal learning, and the local manufacture of essential technology. The erection of cultural difference entails, to some degree, a loss of distinctiveness. Assimilative forces are built into cultural defenses. This, to my way of thinking, is a central aspect of globalization today that is different from the ebb and flow of past civilizations. More than ever before, people are being brought together in global networks and basic institutional resemblances by the very strategies they use to assert their distinctiveness.

There is no clear indication that the economic and technological forces usually associated with globalization are leading to unhindered individualism or a loose kind of transnational pluralism. They can also encourage rigid social boundaries and redefined traditional values. First, there are those approaches to modernity, of which hard line religious extremism is perhaps the clearest expression, that directly refuse integration with the globalizing world. A purified faith becomes a filter that excludes socially-sanctioned individualism (even though the individual stands spiritually alone before the Creator), secular education, secular politics, and freedom of expression.

Then there are those societies that try to protect themselves from assimilation into a wider social and institutional world through the particularist orthodoxies of birth, language, and culture. Many of the peoples and organizations that comprise the international movement of indigenous peoples, for example, are making creative use of international institutions and liberal values to assert distinctiveness based on birth and to protect themselves, as distinct peoples, from assimilation into nation-states. International organizations provide them with defenses against unwanted aspects of globalization. But these tools come with complex user's manuals, with the need to meet basic standards of competence in literacy, use of technology, and the ability to navigate, and even create, bureaucracies. This predicament has implications not only for (re)emerging local societies, but also for the international institutions and regimes of law in which they seek shelter.

Human Rights Pluralism and Universalism

Rationalism, Religion, and Utopia

Most of us are accustomed to hearing human rights extolled as humanity's major resource for freedom from oppression, a source of state-transcending justice to which all can turn when overwhelmed by tyranny. The images we sometimes see of victims of rights abuses on journeys of displacement or in refugee camps, or even the ever-silent victims – corpses piled like cordwood in mass graves – are in one sense inverted images of hope; most of us prefer not to look upon such horror without imagining a way out, and human rights have become, mostly since the Second World War and especially in industrialized countries since the 1960s, *the* most readily invoked escape route to freedom. Any injustice, atrocity, or horror, framed as a human rights violation, contains a subtext of possible remedy: the world's judgment, correction, atonement, reconciliation, and peace. The moral authority of rights has become an assumption so prevalent as to be taken for granted. Jean-François Lyotard, a leading postmodernist philosopher who is usually on his guard against all manner of "metanarrative," nevertheless lapses into rights language in one of his declamations against liberalism and Marxism, neither of which, he says, "have emerged from these bloodstained centuries without attracting accusations of having perpetrated crimes against humanity."[1] Michael Ignatieff correctly speaks of a "rights revolution" in which legal instruments have transcended their juridical function to become expressions of our moral identity, the central way in which humans express their longing to live in a fair and free world.[2]

At the same time, however, the human rights movement faces serious obstacles, including the vacuums of authority and accountability by agencies responsible for them, the cultural incompetence of some of those promoting rights observance, and the occasionally dangerous stridency of those claiming distinct protections. Human rights, it would seem, are caught in more than one paradox, and consequently more than a few problems of implementation. None of the major entities responsible for drafting human rights norms, for observing them, or organized to defend them and extend their application are, as collective bodies, fully accountable to those whose rights most need defending. Some of the most important governing bodies, and even the entities that set themselves the challenge of protesting their abuses and checking their power, have often grown beyond the reach of those whose fates they claim to protect.

The United States, the most important potential source of human rights legitimacy, has seized upon the difficulties and partisan objections that accompany the development of human rights standards and stood alone among liberal states in rejecting important initiatives: it is alone among the world's nations – except for Somalia – in not signing the United Nations Convention on the Rights of the Child, ostensibly because it wants to protect its practice of executing minors accused of capital crimes; unlike 169 other countries, it has not ratified the Convention on the Elimination of all forms of Discrimination against Women, which urges nations to dismantle barriers to women in, among other things, education, health care, employment, marriage, and divorce (the influence of the Christian right, particularly with regard to abortion policy, seems to be at work here); the United States is alone among industrial democracies in retaining an ongoing commitment to capital punishment (the United States federal government, the military, and thirty-eight states currently have the death penalty), and flouts Article 6.5 of the United Nations International Covenant on Civil and Political Rights, which discourages States from applying the sentence of death to those under 18 years of age (perhaps some comfort to human rights advocates can be found in the fact that in June 2002 the U.S. Supreme Court declared an end to the execution of convicted murderers who are mentally retarded); in the same year, the U.S. administration backed out of the Rome Treaty establishing the

International Criminal Court (ICC), over concerns (dismissed by its closest allies and the architects of the ICC as unfounded) that American peacekeepers would be particularly subject to groundless accusations of war crimes; and in July, 2002 the U.S. attempted to block a protocol intended to strengthen the U.N. Covenant against Torture and other Cruel, Inhuman or Degrading Treatment or Punishment by submitting a proposal to reopen ten years of negotiation on the document (voted down by participating Member States) and then abstaining in the final vote (the Protocol nevertheless passed by a margin of 35 to 8, with 10 abstentions). There is growing concern in the human rights community that the U.S. led war on terror will bring about a return of an American Cold War style foreign policy that is insensitive to human rights, that overlooks or strategically encourages the abuses of "cooperative," or "friendly" regimes in the interests of advancing a struggle against a global enemy. One can certainly not point to the treatment of the more than 650 prisoners held anonymously in the U.S. detention camp at Guantánamo Bay, along with lesser-known detention camps such as those in Iraq, Afghanistan, and on the British-owned island of Diego Garcia in the Indian Ocean, as examples of state conduct to be followed by emerging democracies. These camps have come under critical scrutiny by rights experts for an increasingly apparent pattern of violent and coercive interrogation (euphemistically referred to as "stress and duress" tactics) and in some instances removal (or "rendering") of prisoners to the jurisdictions of states in which torture is routine, raising new concerns that the United States is not fully committed to human rights or to the Geneva Conventions governing the conduct of states in international armed conflict.[3] It is widely recognized that without U.S. cooperation, most human rights initiatives are dead letters. Yet the nation-state that is the most important potential source of human rights leadership has in significant instances refused to be influenced by human rights standards.

Many of the obstacles to the legitimacy of human rights, however, are endemic to the human rights system itself. Of the many contradictory features of this system, the most basic and rife with secondary implications is the tension between its reliance upon the formal powers of states (legal, bureaucratic, and occasionally even military) and its legitimation as a source of liberation for the victims of state oppression. Every lesson of history since people first harvested grain on the fertile plains of the Tigris and Euphrates tells us that states are not to be trusted when it comes to protecting the weak and purveying unbiased justice, and such skepticism was confirmed by the unprecedented violence by states in the Second World War, not only externally toward innocent civilians of enemy states but internally toward innocent citizens unwanted by states, especially the Jews, Gypsies, homosexuals and other "deviants" expunged by the Nazis – these are the very horrors that led to the drafting of the United Nations Charter and the Universal Declaration of Human Rights in the mid to late 1940s; yet almost all the hopes of the human rights movement are pinned upon organizations largely controlled by states, organizations in which the most powerful states, and hence the most potentially dangerous, have powers of veto, and in which nearly every state has the ability to obstruct procedure, or, at the very least, take a "devil-may-care" approach to exposure of abuses.

The primary place of states as the parties responsible for ratifying and upholding human rights gives rise to other concerns. For example, to what extent do nation-states, as the principal agents of global rights, represent the will of those who are supposed to be the beneficiaries of those rights? Democratic nation-states there may be, but taken together there is a considerable number of rogues, thieves, and butchers that represent state interests (and that represented these interests during the development of human rights instruments); and the number of governments brought to power by bogus elections, other forms of fraud, or the naked use of power still gives one pause for thought about the globally democratic nature of international state assemblies. Taken together, democrats and despots alike, do the leaders and administrators of nation-states truly represent a universal moral consensus? There is plenty of room for doubt. To the cynical, human rights instruments seem to set forth something like the inalienable rights of hens, drafted and upheld by assemblies of foxes.

More hope is attached to another tier of participants in human rights: nongovernmental organizations (NGOs). In 1840 the organization widely recognized as the first human rights NGO, the Anti-Slavery International for the Protection of Human Rights (originally named the British and Foreign Anti-Slavery Society), initiated its work of sponsoring publications and organizing conferences, with the goal, obvious from its title, of eliminating the traffic, trade, and ownership of humans. In organizing itself in this way with a general goal of human liberation, it preceded the U.N. Charter and the Universal

Declaration by more than a century;[4] and the same kind of civil resistance continues today in many other forms, with organizations like Amnesty International, the Center for Science in the Public Interest, Human Rights Watch, Physicians for Human Rights, and a host of others too numerous to mention, that go beyond the mandates of relief agencies by trying to peacefully engage the forces of social change. But not all NGOs are cast from the same benevolent mold. Some nongovernmental organizations harbor anti-democratic impulses, resist public accountability, are suspicious of the rule of law, and reject human rights as a source of guidance for the use of power. Taking this point further, human rights are themselves sometimes championed as a vision of political virtue by those very entities that would readily violate them in political practice. Whenever rights become an avenue to power, rather than a check on the exercise of power, they are subject to being inverted.

Given the seriousness of its handicaps, one would expect the human rights movement to suffer a major crisis of legitimacy. And while it is true that there are many critics of human rights who, for various reasons, point to their dubious origins, their incapacity to resolve pressing issues, or their failure to protect particular peoples, one of the most surprising things about human rights is how scant the criticism and doubt are, and obversely how resistant the legitimacy of rights has become. If anything, the most vocal demands for human rights reform have centered upon issues of recognition – inclusion of distinct societies as "peoples" in various regimes of rights – or on the need for new protections through new rights instruments, striving for stronger legal affirmation of such widely varying goals as development, anti-racism, peace, housing, and food, or wider ratification of already existing treaties. Other calls for reform look to the ineffectiveness of human rights sanctions and call for more direct and effective deterrents (economic sanctions, for example) to be more often applied against those states that commit the most serious offences, wanting to add some bite to the idea of "soft power." The idea of human rights as a guide to human behavior, as a legal synthesis or compendium of liberalism and the world's major religious traditions, has a wider global reach than any one major religion or system of thought. And, whatever human rights violations states may commit and whatever reluctance they may have to ratify particular human rights instruments, no existing nation-state categorically denies the legitimacy of the human rights movement as a source of guidance for the exercise of power. If human rights are being used by the forces of vice as a way to pay homage to virtue (as the saying by La Rochefoucault goes), that is an indication of success, not failure.

The human rights movement has tapped into a wellspring of hope that draws upon a combination of rationalism and utopian imagination, or rather a tradition in western philosophy, universalized though efforts to accommodate other civilizations, that attempts to apply rigorous logical and scientific principles to the construction of a just, well-ordered, perfect society. This hope is not revolutionary or apocalyptic, but aspires to change the world slowly, like the warming of the day. The human rights system is a legally-formulated moral code that somehow appeals to spiritual sensibilities.

Despite possessing basic underpinnings of rationalism, the human rights movement is not and cannot be dismissive of religious ethics in the tradition of the French *philosophes*, fervent anticlerical revolutionaries like Condorcet and Thomas Paine, or the utopian socialists of the nineteenth century. The central goal that inspired the drafting of the Universal Declaration of Human Rights of 1948 was to assemble a moral charter that identifies and builds upon the values common to humanity, condemning those actions universally understood to be evil and setting out the basic, this-worldly aspirations shared by every civilization and religious tradition. The Universal Declaration is an unprecedented ecumenical blueprint for moral political behavior. In this sense it represents a common religious creed, without reference to scriptures, without invoking the name (or names) of God, and with no promise of otherworldly salvation.

The human rights movement thus combines very different legacies of radical, rational, religious, and at times revolutionary hope. It is part of a great historical oxymoron – a tradition of new beginnings – that has guided the course of western societies for centuries.[5] Despite the skepticism that greeted the Universal Declaration upon its ratification in 1948; despite the continuing incidence of horrifying rights abuses, including those arising from genocidal impulses; and despite the doubts that linger over the universality of human rights and the salience of seemingly incompatible perceptions of them, the human rights movement is carried forward by popular legitimacy and moral authority. A legal historian focusing on the origins and impact of the Universal Declaration has argued that the fall of apartheid in South

Africa and the collapse of East European totalitarian regimes owe more to the moral power of human rights than to any other product of international law.[6] The peace process in Bosnia, while not by any stretch of the imagination an unmitigated success, eventually succeeded in overcoming much skeptical hatred and raised the profile of human rights as the moral foundation of viable multi-ethnic states. Human rights figured prominently in the formation of a coalition government in Afghanistan after the fall of the Taliban, with interested western governments demanding (with either anarchy and isolation or billions in aid in the balance) an ethnically inclusive democracy and improvement in the status and political representation of women. If this effort proves to be untenable, it is because of subsequent compromises with warlords, not the illegitimacy of human rights. State governments that choose to violate human rights often go to great lengths to cover their tracks, more out of concern about international public opinion than the censure of other states; or if states do collectively censure one of their members in the international community it is more than likely because of pressure from popular sources, acting in accordance with the moral beacon of human rights. And, like revolutions and religions of messianic expectation (though tempered by a grounding in bureaucratic pedantry), the human rights movement has its enthusiastic visionaries, apostles, and Quixotes, those willing to pursue a lofty ideal regardless of their own material interests, who are guided by a message of world renewal, and who are sometimes destructively inattentive to the moral complexity of societies in transition.

The origins of the modern human rights movement are therefore deeper than the ideals that emerged from the American and French Revolutions, deeper even than the engagement of Enlightenment political philosophy with ideas of social contract and natural law.[7] There can be little doubt that the human rights movement shares in this rationalist tradition, not so much in its elevation of formal procedures as a way of establishing moral consensus as in its application of legal and scientific methods to arrive at a universal goal: peace, order, and good government for all, an end to the scourges of racism and war, a time (to last for all time) in which the world's peoples can coexist as brothers and sisters, tolerant of one another's differences. These are the same, or at least similar, ideals to those of the earliest utopian visions of the Stoics or the applied reason of the Enlightenment, and are part of the same tradition of calling upon rational methods to achieve an ideal social order in a state of historical finality.

The Limits of Liberal Evangelism

The idea of a universal rights ethic has its origin primarily in a combination of western traditions. Most obviously, it draws upon liberal political philosophy with its emphasis on natural law and contract theories of the state; but it is equally influenced by revolutionary Enlightenment-inspired hopes for a global rational society and Christian aspirations toward an ecumenical brotherhood, two seedbeds of the western utopian imagination. The starting point to human rights, from any angle we look at it, is firmly situated in western conceptions of the ideal conditions for universal peace, justice, and prosperity, at times underpinned by secular versions of world-renewing enthusiasm.

The argument that the origins of human rights are specifically tied to western legal, revolutionary, and religious traditions does not sit well with the prevailing idea that a basic workable consensus is already built into the major human rights instruments, in other words, that the hearts and minds of all people of the world have been won or accommodated, that the task at hand is not so much to convey the truth as to ensure that it is respected and that the temptation to abandon it, especially in troubled times, is resisted.

The task of bringing states to apply in practice those universal moral rules that they have accepted in principle is inconsistent with the perception that the moral consensus supporting human rights is a mere façade, that states (perhaps, indirectly, civilizations) have signed on to rights regimes in bad faith, strategically masking fundamental moral differences and disagreements. But there are lingering doubts about the moral depth of human rights universalism, such as those that arise from the restrictions applied to women in Islamic societies, mainly through the visible imposition of invisibility (especially widely criticized in the wakes of the Iranian Revolution and the rise and fall of the Taliban regime in Afghanistan). This is only the most noticeable area of discord from within the Muslim world with the moral tenor of human rights. The inseparability of faith and politics is more fundamentally at odds with the political freedoms enjoined by the Universal

Declaration; and Islam's strict prohibition against apostasy is in even sharper contrast with the Declaration's call for freedom of religion, and was the principal reason for Saudi Arabia's abstention in the General Assembly's vote for its approval.

An approach to human rights that admits to an incomplete hold over major traditions, however, raises the uncomfortable question of the legitimacy of belief, and the uncomfortable possibility that a world of increasingly integrated civilizations and peoples could fall into moral chaos. The sometimes very wide discrepancies between human rights standards and the manifest teachings and tendencies of major traditions cannot be allowed to stand. Strategies must be developed to change the hearts and minds – and ultimately the behavior – of the non-compliant. This would make the first challenge of human rights not one of ensuring compliance with accepted norms, but the evangelical goal of challenging and altering the convictions of those who are unaware of or repudiate those norms.

The most sophisticated advocates of this perspective, being reasonable doctors of the faith, adopt a gradualist strategy of discourse and progressive emancipation. They seek to demonstrate that in any society, no matter how politically authoritarian, there can always be found, besides the dominant views of the illiberal cultural position, voices of dissent that can be encouraged to develop dialogue more receptive to the human rights agenda. Elements of the agenda can also be deliberately but subtly introduced to spaces of intercultural exchange in order to overcome the most problematic antagonism to it. A broad, culturally sensitive strategy of cultural reform is, according to this view, the only way to effectively substantiate and expand the universality of human rights.[8]

This should not be confused with a popular approach to human rights that builds its strategy (whether self-consciously or not) on more direct and strident principles of religious evangelism. The struggle for flexible (rather than final) universality is the definitive feature of human rights, and this elasticity goes some way toward discouraging the excesses of both opponents and advocates; but even the most accommodating universalism has its radical detractors, those who say it goes too far toward imposing a western blueprint for the social and moral orders on "traditional" societies unwilling to accept it, and those who have their own, more urgently spoken, version of unadulterated

Truth, with or without global aspirations, that denies the validity of a secular moral ecumene. Focusing on such renunciation of human rights can lead radical supporters to take on some of the apocalyptic overtones of proselytizing faith, summoning in rejoinder the almost overwhelming task of convincing reluctant skeptics of the urgent truth as against their own passionately held convictions.

This is indeed the approach taken by the most zealous of human rights advocates. David Stoll provides an example of this in his description of an international influx of human rights activists to north-western Guatemala beginning in the early 1990s in the aftermath of that nation's catastrophic civil war, which led to a realignment of complex local power relations. Simplistic victim/victimizer dichotomies were imposed by human rights internationalists on peasant societies in remote villages in which local land disputes formed the backdrop of years of violence and exploitation at the hands of both guerrillas and state forces. Well-intentioned Catholic clergy and leaders of an array of human rights agencies simply got it wrong when they inserted a kind of Manichean human rights perspective that elevated the claims of some groups while trampling on the land rights – and human rights – of others.[9]

One of the potential consequences of such excessive zeal is its transformation into a protective shell of hate following the experience of disillusionment. Faced with large numbers of peoples who reject universalist aspirations with particularist defiance there is just such an alternative to evangelism: to retreat from the ambitious goal of reaching all of humanity, reconstituting an invigorated *We* with reinforced cultural and political barriers against a different and menacing *They*. *We* are those who respect the liberties and rights of individuals, who above all respect the rights of all persons to choose the life they want to live, as long as that choice does not infringe on the rights of others; but *They* have chosen differently, putting tyranny above freedom, justifying oppression of individuals with self interested piety. That is their choice. *They* must live with it, but cannot ask the same of *Us*. Such an approach to human differences would (if it has not already materialized) bring the world to a point of crisis, not just over the irreconcilability of competing paradigms of the truth, but also through absolutist programs of conveying the truth to the ignorant, the unconvinced, the refusers, and the apostates. The strategic blunders that go along with applied liberal absolutism are every bit as harmful to the achievement of moral reform as the abuses that are the target of liberal intervention.

But even as awareness of such blunders encroaches on liberal consciousness it becomes possible to see how difficult it would be for those committed to liberal identity to accept compromise. It would involve taking the "human" out of human rights. For those convinced of the existence or achievability of universal moral principles this would be tantamount to an intuition that God is dead. Rather than face the torments of disillusionment, the universal identity inherent in human rights (as distinguished from a narrower form of "occidental rights" or "liberal rights") is buttressed, and efforts are doubled to include all peoples and all peaceful aspirations for global unity in the program of "emerging standards."

The Collective Rights Dilemma

The universal ethic of individual rights, which has become the foundation of liberal democracy, is in a state of tension and opposition with collective rights. If the differences between individual and collective rights appear intractable, it is because convincing arguments can be made in favor of each, and the respective positions, which I will now summarize, are held with a firmly set mixture of political and ideological fervor:

The case for collective rights

The prevailing emphasis on the individual as the ultimate beneficiary of rights is beset with dilemmas posed by social reality. No one, it can truly be said, is able to live in dignity apart from a community; the social world is the ultimate source of what it means to be human. A regime of human rights that gives everything over to the individual not only seems abstract, sterile, and alienating, it is in contradiction with the nature of humanity. This was the position taken by the American Anthropological Association (AAA) in a 1947 letter to the Human Rights Commission in response to the proposed human rights declaration. The AAA challenged the Commission to formulate a statement of rights that went beyond "the values prevalent in the countries of Western Europe and America," that took "into full account the individual as member of the social group of which he is a part, whose sanctioned modes of life shape his behavior, and with whose fate his own is thus inextricably bound."[10] Melville Herskovits, the principal author of the 1947 statement on human rights, considered culture itself to be *the* supreme ethical value, and proposed that one of the main goals of anthropology should be the protection of "primitive" peoples from the global reach of "Western" values. To Herskovits nothing represented the extent of this reach quite like the human rights initiatives being undertaken by the United Nations.[11]

There are strong relativistic stirrings in such expressions of doubt about individual rights. If moral standards are defined by and contingent upon communities – in other words, if there is no way to define a universal code of ethics that supercedes distinct cultures – then a regime of exclusively individual human rights would be a danger to human diversity and dignity. Rights must inhere in cultures and communities if the universal essence of individuals is to be protected.

The liberal emphasis on individual sovereignty and equality fits uncomfortably with renewed ethnic and tribal identities, which emphasize the obligations of individuals to their communities, seeing individuals as the bearers of duties more than of rights. The essence of being human (and therefore of human rights) resides in the groups to which individuals belong, their lineages, clans, villages, tribes, or nations. If communities at some level do not have rights, how can individuals truly be protected? How can they find a place in the world if their traditions and the people to which they belong cannot in some way be sheltered and supported? If human rights are intended to end the scourges of racism and social injustice, should not races and societies themselves be the beneficiaries of rights? But resistance to collective rights in international forums reposes more on selfish political considerations than on any noble aspirations toward promoting world justice and the dignity of the human person.

The case for individual rights

Complicating matters, however, some nation-states claim that they, not just their citizens, are or should be the beneficiaries of human rights protections. The strongest incentive to hold the line against collective rights is to keep them from spilling over to rogue states, which could then use them to strengthen their political claims against international government. For example, the government of Zimbabwe – whose record of human rights abuses is among the worst in the African continent, with president Robert Mugabe leading widely-reported campaigns of racial profiling and dispossession of white farmers, using the powers of the state to eliminate political opposition, and detaining legitimate foreign journalists on accusations of "aiding terrorism" – was among the African delegations to the 2001 United Nations racism conference in Durban, South Africa to insist upon a state level of human rights victimization and rights to compensation from Industrial nations for Africa's history of oppression from trans-Atlantic slavery and colonialism.[12] Only when this became an intractable sticking point, threatening the collapse of the conference, was the issue retired. Whatever we might feel about the history of slavery and colonization or the need for global equity in the distribution of prosperity and opportunity, the framing of such issues as the rights of states raises the very real danger that individual rights, the cornerstone of the human rights movement, could be consumed, neutralized, and rendered useless by repressive state governments.[13] Given the fact that human rights instruments were originally intended to protect the weakest members of society from the depredations of those who would abuse power over them, the rise of new regimes of rights granting privileged status to nation-states is chilling.

It is precisely because communities and nations have the potential to take total control of the human person, to define the essence of humanity through the imposition of duty, obedience, and narrow conformity, that human rights are framed as individual rights. If states were to ever become the principal beneficiaries of rights, the entire purpose of human rights would be defeated. The designs of totalitarian governments would once again be accommodated by the world order. Totalitarianism subsumes individuals within collective wholes, and responds to persons according to preconceived notions of their collective membership: their race, class, party, or nationality. It emphasizes the collective aspects of virtue and diminishes voluntarism. It is at the furthest extreme from rights-based society because of its expectation of unconditional obedience, fulfillment of duty, and rigorous commitment to collective interests. The nation makes all claims of rights – rights of development, prosperity, productivity, efficiency, expansion of power, and *lebensraum*; none accrue to individuals.

The human rights liberalism that has developed since World War II sees this kind of collectivism as a perilous condition of modern states, reminiscent of the fascist dictatorships of the Axis alliance and Stalinist-style communism – the kind of states that suppressed civic institutions and wiped out minority communities, grinding internal opposition into the dust under the industrial state's far reaching powers of destruction. Much of the energy of the human rights movement has been devoted to preventing this kind of total tyranny and diminishing it wherever it occurs.

The political origins of the collective rights dilemma are connected to the fact that nation-states generally proved to be extremely poor guardians of rights, especially toward those whom states excluded for their differences or who refused to find a place within the national polity and identity. The stranded minorities of post World War I Europe, the Hungarians, Germans, Jews, Roma (Gypsies), and others who could not or would not fit into the clumsy alignments of national identities and state boundaries, faced states protective of their sovereignty, acting as the keepers and watchmen of rights. At the same time, the mandate system, intended to bring a regime of rights to European colonies, only occasionally acted to reduce the brutality of forced labor. The colonial powers, especially France, were better at communicating the *idea* of rights to their overseas subjects than at bringing about the justice intended to follow from them.

The historical legacy of the twentieth century turns as much upon the regimes of peace that followed its two world wars than upon the wars themselves. Following World War I, the establishment of the League of Nations raised the hopes of those who expected great things from a global institution with a mandate to prevent the recurrence of war and revolution, to usher in a new era of world peace. But the Paris Peace Conference floundered on the issue of racial equality. Japan, backed by an amalgam of thirty-seven different Japanese NGOs collectively organized in the Association for the Equality of Races, sought a clause in the Covenant of the League of Nations that would support the principle of the right of all to racial equality. The idea of building racial equality into international law was also supported at the Conference by W. E. B. Du Bois, the American intellectual and activist, who had already established his international reputation by defining "the color line" as the central challenge of the twentieth century.

Delegates from Asia, Africa, and Latin America held similar views. But Japan's proposal was met with a wall of intransigence from delegates representing the dominant world powers, who referred to their colonial subjects as "primitive," "racially inferior," "savage," and too "backward" for self-government.[14] What emerged from the Paris Peace Conference was a mandate system that regulated existing colonial relationships, keeping them intact largely through a system of rights that did not protect all equally. The League of Nations did provide a new regime of rights, including rights of minorities, to be administered for the first time in history under the umbrella of broadly inclusive international organizations; but the expectations of those who sought racial equality in a new era of peace were disappointed, if not shattered, by an international regime which supported the attitudes and institutions of colonialism.

This could not be repeated after World War II. Retrospectively, the gruesome efficiency of the Nazi campaign of extermination pointed to a new global reality in which the horror of war was no longer manifest only in violent combat between states but also in genocidal violence inflicted by deviant states on their own citizens. The international protection of certain basic human rights had become not just a moral duty but also a matter of collective security. Aspirations for self-determination from "non-self-governing territories" could no longer be ignored. Minorities needed new, stronger protections. The rights of both individuals and minority peoples needed to be strengthened against the claims and duties demanded of states. State sovereignty, everyone agreed, must never again be used as a pretext for genocide.

With decolonization and the establishment of the post-World War II regime of human rights, a collective sense of unrequited rights extended further, to the most marginalized and excluded, some of whom took up a name and identity – "indigenous peoples" – first provided by international law. And with this new global identity came the now familiar feelings of wounded pride and cultural emptiness, of living without a shadow, of being at the same time within the reach of restoration, affirmation, justice, and dignity, while being denied these things by the state guardians of rights.

Even the decolonized states are therefore now included among the refusers and spoilers of collective rights, who gain control of governments through a dominant people and then close the gate on the powerless. The national boundaries drawn to include colonized people within the world's community of nations did not (and to a large degree could not) accommodate complex, indefinite, and interpenetrating contours of ethnic and tribal identities. The transfer of power favored those with large constituencies, western education, and the political wherewithal to engage with colonial power and then to build a government in its absence; it excluded small, subsistence-based societies remote from national capitals and those peoples divided by national boundaries; it especially excluded those whose kinship, trade, and political networks were fractured by an artificial process of nation building that began with lines on a map. Nomads and hunters were marginalized within marginal states. An observation made by Hannah Arendt shortly after World War II now goes far beyond the European minorities with which she began: "Not the loss of specific rights . . . but the loss of a community willing and able to guarantee any rights whatsoever, has been the calamity which has befallen ever-increasing numbers of people"[15]

Demands for collective rights thus come above all from those who have a strong sense of group identity but lack recognition and avenues to power within the state. The process of decolonization did not put an immediate end to the sense felt by many of being dominated by an alien and illegitimate power – it only made that power more proximate and recognizable. It sharpened the feeling that being dominated by one's own local tyrant is still better than the humiliation of being controlled, abused, or neglected by an inferior neighbor. And if the state could not bring itself to share power, recognition must be sought elsewhere. The pursuit of collective rights is for some peoples an answer to renewed identities and unfulfilled longings for recognition and empowerment, exacerbated, not improved, by the long reach of modern independent statehood. It is a strategy of decolonization-once-removed.

This strategy leads inevitably to a number of dilemmas. It is not just that traditional societies are making good use, for their own purposes, of legal formalism; the law itself can be legitimated through irrational hopes; it can repose upon fervent nationalist aspirations of self-actualization, inspired by utopian hopes for a world order brought about through shared values, peace-instilling moral common denominators, the uncorrupted kernels of universal tolerance and love. But these global goals of human rights lead to the convergence of human societies. Human rights are inspired by hopes that far exceed the voices and powers of international treaties. And the specific contents of laws derived from these hopes are forces of global integration every bit as powerful as the autonomous effects of bureaucracy and legal rationality. The integrity of distinct societies is therefore being enthusiastically and innovatively defended using legal mechanisms and standards that act to reduce cultural possibilities.

There is a more complicated way of expressing the dilemma stemming from the pursuit of collective rights: the more nation-states insist on being the sole arbiters of individual rights, including overseers of human rights compliance by minority cultures, the more they are encouraged to intervene in the rights violations of distinct minorities, and hence the more they inflame the cultural resentment, collective grievances, and separate identities of minority peoples. But the more political autonomy nation-states surrender to collectively-oriented minorities, the less control they have over compliance with the rights of individuals. Rights compliance is either effectively imposed at the expense of collective identities or ineffectively fractured through unconditional pluralism.[16] The choice is between monolithic states that impose equality through rights mechanisms and justifications, or pluralist state regimes in which minority peoples are not accountable for the rights of their members and states lack the authority to enforce compliance. Either way, the general orientation and effect of human rights is toward a reduction of cultural possibilities or, seen another way, the creation of a single human social type or personality, one world out of many.

The progressive integration of the world's nations, peoples, and cultures is bringing into prominence an issue that has until now mostly occupied democratic states: how do liberal societies accommodate, assimilate, or dominate those illiberal societies that flout the principles of individual freedom and the dignity of the person? One of the points at which rational/legal and Christian influences on human rights converge is their emphasis on the individual as the ultimate beneficiary of rights. Some states therefore have taken on a new responsibility toward their citizens: to protect their ability as individual actors to choose their fate, to decide for themselves what their contribution to society and nation will be, and to determine for themselves how they will develop as moral actors.

Faced with collective claims of rights and justice, strident interpretations of the mission and scope of individual rights, or of any liberal creed for that matter, can easily lead to the kind of malaise that occurs in conditions of frustrated evangelism. The receding possibility of conveying the Truth to recalcitrant nonbelievers calls for explanation, one that is often found in a reinforced conviction of the doubters' inherent moral inferiority. The goodwill of misguided cultural patronage transforms easily into self-defeating intolerance.

Now that menacing forms of collectivism have taken the form of international networks, state commitments to universal human rights are being replaced by the need for security and secret justice. One of the profound transformations of the world marked by the war on terrorism is a shift in the direction of liberal hostility toward absolutism from totalitarian states to smaller "totalitarian" communities and their networks. No longer does the threat to liberty come exclusively from rogue, freedom-hating dictatorships; it also, more than ever, comes from uncontrollable tribesmen or organizations upholding faith, honor, and loyalty to kinsmen – or what many now see more generally as the narrow, oppressive values of tribal societies – through modern tools of communication and violence. Tribal societies and their migrant extensions in the United States and Europe are now seen as the principal source of resistance to liberal democracy and the greatest danger to state security. Perhaps it is not tribes as such that are suspect, but only those that have developed international networks or that have been artificially made into nations ("tribes with flags") or that are consumed with the misdirected passions of radical Islam, or worst of all, that combine these defective attributes; these are the entities that pose the greatest danger to the universal values of freedom and democracy. The threat comes from those who impose ascribed identities upon individuals and turn them into integral parts of the social sub-unit, and who now have this as a model for the world to follow.[17] In the Muslim world, this is not a product of Islam as such, but of Islam used as a support for what many in North Atlantic civilization see as an atavistic, repressive social order based on systems of honor and collective moral reckoning, out of keeping with the nation-state and completely at odds with liberty and democracy. The new barbarians are at the gates. And the freedom of freedom's enemies must be denied. In such societies individuals are seen to be an asset or threat in more ways than through their behavior or ideas – conformity is almost a given; moral makeup is especially a product of blood and belonging. This is a new form of the ancient decentralized tyranny that has throughout history struggled against the imposition of centralized state power; only today, with new weapons at its disposal, it also struggles against modern conceptions of liberty.

Human rights have thus become more than the expression of a general resolve to protect the innocent by condemning the wrongs of states; the emphases on individualism, equality, and security reinforce the urge of nation-states toward cultural and constitutional homogeneity. A climate of insecurity, in which tribal societies are identified as threats to democracy, progress, and peace, can lead to the renewal of once discredited state-sponsored programs of assimilation, oriented toward constitutional and cultural homogeneity. Cultural differences enshrined by law are seen to be contrary to the basic principles of equality. Those who have made their identity attachments politically uncomfortable and indigestible must somehow be neutralized and absorbed. The forms such efforts can take are not just those that overtly manifest the state's powers of repression, but also those that include more philanthropic intervention. Efforts to "develop" a people or impose on them particular visions of "freedom" raise new possibilities for inter-cultural misunderstanding, ineptitude, and frustrated yearnings to find one's cherished values in others.

For those who want nothing to do with the philosophical and practical conundrums of human rights universalism, there is at least one basic option: to abandon altogether the Enlightenment project of a reason-based social order, to accept the view that all thinking aspiring toward universal good, in fact all effort to achieve cognitive or institutional stability, leads to a loss of spontaneous freedom. Every call to the fold of a community – especially to a global community – reduces the range of human possibility. There is no progress. There is no world Utopia. The moral universalism of rights regimes and the promises of techno-scientific development are illusions, products of a social malaise, known in the most general possible terms as "modernity."

Such sweeping rejection of the western heritage is unprecedented. Today there is a new armature of social and political thought, and even though the ideas that inspired liberation movements in the past are being dusted off and applied to new circumstances, they cannot be understood in the same way as before. Just as the global political and institutional transformations now taking place should not be seen as mere extrapolations from past transitions, there are new qualities to ideas of liberation that cannot be understood by looking exclusively at their philosophical antecedents. In the next three chapters I will consider this revolt against western ideas of universal human good – a rejection, as we will see, that leads some to favor a borderless world of featureless identities and incognizable tribalism.

6

Postmodernism's Revolt Against Order

Postmodernism Ill-defined

Anyone wanting to assert that overt utopian longing has faded from view in the course of late modernity could probably strengthen their argument by considering the influence of postmodernism in the last decades of the twentieth century. Postmodern critique elevated the status of relativism to a new, possibly unprecedented level with its sweeping, uncompromising rejection of classical positivism, scientific objectivism, instrumental reason, and, most forcefully, the kind of social engineering that follows from political idealism. The planned societies of Owen and Saint-Simone would not have found fertile soil in an intellectual climate dominated by postmodernist skepticism. Yet, as I intend to show in this chapter, the vagueness of postmodernism's depiction of possible futures resulted in a different kind of radical hope, not an instrumental, rational utopia of the kind that emerged from Enlightenment thought, but rather a loose, permissive, pluralist idealism, a kind of heterotopia of unlimited possibilities.

There are few today who adhere unquestioningly or unwaveringly to postmodernist nihilism – almost as though the approach of radical dissent eventually turned to consume itself. The most sweeping abandonment of "modernist" approaches to social thought had a particularly uncomfortable fit with those fields once (before the advent of postmodern critique) uncritically referred to as the "social sciences." How does one build a profession as a scholar if one emphasizes the contingency of knowledge and has rejected all possibility of sustained insight in the context of "cultural difference"? Most scholars have therefore reached some form of accommodation between the so-called modernist and postmodernist approaches to social knowledge, and many would say that the ability to reason, argue, and understand is not precluded by the recognition that reason, argument, and understanding are positioned in the social world and in history.

In this chapter I look in particular at what might be called the original, uncompromising versions of postmodern critique in an effort to show how this form of counter modernity or "a-modernity" has influenced current imaginings of global collective life. In some ways, contrary to the accommodation many have made with the restless identification and critique of modernity, I have spotlighted the contrast between the modern and the postmodern, but this is largely for heuristic purposes and to make more clear postmodernism's influence on other approaches to globalizing modernity. I do not consider postmodernism to have been a fad that has now and forevermore receded from our intellectual lives. Its influence remains, and remains to be fully understood.

A certain amount of complexity arises immediately from the question raised by topic of this chapter: what is postmodernism? The question is beset by difficulty because postmodernism is not only difficult to define but actually refuses to be defined – and sets upon anyone who makes the attempt. The intellectual network of self-styled "postmodernists" is connected by dedication to an uncompromising rejection of all "grand narrative," and sees any effort to "fix" or "capture" this pattern with tools of analysis as yet another "grand narrative," similarly to be rejected. It is impossible to delve into postmodernism like an intellectual ethnographer, to participant observe and later report one's findings. One either is a postmodernist who has taken a leap of faithlessness, who understands the intellectual culture intuitively from the inside, or one is not. The very project is suspect, the tools of *reportage* somehow hegemonic, playing into the hands of dominant cultural and political interests. It shares this reliance on such a criticism-rejecting device with other closed philosophical systems, such as "false consciousness" in Marxism, "resistance" in psychoanalysis, and "bad faith" in Sartre's existentialism.

Despite postmodernism's built-in rejection of critical scrutiny, the task remains to isolate its starting point and essential features. In attempting do accomplish this, I do not aspire toward a uniform definition so much as an understanding of some of postmodernism's main currents and qualities, starting with its most general features, which I will first outline before going on to consider some minor variations:

1. Postmodernism is principally an intellectual movement of criticism and counterpoint, which cannot be understood without reference to *a fatalistic theory of modernity*. The "modern" of "postmodernism" is essentially everything in industrial societies or the "Occident" that tends toward centralization and social control, especially subtle forms of control-through-conformism. The modernity of postmodernism is a huge, impersonal force that can be neither thoroughly investigated nor deflected from its trajectory of domination. The heritages of the Enlightenment, Christianity, and Communism are all similarly suspect because they aspire toward universal goals of peace and progress – goals that cannot be worked toward without invoking powerful energies of social control and homogenization, eradication of small traditions and canalization of individual self-expression, especially of dissidence. These are all based upon what Jean-François Lyotard calls "metanarratives," those grand religious or philosophical ideas of liberation that "look for legitimacy, not in an original founding act, but in a future to be accomplished."[1] The main historical reference points for this position are the holocaust, the breakup of colonial empires, and the de-legitimation of communism in the aftermath of Soviet expansionism.

It is no mere coincidence that philosophical postmodernism first found a secure place among those French intellectuals who, in some cases against their better judgment, participated in the failed communist-inspired university uprisings of May 1968. These are the so-called *soixante-huitards* who were subsequently disillusioned with *everything* states or rebels had to offer: not just liberalism and communism, but all other world-historical paradigms of truth-in-politics. Such paradigms were, as they saw it, just so many variations of the forces that brought the holocaust into being. In a post-Auschwitz world, "how could grand narratives of legitimation still have credibility?" Lyotard asks.[2] And "how could the ideal of mastery persist?"[3]

2. The first order of business, therefore, is to reject all manner of grand narrative, without erecting a replacement paradigm of universal emancipation, to avoid at all costs the temptation to construct real or imagined utopias, to take up an orientation to liberation based almost entirely on *criticism of universalizing values and institutions*. This objective is most clear in architecture, the field in which postmodernism originated, specifically in post-fascist Italy, well before its philosophical incarnation, as a counterpoint to designs intended to celebrate the authority of the state. In the architectural postmodernism of the 1960s, the first premise was to reject the grandiose, impersonal structures that celebrated power over individuals, the designs that celebrated the arid, anonymous regularity of bureaucracies and bureaucratically organized living space within totalitarian states or capitalist empires. In building – quite literally – resistance to the structural forms of domination, it sought to recover the lost patrimonies of individual cultures, to celebrate human diversity by representing each milieu in its own space, through its own socio-architectural forms, symbolism, and materials. It responded to the dominating representation of universal forms with a celebration of eclecticism, a diminution of scale that permitted expression of local values, attempting to heal the cultural amnesia of modernity with a recovery of collective local memory.[4]

If one applies this general thrust of architectural postmodernism by analogy to its more abstract forms in philosophy, sociology, and anthropology, the entire "movement" becomes easier to understand, provided one recognizes that in its social-theoretical forms fatalism is more salient. Postmodernism stands opposed to grand structures of liberation in all their varieties because they come to be controlled and corrupted by powers that dominate individuals and distinct communities. Emancipation promised through duty and obedience is an illusion; even efforts of critique can coalesce into false promises of liberation and nightmarish revamping of centralizing tendencies. Therefore, to avoid becoming an unwitting apologist for what exists, one must renounce the very project of directly confronting it; or if one does hazard the elaboration of an alternative to existing forms of modernity, these in their turn must be dismantled. "Everything that is received must be suspected, even if it is only a day old," says Lyotard.[5] Radical postmodernism involves a "war on totality" in which the fundamental premise of dismantling modernity is the only thing that must remain secure – and hence must always remain incomplete.

3. The uncompromising rejection of universals has led postmodernism to become the currently fashionable form of a fairly old idea: *relativism* – that is, radical skepticism toward any claim that it is possible to achieve or approach universally valid truth or, put it another way, the theory that "objective," universal truth is unattainable and unapproachable.[6] In fact, postmodernism goes one better, with the idea that efforts to apply false ideals of universal truth to human life oppressively constrain the human spirit. Hence, not only do the structures of state domination and legitimation come under the critical gaze, the very enterprise of scientific truth seeking is suspect, just another form of Occidental cultural imperialism.[7] There is no way to achieve truth-consensus without narrative sleight of hand and the authority structure of experts. Postmodernism is largely built upon the argument (or arguments like it) that all scientific and philosophical absolutism is repugnant, since it uses a dogmatic and authoritarian claim to possess the truth as a principal criterion of the truth.[8]

Postmodernism's radical skepticism toward truth and social order usually takes the form of what I would prefer to call *critical relativism* or, because it is critical of almost everything, *negative relativism* – not the optimistic form of relativism common, for example, to postwar anthropology, promoted most effectively by Margaret Mead, in which all standards of truth and forms of life were seen to be equally valid – or more precisely, those who were marginalized and lacking power were seen as equal among themselves, in some ways superior to industrial or bureaucratic societies, and therefore not to be judged. Negative relativism is rather the idea that all standards of truth (except, perhaps, those of postmodernists themselves) are equally to be distrusted and, if possible, exposed as equally oppressive forms of deceit. The difference is perhaps only one of emphasis, with anthropology focused on the relatively powerless and postmodernism on the powerful or, what amounts to the same thing, on the legitimizing sources of their power.

If there is no legitimate meta-narrative, no grand social construct that can command respect and order, what is to keep societies from disintegrating into anarchy? The solution most commonly posited by postmodernists (at least by the minority which makes the attempt) involves a return to some form of small-scale society, a social form that does not dominate because it does not have the power to do so, one that provides individuals with the minimal shelter of a world view, without imposing an alienating vaulted edifice of truth and liberation.

Although it is sometimes difficult to disentangle the great variety of philosophical influences that can be found in the work of postmodernists, this nostalgic, neo-traditionalist quality strongly evokes the eighteenth-century critique of the Enlightenment by the German Romantics. The Romantics categorically rejected the views that a perfect pattern of life was attainable and that reason was an avenue to the truth. The typical romantic nostalgia was opposed to the attainment of fulfillment; but, oddly enough, they were not at all opposed to the quest for it, because it was principally through the inexhaustible yearning for an undiscoverable state of completion that the Romantics expressed themselves.[9]

This seems also to apply aptly to the postmodernists, except that for the latter, even the unfulfilled *Sehnsucht* of the Romantics is disqualified as a source of futurism, hopelessly bound up in the project of modernity. The quest for truth, perfection, harmony, and fulfillment can only result in disappointment or, worse, legitimation of the great projects of domination. Ideally (and, as we shall see, this ideal is not always followed), postmodernism expresses its yearning through criticism – not of an instrumental kind intended to make incremental improvements to the social order, but a "deconstructive" effort to peel back the layers of hegemony. It is this ever-unfulfilled task that characterizes postmodernism, a new kind of quest-abandoning critical romanticism, which combines unconsummated yearning with paranoia toward modernity.

4. Hegemony, most postmodernists agree, is not only manifest in the institutions of modernity; it permeates, or even originates in, the *meanings* of modernity; *Hegemony is built into the language of domination.* The words and symbols we use are imbued with an almost inescapable, conformity-enhancing power, which we must struggle to transcend. In particular, clear hypotheses and generalizations are products of the Enlightenment's project of world-historical-domination-through-progress. To nullify this effect, postmodernists must refuse the "consolation of correct forms" and the consensus of taste; they must instead develop new forms of presentation, and enhance the mystical, unknowable qualities of so-called reality, "to better produce the feeling

that there is something unpresentable."[10] The ultimate act of resistance is the interpretation of interpretation.[11]

5. The relativist idea that universals are inseparable from oppressive "metanarratives" leads postmodernism in the direction of *methodological looseness and irregularity*. Stylistic rebellion is a complement of its negative relativistic approach toward "techno-science" and instrumental reason. Up to a point, it is possible to draw up a reasonably cogent argument in favor of this absence of cogency. If there is no such thing as a secure truth, and if all efforts to arrive at it are inherently hegemonic, then the study of human society must be approached with reduced expectations, with the use of metaphor rather than "evidence," tropes rather than description, intuition rather than analysis, and, in an extreme anthropological form, a surrender to the unfathomability of the "Other" in subjective musings about the trials and tribulations of cultural encounter.

This, at any rate, is the main thrust of an argument justifying postmodernist meanderings, intentional ambiguities, and verbosity – an argument which posits almost insurmountable difficulty in overcoming the limitations of meaning and constraints of power (the part of postmodernism's case that might be understandable), the antidote to which is obscurity of style and self-reflexive musings on the inescapability of meaning and the ineluctable unknowability of the "Other" (the part that is not).

As I mentioned earlier, this general quality of postmodernism provides it with a certain degree of protective cover from criticism – of which it has nevertheless attracted its fair share. Postmodernism has been called irrational, neo-conservative, simpleminded, nihilistic, anarchistic, cynical, intellectual terrorism, and a variety of other not very nice things, none of which quite seem to stick. The harshest critics of postmodernism have tried to extinguish it without, it seems, being quite able to point toward the base of the flame. But it is this very quality of critical imperviousness that ultimately undermines it because the only way to avoid *all* labels and *all* philosophical confrontation is to be vague and noncommittal, to treat the most important political questions of the day with poetry and paradoxes. Properly speaking, postmodernism is not irrational, it is *a*-rational. Its major flaw is not the presence in its leading authors' work of logical inconsistencies or contradictions (though they are certainly not lacking these), but in its extreme form the elaboration of systems of thought in which logic is suspended, in which clear, orderly, and systematic presentations of ideas are rejected as mere byproducts of "positivistic hegemony" and the subtle intrusions of Enlightenment forms of "grand narrative."

But the very barrier of indeterminacy that in some ways protects postmodernism from its critics at the same time prevents it from launching effective criticism of its own. By rejecting reason, organization, and clarity as products of the hegemonic Occident, postmodernists push the most effective tools of critical thinking beyond reach, relying instead on metaphor, intuition, "poetics," awkward neologisms, and broken narrative to make the (usually implicit) point that *they* at least cannot be accused of marching to the tune of a homogenizing paradigm of domination.

This, it must be confessed, has a certain appeal. It leaves room for a certain kind of intellectual creativity, even playfulness. The very term "postmodern" is sometimes used with a sideways wink, suggesting that nothing one teaches or writes in the academy should really be taken all that seriously.[12] It can be amusing to learn a form that rejects formalism. But when it comes to reaching the uninitiated, and in particular having an impact on those in control of the structures of domination, postmodernism makes itself small and melts into the background, content with a kind of inscrutable quietism. It is so overpowered by its perception of the scale of oppression in modern society that it is satisfied with merely exposing the conspiracies of modernity to the circle of the initiated. Postmodernism, for all its rejection of power-elitism, is, in the words of Michel Maffesoli, for the "happy few" who possess a "certain aristocracy of the mind,"[13] not (by implication) for those common, misguided souls who would actually like to have an impact on their world.

6. Those postmodernists who do venture to depict an alternative political reality usually arrive at a version of what might be called *emancipation beyond hegemony*. Postmodernism's most successful argument is that hegemonic calls of duty, obedience, and public virtue are not limited to aberrant dictatorships. Liberal individualism has never been distilled in pure form, even though it is often presented as the virtuous side of an us/them dichotomy. Every civilization, every nation-state, every society has the potential to require of its members

a level of obedience that shades into conformity and hostility toward innocent differences. This view is not a unique possession of "classic" postmodernism. It is commonly attributed Michel Foucault (often considered a proto-postmodernist), whose approach to governance and power from below was grounded in the historian's craft and did not lapse into a global paradigm of liberation. It can also be found in the work of some of the leading figures of the Frankfurt school, notably Herbert Marcuse, Erich Fromm, Leo Lowenthal, Max Horkheimer, Walter Benjamin, and Theodor Adorno, particularly their depiction of the moral and political ambiguities of the Enlightenment ideals of social and technological progress and of the gap between the promises of bourgeois ideology and the disappointingly vacuous everyday reality of bourgeois society.[14]

Postmodernism takes on much of this critical project, while hiding its emancipatory ideas deep within more visible, attention-consuming methodological critiques. Its ultimate appeal, however, still derives from the sense that the power of words can break down barriers; set back the limits to human liberty; make the way people are dominated more humane, or if unjust domination is inevitable, find other ways humanity might become free; penetrate structures of thought; and push the limits of language and cognition that they might somehow be transcended.

What would happen to postmodernism in a world in which democratic/liberal hegemony was not at all corrupted but somehow managed to fulfill every one of its ambitions; in which almost all the aspirations of the rights movement had been realized: peace and stability among all nations, achieved through regular and productive mechanisms for negotiating differences between nation-states and national minorities; democratic state governments brought to power everywhere through regular, fair elections; a strong, independent judiciary in every nation-state, promoting civil liberties while bringing about a virtual end to state-sponsored torture and repression of civic organizations; and success in the development and implementation of redistributive or "third-generation" rights – effective elimination of global hunger, homelessness, preventable illness, and poverty, in large measure through redistribution of the world's wealth, services, and opportunities. Imagine (and this may be more of a stretch) that a relatively even level of global prosperity and general fulfillment of nationalist aspirations leads to a decline of religious extremism and an end to organized terrorism. Imagine that there remain just enough social challenges to provide an outlet for extroverted political passions, but without leading to hatred, violence, or instability. This is the unachievable paradise that lies behind a great deal of liberal-oriented political activism, part of a realm in which postmodernism either disavows practical effectiveness or fails to achieve it. But would this kind of fulfillment lead to an end of dissidence? Would civic organizations have nothing of substance to declaim against? Would ink dry in the pens of those who, in a more turbulent world, would by skill and inclination devote themselves to social criticism? Curiously, the answer that comes immediately to mind is "no," perhaps even an adamant "of course not." A liberal Utopia would not spell the end of the almost infinite human capacity for dissatisfaction. Expressing a lack of fulfillment seems to be, for some at least, a main source of fulfillment.

This brings us to a quality of postmodernism that I consider essential for a proper understanding of its contribution: Postmodernism inhabits the area of social and cultural criticism left over from struggles to fulfill basic freedoms and equalities. If the human rights movement strives to break down the walls of torture rooms and concentration camps, the main targets of postmodernism are the walls of conformity and cultural hegemony.

Pomotopia

We can probably credit the sociologist C. Wright Mills with the obvious but significant point that the process of transcending modernity means by definition to construct or anticipate a social state of postmodernity. In 1959, at least a decade before anything that could remotely be called a postmodernist movement had emerged, Mills made an intriguing observation: "Just as Antiquity was followed by several centuries of Oriental ascendancy . . . so now the Modern Age is being succeeded by a post-modern period. Perhaps we may call it: The Fourth Epoch." This is a currently unfolding period in which "the ideas of freedom and of reason have become moot [and in which] increased rationality may not be assumed to make for increased freedom."[15]

What has in fact arisen, however, is a sociological postmodernism that, in this time of restricted freedom, exaggerates and exacerbates the limits of rationality and avoids direct engagement with political realities. The postmodern condition is one which declines even the comfort of amassing convincing evidence of epochal transformations, preferring instead the solace of paradox: the permanence to be found in dismantling everything that aspires toward permanence, the ideal to be found in the negation of ideals and an "end of history" in the rejection of grand historical narrative. There is no steady state of post-modernity and no intellectual anchors that would enable one to be secured, only what Gianni Vattimo, without a touch of irony, calls "weak thinking" (*pensiero debole*), a kind of self-avowed nihilism in which all forms of intellectual dogmatism are supposedly avoided and history, in particular, ceases its concern with the idea (or illusion) of progress.[16]

Vattimo at least deserves some credit for honesty; some of those who call themselves postmodernist would not accept the label "nihilist." Theirs is a noble way of thinking that really does aspire – though never dogmatically or universally – to something better than the present. True, the obstacles of modernity may be overwhelming, the chances of success, of even making a dent in the edifice of domination, slim to none, but the challenge is there for the intrepid few to take up.

This leaves unanswered the question of what kind of society or state of being one is anticipating or being asked to struggle for. If we are not to revel in impotent pessimism (as indeed some do) what is the alternative to the ills of the modern condition? Or, if we abstract from what postmodernists say or don't say, if we violate the rules of disengagement by reading between the lines a little, what sort of society is being called for? What really is the Fourth Epoch?

Gilles Lipovetsky, in *L'ère du vide* (The age of emptiness), first published in 1983, is one of the few so-called postmodernists to take up this challenge.[17] The new era of "postmodern society," he begins, is inseparable from the conditions of modernity. Liberty is emergent from a state of oppression. In a way, it builds its liberating energy by feeding off the constraints of disciplinary society. Modern society, for Lipovetsky, is based on a revolutionary eschatology that leads to the erosion of individual identities, destabilization of personalities, widespread ideological and political disaffection and malaise brought about by inherent social contradictions: disciplinary democracy, the conventionalized revolutions of a permanent state of impermanence, all within the "air-conditioned hell" of consumer society. Then there is

the "global sociological mutation" to be found in scientific and technological (over-)optimism – in fact a parallel form of permanent revolution. The future is approached by modernity in all its forms with a
conquering ideology and is defined by an expectation of ineluctable
progress.

But the ideal of forging a new humanity does not sit comfortably
with a consumer society based upon instant or imminent gratification.
Modernity is accompanied by a state of emptiness (*vide*), in which the
promises of historic mobilization toward an ideal end are abandoned.
There is no longer an apotheosis, a divine or historical ideal, to release
us from the confines of the modern state of being.

Lipovetsky finds this very condition of emptiness to be a source of
contemporary promise. Liberation is occurring in the present. A form of
socialization and individualization is emerging which breaks with the
Enlightenment anti-tradition. A process of "personalization" is taking
place, which rejects (*"pulvérise"* is the hyperbolic word Lipovetsky uses)
the rational collective rules that attempt to subordinate individuals to
homogenous social wholes. Instead, social legitimation is based upon
hedonistic values, respect for differences, on the "cult" of personal liberation, the values of which include (in no particular order): humor,
sincerity, freedom of expression, and the absence of sexual inhibition.
In a way (though Lipovetsky might not agree), this is an expression
of Enlightenment hopes taken one step further: not just upholding the
liberty of the individual, but the freedom to be *absolutely* oneself; not
just placing cardinal value on the right to life, but the right to *enjoy*
life to the fullest. The consumer revolution is almost solely responsible for this new development of expectations (occasionally expressed
by Lipovetsky in the language of "rights") and desires; having stimu-
lated new forms of expression, it has simultaneously brought about a
criticism of "bulimic" excess, placing emphasis instead on quality of
life. Individuals and groups are expressing an unprecedented will to
autonomy. The challenges of "neo-feminism," the claims of linguistic
and regional minorities, and the search for alternative lifestyles in new
social movements are all expressions of personalized identity, the
search by individuals and groups for autonomy and self expression,
and a corresponding rejection of all forms of universalism. Postmodern
society is part and parcel of modernity, built into the logic of consumerism, which makes the autonomous individual the ultimate
source and marker of liberation.

This is vaguely reminiscent of Marxism, except that in Lipovetsky's postmodern society, hedonistic consumerism, not the increasing immiseration of the proletariat, is capitalism's source of inherent contradiction; and the goal or expectation of revolution, of dismantling the entire social edifice, is discarded. Revolution has shown itself to be inseparable from civilization's tendencies toward domination, to be cast off together with other forms of hegemony.

One would naturally expect the ardor of this vision to diminish with time, or at the very least with the rise of radical right-wing nationalism, but in a ten-year retrospective to *L'ère du vide*, Lipovetsky is on the whole unswayed by events that seem to run counter to his account of critical consumerism. He notes with approval the higher rates of voter abstention in general elections, but neglects to mention the unexpected success of Jean-Marie Le Pen and the Front National. His assessment remains that, "the kaleidoscope of the post-modern individual is more than ever the order of the day."[18]

Let us now consider a rival interpretation of postmodern society. Michel Maffesoli, using a similarly loose method (which he explicitly calls, "*une sociologie vagabonde*") in which the truth is relative, "situated" in complex ways, unknowable, and only approachable through metaphor, imagination, and spirit, emphasizes quite a different definitive phenomenon of postmodern societies: "tribalism."[19] The traditional bugbears of postmodernism – Enlightenment universalism, Occidental triumphalism, and hierarchical patriarchalism – are in the process of giving way to a horizontal, fraternal form of sociability. Or if they do affirm a hierarchical dimension of social existence, it does not take a rigid form that excludes outsiders, but a vital form of "spontaneous regulation," a kind of pluralist or polycultural hierarchy with no use for boundaries or xenophobia. "As opposed to the periods that accentuate rational activity," Maffesoli writes, "this regulation is the result of those who have greater confidence in the intrinsic sovereignty of each group."[20]

Social groups, as Maffesoli sees them, are mobilizing through common desires to return to nature, to human origins, to the "humus of existence" – the odors, and textures of human animality – expressing themselves in play, the feeling of brotherhood (and sisterhood), a self-conscious reawakening of barbarism and savagery (*ensauvagement*) and nostalgia for fusion in community existence.[21] This "tribalism" is not something that leaps out at you. It is more or less hidden, ephemeral, intruding subtly into society. And yet it is something on which the health and livability of our existence depends, a kind of Reichian regression therapy for the collective soul.

One man's emancipatory individualism is another man's freedom-instilling tribalism. Lipovetsky claims to intuit a growing individualist rejection of duty and conformity, while Maffesoli senses a decline of individualism in a resurgence of savage micro-collectivism. These contradictory sociologies of liberation reject the methodological limitations inherent in the fact that industrial societies are of such complexity that virtually any set of vaguely complementary facts can be plucked from the mass of available information and emphasized as a significant trend, especially when contrary tendencies are selectively ignored.

But, it could be argued, the two perspectives can be seen in some ways to overlap; there is no necessary contradiction between individualism and a kind of restorative tribalism, except perhaps in the way each perspective invests its favor. In fact, they might even be vaguely complementary, with individualism creating the kind of "emptiness" that encourages many small efforts toward tribal renewal. Even this, however, would amount to little more than the platitudinal truism that industrial society includes self-expressing individuals and groups, both of which are occasionally resistant to dominant culture and organized power.

The most interesting question, though, is not the degree to which this kind of postmodern view of the world corresponds with reality or, alternatively, is an edifice of fantasy (how exactly does one set out to determine, even approximately, how many kaleidoscopic individuals or tribes are in our midst?); it is more revealing to consider these postmodern perspectives as material in themselves for sociological inquiry, especially to consider the near-utopian dimensions of such descriptions of modern/postmodern society. For, judging by their cumulative investments in sociological imagination and metaphor, it seems clear that they are presenting us not with social reality, but with social promise. Postmodern society, according to those postmodernists with the most optimistic bent, embodies the greatest possibilities for freedom and pleasure of any social order, past or present. It is emergent. It is irrepressible. And it is here, within our grasp. There is, it is true, no call to action, no recipe for bringing about a higher ideal. After all, revolution is the stuff of modernity and postmodernists are beyond *any* deep political commitment. Maffesoli explicitly makes a virtue of political disengagement when he describes the values of citizenship, Republic, State, social contract, liberty, civil society, and mechanisms of representation as no longer having any "relationship with that which is lived."[22] In other words, he de-legitimates every conceivable avenue of democracy, offering nothing in its place except the vague hope that he pins on tribal effervescence.

Postmodernists like Lipovetsky and Maffesoli, who exercise a certain amount of sociological candor – to the extent that they set out to isolate the emancipatory aspects of industrial society – provide an important service because their work serves to highlight a wider quality of postmodernism that might otherwise escape notice: an opaque and dishonest dedication to radical hope. This propensity is obscured by postmodernism's consistent rejection of Enlightenment conceptions of liberation, of rational political engagement with the goal of universal prosperity and peace. The postmodern social ideal, if it can be seen at all, is almost always implicit, a mere shadow on the screen of metaphor or "deconstruction." Paradoxically, this in itself leads to a vision of emancipation, of universal deliverance from universal paradigms of deliverance.[23] Postmodernism's injunction against futurism is uncompromising, but freed by methodological permissiveness, it is also sometimes able to describe utopia – though only in the present tense – as a secure trend or accomplished reality.[24] The ideal society becomes a presentiment of culture-in-the-making.

Civil Society and Extraparliamentary Democracy

One of the ways postmodernism has influenced many people's understanding of society and political virtue – whether they acknowledge this influence or not – involves the perception, in some cases the overpowering conviction, that power in modern society has greatly transcended public will, that individuals possess a greatly diminished capacity to be governed by their own consent, in part because one of the prevailing tools of power is the ability to manufacture or manage political consent, in other words, that significant power is situated outside the realms of party politics and voting stations and even lies beyond the reckoning of those who are controlled by it.[25]

More recently, postmodernism has also lent a great deal of credence to the idea that the arrangements under which people live – even in democratic societies – are no longer controlled by them, that capitalist societies have largely transcended the need for legitimation, that "the free society is no more demonstrable than the free act."[26] By opposing all forms of universalizing domination, postmodernism garnered strength from the decline and dismantling of the Soviet dictatorship. Then, without attacking the enormously appealing *idea* of democracy, it could lay claim to being the only viable avenue of sweeping criticism of democratic/capitalist mass society. Without committing itself to the construction of alternatives, it situated existing democratic institutions in the camp of hegemony-producers; and in doing so it attempted to undercut commitment to the existing political frameworks of western democracies. (How far it may have succeeded is more difficult to say.) At the same time, the postmodernist critique of capitalism (or premise of its fragmentation) challenged the central virtues of commercial society, as extolled early on by David Hume and Adam Smith: that capitalism was capable of softening the harsh subordination of individuals characteristic of rural societies in earlier centuries, that it eroded personal dependence on superiors with inherited authority as one of the main organizing principles of human society.[27] Postmodernism, in some of its iterations, has instead looked for new forms of "tribalism" and new ways to express the reassertion of the color and intimacy of community. It did all of this elliptically, through an obsessive concern with hegemony-in-meaning rather than the failings of democracy or the proliferation of supra-democratic institutions and sources of power.

But if modernity's constraints on freedom are so insidious as to often go unperceived, if the tyranny-engendering force of universal idealism is so pervasive and the idea of social mastery is so persistent, how can there be liberation? Clearly such an account of our social lives, and particularly our political thoughts and arrangements, does not call for carefully reasoned, piecemeal reform – for to do so is in postmodernist terms to be either thoroughly corrupted by the superficial promises of democratic modernity or lured by the illusions of technoscience, in the form of social engineering. Nor does it call for revolution, which inevitably results in such universalism-gone-awry as that exemplified by Jacobinism or Stalinism. Instead, those who have not succumbed to fatalism look for signs indicating that, independent of any kind of social reform or emancipatory effort, modernity is failing. And what they usually see in this present-oriented oracularity is the rise of new interest groups, new forms of collectivity, new kinds of identity politics, forms of social effervescence that mark a shift from the modern to the "postmodern."

Insofar as postmodernism does articulate alternatives to the oppressive conditions of mass society, it is situated in informal resistance, in what might be called "extraparliamentary democracy" or in an unceremonious approach to the concept of civil society. Yves Boisvert cites a wide range of postmodernist literature to argue that there are inherent political possibilities in the postmodern corpus, characterized by a democratic will.[28] Then there is the approach of Gilles Lipovetsky, who argues that democracy is "second nature" to the postmodern individual. We can be thankful, he informs us, that we live in a time of such individualism and hence such counter-hegemonic vitality.[29] And Michel Maffesoli finds an answer in self-avowed relativism, sharply reducing the expectations of equality-based democracy, recognizing the inevitability of hierarchies in social systems while leaving the correction of its harmful effects to local orders. (Appallingly, the Hindu caste system is an example he uses of "corrected" hierarchy.) Again, this is a process that happens on its own, that does not require nurturing, only non-interference, and he thus enjoins us to "leave it to the groups concerned to find their own forms of equilibrium."[30] It is hard to see democratic will in this, except perhaps in the form of an exclusively collective approach to social justice, one that sees freedom and democratic voice as being manifest in autonomous "tribes."

According to the postmodernist perspective, civil society (in the instances its presence among us is acknowledged) is therefore seen as an almost spontaneous outgrowth of mass society. There are no conditions in which it develops more readily, nothing to be done to nurture it – and little that can be done to kill it either. The humus of civil society simply *is*.

The reason for such sociological detachment and reticence is reasonably straightforward. If some forms of modernity really are better (or less bad) than others – if some really do foster a climate that is at least tolerant of criticism and peaceful civic resistance while others specialize in mechanisms of repression – then postmodernism's disengagement from the public sphere and its sweeping rejection of everything with the faintest odor of modernity are called into question. Postmodernists are then forced to make distinctions and choices, and thus to give up much of that rebellious allure that comes with setting out to expose *every* form of strong-thinking universalism as a sham, a delusion, and a constraint on what, in imitation of their verbosity, might be called "the spontaneous expression of creative subjectivity." Once the premise that there are conditions that foster the growth and dynamism of civil society is accepted, it becomes a scholarly task of the greatest importance to identify these conditions, encourage them, and, if necessary, defend them.

It is equally clear that not all entities that can be called "tribal" or collective are equally committed to the welfare of democracy, the benefits of civic institutions, or even the lives of innocents. Some are self-destructively dedicated to undermining the conditions in which all forms of civil society come into being. Postmodernism thus tends to overlook the ways that some forms of resistance to modernity can embody the worst qualities of both modernity and pre-modernity. A terrible deficiency of postmodernist relativism (or of all stark relativisms, for that matter) is its blindness to the potentially oppressive power of the oppressed.

Because postmodernism has no use for any kind of hegemony, it tends to ignore or to be shy about the employment of universal paradigms of liberation by the relatively powerless. It has become increasingly difficult to advocate for a distinct peoples' survival, reawakening, or protection from outside interference, however, without ultimately drawing upon ideas of global salvation or emancipation. There are many who have made good use of conditions that encourage the growth and influence of civil society, have "reverse engineered" the organizational structures, networking patterns, and lobbying strategies of nongovernmental organizations.

Yves Boisvert cites the James Bay Crees' political lobbying effort of the early 1990s, an effort to prevent unwanted hydroelectric development on their northern Quebec territory, as a "perfect example" of postmodern-style peaceful resistance: the use of social partnerships and language games in confrontations between interest groups.[31] But what the Crees themselves have done to further their liberation is especially noteworthy. The most significant "language games" they engage in do not involve resistance to hydroelectric development – in fact they have recently reached an agreement worth $3.5 billion over 50 years with the province of Quebec and its state-owned utility,

Hydro-Québec for the construction of new dam projects in their territory. The issue of ultimate concern to the James Bay Crees, and Canada's aboriginal leadership generally, is sovereignty, or their rights of self-determination, a concern frequently expressed in a wide range of national and international forums. By invoking only the critical side of the Cree campaign as an illustration of the potential of postmodernism, Boisvert is denying credit to the real source of the Crees' inspiration: a very modernist form of liberal pluralism, above all a regime of human rights grounded solidly in the Enlightenment's promise of human emancipation from slavery, servitude, poverty, and injustice through recognition of basic human endowments, especially a universal capacity to communicate across cultural boundaries.

The important, connected issues surrounding identity politics and civil society can neither be attributed to postmodernist strivings toward critical disobedience, nor convincingly explained by its forms of analysis, nor reliably captured by its style of description. Postmodernism provides neither an effective method of analysis nor a viable strategy of resistance.

In a roundabout way, postmodernism is historically important because of these very failings. The postmodernist version of extra-parliamentary democracy, for those seeking any form of *political* emancipation, is de-clawed and empty of promise. One could even say that it has, at a critical time in history, distracted attention from the significant responsibilities of effective social criticism and thereby given an advantage to those manifestly oppressive aspects of modernity that it consistently rejects.

In the context of an effort to clarify the nature and significance of ideas about globalization and anti-globalization, postmodernism is an example of a theoretical paradigm that, oddly enough, replicates the basic paradox that I described in chapters three and four: postmodernism's chosen method of resistance to forces of global domination and social convergence ultimately creates conditions that make it easier for those forces to assert themselves. If we accept the initial premise of the postmodernist critique, that hegemony especially pervades those institutions with global agendas, then the intellectual abandonment of efforts to imagine practical alternatives would ultimately contribute to the global insinuation of that hegemony.

In saying that postmodernist fatalism shares this quality, this basic counter-intentional elaboration of a process of global convergence, with the collective efforts of peoples that are manifestly marginalized and oppressed, am I not thus expressing a similar fatalism? Am I not a postmodernist *malgré moi*, conceding to a view of globalization in which hegemony is all pervasive and ultimately unstoppable? In a sense this might be true. But there is an important distinction to be made between those forces of "globalization from below" that occur as a paradoxic side-effect of transnational efforts to (re)define communities and secure their self-determination and those that give comfort to the forces of "globalization from above" by advocating sweeping critical disengagement, even from the social impacts of decisions made by institutions of global industry, trade, and governance.

Meanwhile, there are still paradigms of global liberation that have not given up on the possibility of developing an engaged sociology that strives toward advocacy and reform. Even hopes of world revolution, though certainly overshadowed and cast to the periphery by the decline of state-sponsored communism, have not been eradicated from the sociological imagination. Neo-Marxism, the topic of my next chapter, remains an approach to oppression, liberation, and the reconciliation of human differences that serves as a starting point for a variety of efforts to understand a shrinking world.

7

The New Neo-Marxism

The Moment of Disillusionment

The year 1989, marking the fall of the Berlin Wall, has become short-hand for tremendous changes in the way our world is constituted, above all the end of a bipolar world order, but it still remains difficult to see events clearly, to prioritize them, and maybe to discard some hasty assumptions. Notwithstanding the great certainties that went along with the "end of history" debate initiated by Francis Fukuyama,[1] we are still too close to the happenings of this time to make much use of hindsight, and whatever we say still risks being proven wrong by unforeseen events. It seems reasonably certain, however, that 1989 marked a major realignment of the global economy through a sharp decline in the legitimacy and political fortunes of state-sponsored communism, and, conversely, a major boost to the close interdependence of capitalism and liberal democracy. An optimistic implication of the Soviet breakup, as seen by John Dunn from within the swirl of events in the early 1990s, was the birth a new world order marked by an absence of any "specifiable and categorical alternative to modern capitalism, with its own special and historically privileged political setting." The different political circumstances we now face are marked by the fact that "until 1989 the history of socialism had been the history of the presumption in some version or other that there is indeed such an alternative [to capitalism]. Now that this presumption must be abandoned as a matter of historical right, it will be interesting to see which aspects of it (if any) can be resuscitated as a matter of responsible and causal judgement."[2]

This is probably expecting too much out of both the extended reach of post-1989 global capitalism and the possible neo-socialist reactions against it. But it does suggest the need for a task that seems to have been neglected in the rush to express hopeful appraisals of (once) current events: an inquiry into the current theoretical state of neo-Marxism, whether it be responsible or irresponsible, whether grounded in sensible causal judgment or paranoid fantasy.

This task, which I will begin to sketch out in this chapter, requires the suspension of two, usually implicit, assumptions of the capitalism-as-victor approach to the post-Soviet era. First, this approach sometimes assumes the Soviet breakup to be *the* defining moment of the grand disillusion with Marxism, and hence overlooks the many ways neo-Marxists had already been challenged by state-centered communism and answered, with varying degrees of success, the philosophical challenges posed by Soviet tyranny. As we have already seen in the background of the postmodernist movement, the greatest challenge to the legitimacy of Marxism was not the dismantling of Soviet state socialism but the abuses it committed at the height of its power; and the stiffest intellectual opposition to neo-Marxism has not only come from supporters of free-market liberalism but from the critical usurpations of postmodernism. Committed neo-Marxists have had a long time to stew over these two challenges, and, as I will show later in this chapter, a few in recent years have tried to articulate a reply to both.

Second, the celebrationist view assumes the opportunities for development through capitalism in the new world order to be an irrefutable practical reply to the far left, an ever-effective counter-spell against the specter of Marxism; conversely it overlooks the possibility that the painful transitions brought about by globalization among the so-called developing nations could inspire restless compassion and discontent in at least some world regions; and in the realm of ideas, it assumes that Marx's philosophical paradigm, hammered out of shape to suit the ideological purposes of Soviet statism, shared the sorrowful plight of the Soviet breakup and now has nothing more to say – *ever* – nothing which anyone could possibly use to build a critique of capitalism; it assumes that Marxism was as inherently ossified as the politburo, and that the philosophy of Marx and his state-socialist epigones were definitively and irrevocably discredited with the practical victory of capitalism. It mistakenly ignores the possibility that globalization, for reasons I will explain later, actually creates new conditions for a revival of Marx-inspired discourse, albeit in sharply attenuated, even liberalized form, in which the idea of imminent proletarian revolution has been replaced with what might be called cosmopolitan socialism. I will suggest several reasons for this shift in emphasis later in this chapter.

The 1930s were the years when young writers and academics in Europe and the Americas felt the greatest sympathy for communism in general and the Soviet model in particular. For an entire generation between wars it became de rigueur to position oneself somehow in relation to Marx and Engels or their reinterpreters, to play with the ideas of dialectics and revolution, at the very least to apply radical philosophical positions to critiques of power. Octavio Paz, reflecting in the early 1990s on his long literary career, was quite certain that if he had written his famous essay on Mexican national identity, *El laberinto de la soledad* (The labyrinth of solitude), at the height of his infatuation with communism in 1937, he would have concluded with a call to channel Mexico's revolutionary fervor – then referred to as "the search" (*la búsqueda*) – into the adoption of communism.[3] What prompted such commitment was a combination of compassion for those on the economic margins, indignation at the injustices and abuses of power that kept inequalities in place, and ignorance of the real nature of the Soviet regime. As it was, Stalinism disabused him of this revolutionary inclination, and his thoughts on Mexico moved more towards a complex analysis and appraisal of national character.

For many the romance lasted longer. Jean-Paul Sartre was among those in the early 1960s who admired the Soviet and Cuban communist dictatorships, who found "seeds of menace within the representative system" and extolled the virtues of state politics run by "a single, same man everywhere at once."[4] But this position by then required willful ignorance of the abuses of dictatorship, in particular the convoluted political logic and horrors of Soviet totalitarianism.[5] For those whose thinking was at all critical, this kind of state-centered communism already involved an untenable descent into dogma and tyranny.

There is no period in the history of radical Marxism in which there were not illustrious apostates. Octavio Paz, without specific explanation, cites 1939 as the year of his disaffection with communism – we can assume this came as a result of the non-aggression pact between Hitler and Stalin and the escalation of war in Europe. Once disenchanted, he saw Soviet communism as: "a bureaucratic regime, petrified into castes, and witnessed the Bolsheviks, who had decreed 'obligatory communization' under penalty of death, fall one after the other in those public ceremonies of expiation – Stalin's purges."[6] From then on he rejected the idea of revolution, much to the dismay of his erstwhile communist friends and supporters.

The technocratic, bureaucratic nature of communist states was not just an aberration or an abuse of an otherwise unassailable model of history; it exposed an inherent flaw in Marx's paradigm: a failure to anticipate the universal legitimacy of nation-states. A common denominator of disillusionment with Marxism seems to be the revolution's inability to avoid this kind of usurpation, to prevent itself from becoming yet another of the Enlightenment's "grand narratives of emancipation," one which exposes an element of hypocrisy when it becomes tied to particularistic visions of national identity set upon a course of crude, xenophobic imperialism.

The 1960s are usually cited as the twentieth century's most radical decade, but even then, participating in an "avant-garde" uprising at the University of Nanterre in 1968 (subsequently given the heroic appellation, the "movement of March 22"), Jean-François Lyotard felt a certain post-Marxist malaise, claiming, "I performed without enthusiasm the practical–critical tasks that honor and the situation demanded."[7] Is this an autobiographical rationalization, an explanation of the failure of Marxism with the claim that one never took it seriously in the first place? Perhaps. But given the postmodernist direction Lyotard later took in his thinking, the "victors" of the Cold War certainly cannot claim a convert.

For Jacques Derrida there was both a philosophical and political disillusionment at work behind his abandonment of communist orthodoxy and search for an alternative paradigm that rejected all orthodoxies. A "canon of the modern apocalypse," announcing the end of history, of man, of philosophy, took much of the luster away from communism long before Francis Fukuyama proposed an American version of the "end of history" debate inspired by the fragmentation of the Soviet empire. At the same time, Derrida shared with Paz, Lyotard, and many others revulsion toward Stalinism, above all toward its socio-economic disasters and totalitarian terror. At a minimum, the invasion of Hungary was enough to expose Moscow's expansionism, leading to a widespread rethinking of commitments. Those once devoted to Marxism had long ago turned their backs on Soviet communism and moved on.

Postmodernism's Post-Marxism

One of the side-benefits of the post-1989 celebration of the defeat of communism was that it provoked a response from those for whom Marxism continued to hold significant promise in shaping the social order (or predicting its future form). It is almost as though the provocation were actually an inductive experiment designed to see if and how a defense of Marx could be mounted. And the results, so far at least, confirm that a return to "orthodox" Marxism is a difficult proposition at best and that its dilution into postmodern immaterialism renders it self-negating, ineffective, and harmless.

This failure, though evident in works of philosophy that have not become part of any mainstream canon, should still be of concern to us, however, if only because the healthy functioning of any liberal society, particularly one that is simultaneously centralizing and extending its global reach, depends upon an *effective* body of social criticism, not just from the media, lobbies, and opposition political parties, but from those who stand fully outside the corridors of power.

Yet one of the first "neo-Marxist" replies to the victory parade of global capitalism involved an immersion into a strange admixture of Hegelian idealism with a disjointed rejection of systematic thought, inspired, it seems, by such stream of consciousness fiction writing as can be found in James Joyce's *Ulysses* and Hermann Broch's *The Death of Virgil* – not a promising foundation for a new approach to the critique of new power. Jacques Derrida's *Specters of Marx*, as one would expect from a postmodern *apprécie* of Marxism, finds fault with Marx's scientific project, with his universal history based in a "messianic eschatology." At the same time, however, the supposed decline of Marxism marked by the fall of Soviet communism was accompanied by an unexpected twist: it paradoxically brought about the reduction of obstacles to it, especially through the discrediting of pseudo-Marxist ideologies of states, parties, and trade unions. With such chaff removed, Derrida finds something irrefutable in Marx's paradigm, a kernel that remains vital for our times: a lucid analysis of global capital's political and ideological supremacy. Politico-economic hegemony, together with its new technological, intellectual, and discursive domination, is conditioning and putting in danger all possibilities for democracy.[8] Thus for Derrida, despite, or more correctly because of, the reversals of communism, a future without Marx is "unthinkable."

But the difficulty then lies in the way a future *with* Marx is to be thought. If the Marxist system of critical analysis is radically insufficient because of its "metanarrative" of historical inevitability, how can it be rendered meaningful? What remains of Marx's system that can be applied to modern capitalism? And in what ways did Marx's prophecy turn out to be accurate and his solution to the anticipated conflicts of global capital of continuing relevance? In answering such unavoidable questions (though not posing them directly himself) Derrida is drawn to the idea or image of Marxism as an ever-returning specter, a counterpoint to hegemony, never to fully disappear from the presence of capitalist society, nor, in corporeal form, to fully and predictably return; never, in other words, to be cathartically mourned.

But what is the essence of this counter-hegemonic specter (in Marx's terminology, an ever-returning *Gespenst*)? It can be found in one realm that remains impervious to the critical gaze, that remains, in Derrida's words, "as un-deconstructible as the very possibility of deconstruction," that continues to haunt us as, "a certain experience of the emancipatory promise," which we manage to glimpse only in negative terms when he sets out to describe the "New International" of the future, which will continue to draw inspiration from Marx: "a link of affinity, suffering, and hope, a still discreet, almost secret link . . . an untimely link, without status, without title, and without name, barely public even if it is not clandestine, without contract, 'out of joint', without coordination, without party, without country, without national community (International before, across, and beyond any national determination), without co-citizenship, without common belonging to a class."[9] His more positive description of the ultimate source of hope provided by postmodernism via the guidance of Marxism is scarcely more intelligible: "a structural messianism, a messianism without religion, even a messianic without messianism, an idea of justice – which we distinguish from law or right and even from human rights – and an idea of democracy – which we distinguish from its current concept and from its determined predicates today."[10] Derrida's postmodernism therefore does not abandon the possibility of truly emancipatory rights or truly democratic democracy – in fact, all hope is pinned on these things. But neither does he provide any inkling as to what such rights or such democracy might look like. How are they different from existing forms? How can a postmodern regime of human rights be arranged, especially given the fact that a community of nation-states has already cooperated in establishing one? By failing to provide anything concrete (in his terms, hegemonic), by rejecting even those suggestions that could help us distinguish the needs of reform from those of revolution, Derrida falls back upon mere negation as the ultimate source of emancipatory promise, and offers only a nebulous form of messianism that denies even the illusions of messianic hope. What he takes from Marx is one of the most significant flaws of Marxism: its vague promise of liberation in a terminus of history – except that his version of postmodernism fragments Marx's historical, post-revolutionary eschatology into multiple ideals (such as ideal rights and ideal democracy) in an effort to avoid a narrative of historical destination.

By avoiding any commitment to specifics of liberation, postmodernism bows to the inevitable, leaving to others the tasks of order-maintenance, resistance, and reform. And by leaving tyranny more room to maneuver, opting out becomes an acquiescent act. Deciding not to decide is still a moral choice. If postmodernism retreats from the world by limiting itself to convoluted or entirely meaningless forms of critique, deconstruction, and negation, it cannot then avoid all association with things-as-they-are. A philosophy that excuses itself from participation in worldly affairs cannot legitimately claim it has had no part in creating them. Hegemony is built into the very idea of non-participatory social criticism of hegemony.

From Empire to Earthly City

The great influence of Marx's vision – to the extent that he inspired people to action and changed the course of history – can largely be explained by two main qualities of his work. First, he was extremely meticulous, to the point of fastidiousness, in his account of the forces of oppression. His description of the English factory system, presented in greatest detail in *Capital,* was unlike anything that had appeared until then, with its hard-hitting facts about the routines of the working life of laborers, the mind-numbing monotony, the dangers encountered regularly, even by children, in order to spare factory owners minimal cost in the production process, the degradation of working-class neighborhoods, in which alcohol had become the only escape from a meaningless and hopeless existence. These kinds of accounts, written by Marx with an angry pen, probably did much to strengthen the workers' movements that successfully campaigned for reform of labor conditions, thereby reversing the slide into ever-greater misery that Marx anticipated as an inevitable precondition of world revolution.

At the same time, however, Marx gave energy to radical socialism through the fact that he scrupulously avoided engaging in specific description of the future he hoped for. One of his great, history-shaping innovations was a conception of the perfect state which relied exclusively on the historical process leading up to it, thereby sparing his work from the inevitable discrepancies between a particular vision and the immense variety of human conceptions of the perfect world. Marx saw class struggle as the pivotal force of history, moving humanity toward ever more generalized, stark, and simplified opposition between small numbers of capitalists and a global mass of desperately impoverished workers. The famous rallying cry from *The Communist Manifesto,* "workers of the world unite!" was meant only to hasten the inevitable movement of history. As the contours of class struggle sharpened there would be less room for different modes of existence, and even less for different forms of class antagonism. Global sameness of experience along the lines of capitalist class structure was what really mattered. The conditions for revolution would be in place when the reach of capitalism had extended to all corners of the globe, overwhelming all other modes of production. Then and only then would the proletariat be ready to liberate itself and bring about a classless society free from the oppressive confines of history.

This use of a teleological conception of history endowed the new world society with greater firmness and solidity, while leaving its final state undescribed, and indeed beyond all necessity of description. The promise of a communist utopia, without a solid engagement with reality, gave free rein to hope. Rather than matching the supposedly emergent proletarian order with the desires of some, while setting it against the fears of others, Marx was entirely vague about what kind of society was to emerge from the ruins of capitalism. Post-revolutionary proletarian society was to be whatever anyone wanted it to be. With the end of capitalist exploitation and with its coercive systems of power having withered away (leaving aside the intermediate dictatorship of the proletariat – Marx's nod to the untidiness of political reality) all that would remain in the end would be a free existence that accommodated all tastes and inclinations.

One of the recent tendencies in neo-Marxism is to reverse the emphasis placed on the before and after of conditions in the world, to depict the forces of oppression nebulously and imprecisely, while devoting greater attention to the perfect society supposedly within our grasp. There is greater readiness to portray a world order in which the forces of capitalism have become mysterious and ever more potent, combining in ways that are beyond the reckoning of all but the most critically enlightened, while sketching (at least with more detail than Marx ever did) a possible, even imminent, postrevolutionary world. Utopian dreams are once more being called upon to shape opposition to present conditions, above all the growing opposition to free trade liberalism, to rekindle our commitment to socio-ecological change through a radically hopeful conception of the future.[11]

The powers that shape the world and determine our destiny are sometimes seen as united in a complex, overwhelming conspiracy. The conspiracy theory of globalization is an approach to the study of world integration in which the manifold forces of capitalism and globalization are seen to act in concert and are simultaneously presented as tremendously powerful and cunningly indistinct. The conspiracy theory of history was an important aspect of Karl Popper's famous critique of Marx and Marxism in the second volume of *The Open Society and Its Enemies*, lending support to his conclusion that historical prophecy runs counter to the interests of freedom. "People who sincerely believe they know how to make heaven on earth are most likely to adopt the conspiracy theory, and to get involved in a counter-conspiracy against non-existing conspirators. For the only explanation of their failure to produce their heaven is the evil intention of the Devil, who has a vested interest in hell."[12] The overwhelming, yet indeterminate, forces of oppression and destruction are more than byproducts of messianic Marxism's disappointed expectations; they are a significant feature of all social–theoretical constructs that call for radical change or world revolution. For revolution to be justified in an age that, for very good reason, is shy of revolutionary promise, or for that matter any form of radical political universalism, the combined forces of oppression must be portrayed as completely overwhelming and the end point of history as a gentle, joyful, frictionless, egalitarian paradise.

Michael Hardt and Antonio Negri, in *Empire*, provide what is probably the most immediately recognizable example of this conspiracy-centered approach to globalization. Empire's reach of power is quite unlike any expansionist entity that has hitherto existed. There is no limit to the number and variety of individuals who may unwittingly play into its hands or, in full awareness, act as its apologists, servants, or zealots. Almost all thought and action is either an indirect betrayal of freedom or a direct attempt by the hegemonic enemy to outflank its opposition. This conception of domination relies heavily on the historical (and futurist) orientation of Hegel and Marx, while doing great disservice to Marx's grounded, detailed, and compelling description of the social conditions resulting from the capitalism functioning in his time. There is nothing of even remotely similar stature to this accomplishment in the new neo-Marxism, just a kind of non-methodological sociological paranoia that resolves itself into a vague, promise-filled expectation of earthly paradise.

No one could seriously argue that real conspiracies do not exist. Antonio Negri, in particular, is no stranger to the dark side of politics. In 1979 he was arrested in Milan, accused of being head of a terrorist organization, the Red Brigades and, in that capacity, of organizing the kidnapping and murder of former prime minister Aldo Moro; he was later acquitted of direct involvement in terrorist violence, but convicted and sentenced to thirteen years in prison for "membership in an armed band."[13] Either Negri really went so far into the fringes of left wing radicalism that he abutted on the Red Brigades or his politics are merely distasteful and he has been victimized by a witch-hunting judicial system desperate to make convictions in a high-profile case. In any event, Negri must have first-hand experience with very real, very sordid conspiracy. But the political philosophy that he has taken part in elaborating takes the unseen forces of domination to an altogether different level. This comes through loud and clear in *Empire*, despite what appears to have been a moderating influence from his collaborator Michael Hardt, a specialist in literary criticism at Duke University.

"Empire" is the catchword Hardt and Negri use for a power that orchestrates the world's many forces of domination, not only the visible market forces and global institutions of capitalism, but also the less apparent, and perhaps more sinister, forces of nationalism and fundamentalism. The shift in capitalist production toward global reach, and above all global relations of power, "makes perfectly clear and possible today the capitalist project to bring together economic power and political power, to realize, in other words, a properly capitalist order."[14] In the "totalizing social process of Empire"[15] a single power now overdetermines all other sources of power, inscribed by a new, far-reaching production of legitimacy. A single social force has taken shape that draws all other forms of power into its orbit.

What is this entity hurtling unopposed toward world domination? What pushes it forward? Power? Wealth? If such banal and sordid motivations are at work, who are the human actors driven by them? And if Empire is part of a terrestrial, human reality, who is (or tries to be) in control of it?

The conspiracy theory of Empire is sustained by casting aside all phenomena normally recognized as impediments to global order. If there are irrefutable facts or moral positions that run counter to the conspiracy approach, they are simply not mentioned. Every conceivable political entity is implicated in an increasingly cohesive, single structure of domination. To most people all that is visible are discreet institutions, organizations, corporations, nations, etc., but for those who know what to look for the ubiquitous signs of Empire are unmistakable. Such NGOs as Amnesty International, Oxfam, and Médecins sans Frontières (Doctors without Borders) are merely the compliant "mendicant orders" of Empire, conducting "just wars" without arms or violence. "Moral intervention has become a frontline force of imperial intervention."[16] Intervention in genocidal ethnic conflict is similarly cast as an act of repression that serves the interests of global social control. "The conflicts among ethnic groups and the consequent reenforcement [sic] of new and/or resurrected ethnic identities effectively disrupt the old aggregations based on national political lines. These conflicts make the fabric of global relations more fluid and, by affirming new identities and new localities, present a more malleable material for control."[17]

Hardt and Negri invert postmodernism in much the same way that Marx and Engels inverted Hegelianism, replacing a grandiose, meaning-saturated idealism with an effort to unveil more concrete social forces. This is not immediately apparent because Hardt and Negri emphasize that postmodernism is yet another sign that Empire has vanquished the opposition. Postmodern criticism has been appropriated by Empire, an effective civil society has withered away, and the multitude has been segmented by the recognition of differences. There is much to be said for the view that postmodern and postcolonial critiques of modernity have been self-defeating, because their emphasis on pluralism and multivocality has acted against the unity and effectiveness of social opposition. What Hardt and Negri appear to have borrowed from postmodernism, though, is its *pensiero debole*, its rejection of reason-based method in favor of intuition, suspicion, and conceptual and stylistic looseness, turning postmodernism's endless horizon of meaning into an equally limitless structure of domination.

At the same time, however, Hardt and Negri are perfectly willing to associate themselves with the democratic impulse behind criticism of global institutions, and to add their voices to the censure of these institutions on the grounds that they are fundamentally anti-democratic. They extol the protesters' will to democratize the globalizing process and appear to earnestly desire the kinds of reform that would make powerful international institutions more accountable to those whose lives they affect. They argue in an opinion piece carried by the *New York Times* that such international and supranational organizations as the G-8, the World Trade Organization, the World Bank and the International Monetary fund, have no popular legitimacy, no grounds on which to base their control of world finance and the destinies of billions other than illegitimate power. "This new order has no democratic institutional mechanisms for representation, as nation-states do: no elections, no public forum for debate."[18]

But how does this democratic will match up against Hardt and Negri's vision of future society and the transition toward it? How do they propose to channel such democratic impulses toward an effective dismantling of the worst forms of global imperialism?

In fact, democracy has very little to do with Hardt and Negri's answers to the ills of modernity. Instead, they formulate the problem of transition to the future in terms very close to orthodox Marxism. What Georg Lukács saw in the early 1920s as the essence of orthodox Marxism, the concept of "totality" to be achieved through the "subordination of every part to the whole unity of history and thought"[19] is echoed by Hardt and Negri as a source of radical hope. The grip of nation-states is giving way to the global expansion of Capital, and with this come new possibilities for "proletarian science," greater need for opposition to bourgeois society, and a new life for the movement toward world revolution. The basic incompatibility between the Marxist revolutionary paradigm and nationalism, which in some ways troubled the ideological and political career of Soviet communism, is less stark than it ever was. Peasants have been proletarianized and Asia industrialized. Revolution seems less menacing as global integration approaches – much of the dirty work has already been done. Globalization is an indication that the forces of capitalism have converged, just as Marx anticipated, as the central world-historical precondition for the communist revolution.

There is a basic sense in which Hardt and Negri's vision of Empire reproduces the errors of Marxism. As I pointed out in chapter 2, Marx and Engels, in *The Communist Manifesto*, find very clear signs of global integration through capitalism and the class interests of the bourgeoisie.[20] Their failure to anticipate the tremendous strength of national attachments is one of the most salient lapses of Marxist prophecy, one that is, so it now appears, faithfully repeated by Hardt and Negri. "What Marx saw as the future is our era," they announce.[21] The conditions favorable to revolution were only delayed by the appropriations of nationalism, in particular by Soviet communism; but now the boundaries of nation-states are crumbling and for the first time a complete global power has formed. This means that there is a new potential for the revolution to occur. "The passage to Empire and its processes of globalization offer new possibilities to the forces of liberation."[22] This is not to say that their alternative vision can in any way be called "anti-globalization," because, more than any form of global hegemony it rejects, it represents total "cosmopolitan hybridization." Antonio Negri, more radically high-flown when untempered by a coauthor, concludes his recent *Time for Revolution* with just such an expression of the virtues of "extreme deterritorialization": " 'Proletarians of all countries, unite' is an injunction that today means: mix up races and cultures, constitute the multicoloured Orpheus who generates the common from the human."[23] For Hardt and Negri, this revolutionary moment arrives when "the set of all the exploited and the subjugated [forms] a multitude that is directly opposed to Empire, with no mediation between them."[24] The conditions for humanity's liberation, outlined by Marx and Engels in *The Communist Manifesto*, are, according to Hardt and Negri, finally here. And, as Marx himself made clear, clarity is achieved by the march of history so there is no real need for precision in one's vision of a future society.

Except that some things are not quite as Marx and Engels predicted. In Hardt and Negri's version of communist prophecy, industrial labor is not the only, or the most important, form of exploitation. Disembodied, nonmaterial varieties of exploitation have arisen through the new powers of information technology and communication. The proletariat now takes the form of a "multitude" – a loose confederacy of all those who are oppressed by Empire, not only industrial laborers, not only peasants, but more commonly those who labor without personal fulfillment in offices, behind desks and computer screens. This "multitude" will act upon its right (from whence this "right" originates, we are not told) to reappropriate the means of production through "constructive militancy." Destruction of the enemy and creation of a new society means, for the mobile multitude that accomplishes this miracle, reappropriation of the means of production, control over knowledge, information, and communication, unstructured education, deregulated culture, equality and solidarity, autonomous self-production, the continuous creation of "common constructions" (i.e. communities), while that which is common becomes singularized in an "expansive commonality." In the moment of truth, the power of this multitude, united by the call of revolution, will be simply too overwhelming for the forces of Empire to withstand. Oppressive global capitalism will give way to an earthly paradise, described in terms that hearken back to Zeno's first account of a frictionless community encompassing all of humanity. "Certainly, there must be a moment," Hardt and Negri write, "when reappropriation and self-organization reach a threshold and configure a real event. . . . This is the founding moment of an earthly city that is strong and distinct from any divine city . . . [instigated by] the construction, or rather the insurgence, of a powerful organization. . . . We do not have any models to offer for this event. . . . Only the multitude through its practical experimentation will offer the models and determine when and how the possible becomes real."[25] But there are some things we can expect with greater certainty from this new world order. This is to be a world of global citizenship, with a working class empowered by a guaranteed social wage, with a rehumanization of decayed, alienating urban space, and with enlightened popular control over knowledge, information, and communication. The geography of the world will be at last liberated from arbitrary power. "The cities of the earth will become at once great deposits of cooperating humanity and locomotives for circulation, temporary residences and networks of the mass distribution of living humanity."[26] With no more national boundaries, no attachments to the old order of nation-states, the world will take the form of one united, habitable space – an earthly city. This earthly city, like others imagined before it, resolves common human dilemmas in quasi-spiritual oxymorons: a restless, mobile humanity bounded by community, destruction without sacrifice, spontaneous order, and a communist global power that permits anarchistic license. This is to be a world in which, "communism, cooperation and revolution remain together, in love, simplicity, and also innocence."[27]

The basic premises of Hardt and Negri's cosmopolitan socialism would lead inevitably, though perhaps unintentionally, to violence as the principal way to effect political change and to totalitarian dictatorship as the only end of political action. If nation-states have new transnational masters, if there is no hope for wide international enfranchisement under existing institutions, if even international civil society – the organizations and processes of extraparliamentary democracy – has been emasculated and co-opted by the forces of Empire, then what hope can there be for the realization of the earthly paradise? How can the multitude self-actualize without destroying all that exists and making the world anew? How might persistent attachments to local cultures, traditions, and territories be overcome? The future society that Hardt and Negri predict and celebrate is in many ways more terrifying than anything the World Bank or the IMF could possibly muster, reposing as it does on the popular will of the multitude, bringing to mind a new form of Jacobinism cut loose from national boundaries. When postmodernist conceptions of unlimited (conceptual/political) domination and fatalism toward the possibility of meaningful change are applied to global institutions, the obstacles to freedom become overwhelming. Everything seems to conspire against it. There is no regular, reliable countervailing force of criticism or political action capable of resisting domination by Empire. This clearly implies that only an extraordinary struggle led by the enlightened few would be capable of rousing the multitude and initiating the great transformation that will bring history to its inevitable, shatter-ing, glorious conclusion.

The End of Revolution

The most significant thing about the Hardt/Negri paradigm of cosmopolitan emancipation is that it stands virtually alone in its advocacy and expectation of a global revolutionary workers' move-ment. In other circles it has become acceptable, if not fashionable, to remove sweeping socio-political criticism from both classic world-revolutionary paradigms and from concern with the postmodernist under-the-surface nature of things. The tricky thing about such liber-alization of radical politics is that at a certain point it disappears into the mainstream, or at least falls outside the purview of this discussion of neo-Marxism. It remains possible, however, to find a few social critics, those who might still, though sometimes only loosely, be called neo-Marxists, and who have at the same time attached themselves (but in suitably obstreperous, unorthodox ways) to such liberal uni-versalisms as human rights and democracy. Ulrich Beck, for example, a leading voice of the German left and the environmental movement (the latter tag is less definite but he accepts, to some extent, the asso-ciation between being "green" and German national identity), sees oppression taking new forms in a "second modernity" marked by looming economic and ecological risks and the insecurities, ambigui-ties and loss of boundaries that accompany the rise of "post-national," transnational, "despatialized" power. Neoliberal utopianism is favoring conditions, even in Europe and America, which are usually considered characteristic of the "South," of endemic job insecurity, rootlessness, environmental degradation, and old age poverty.

Beck's bleak perspective on global transformations, however, is offset by buoyant optimism toward possibilities for change. "A new cosmopolitan reality is in the air!" he triumphantly proclaims.[28] The same corporate entities and policies that are eroding democracy and security can also "help to create the foundations for equality, justice, freedom and democracy on a world scale because their investment decisions are central to the distribution of work and income."[29] The catalysts for this era of global responsibility are new forms of transna-tional civil society engaged in democracy-enhancing transnational "subpolitics." Where Beck does make reference to Marx, he does so in a way that emphasizes the democratic possibilities inherent in creative disobedience. He adorns his "Cosmopolitan Manifesto," for example, with Enlightenment ideals of dynamic criticism and self-criticism, of flux and uncertainty coupled with the realization that "we do not have *enough* reason (*Vernunft*)" to live and act in an age of Global risk manufactured by experts and industries.[30] For Beck, a central goal of our critical faculties should be the "democratic scrutiny of the previously depoliticized realms of decision-making" in realms that are transcultural, transnational, and global.[31] Such criticism should be oriented toward a new, "complex architecture of sovereignty and identity," a "countermodel to the container theory of state and society," a "realistic utopia" to be found in transnational, non-territorial states.[32]

David Harvey, who has for many years bravely pursued the study and teaching of Marx from within the communist-hostile American campus environment (hidden from university administrations in the largely ignored recesses of geography), exhibits somewhat less commitment to democracy in his recent book *Spaces of Hope*, with his vision of a "long revolution" led by a cadre of "insurgent architects" committed to combating the "degenerate utopianism of neo-liberalism" with a radically different political consciousness, to be realized through the design of collectivized cities. Rebellious designers are those best qualified to resist the decay, corruption, and injustice of things-as-they-are through their own "utopian schemes of spatial form" that will embody "entirely different systems of property rights, living and working arrangements, all manifest as entirely different spatial forms and temporal rhythms."[33] To successfully implement such designs, however, insurgent architects must circumvent "formations of collective governance" which have the effect of preserving and sustaining the existing system. They must offset "the rule-making that ever constitutes community [with] the rule-breaking that makes for revolutionary transformations."[34]

Yet when it comes to attaching himself to a universal paradigm of liberation, Harvey turns to the possibilities inherent in human rights, presenting a plan for a utopia-accommodating system of rights and indicating where it overlaps with existing human rights, while overlooking the stark contradiction between upholding the will of the people as the basis of authority in government (as articulated in Article

21.3 of the Universal Declaration of Human Rights) and negating the community-based processes of rule-making that would probably stand in opposition to the noble visions of specialist, insurrectionist city designers. If local democracy is to be circumvented by insurgent architects who are not bound by community rules as they realize their unorthodox visions of urban space, then what use is the right of citizens to freely elect their government? Leaving aside those aspects of Harvey's self-avowed utopianism, however, one of its most significant features is that it relies ultimately on acceptance and advocacy of the idea of universal human rights. There is, of course, a caveat. Even with sweeping changes, Harvey insists, the system of universal rights would be imperfect and merely "a formative moment in a much more complicated social process directed towards socio-ecological change." But some system of universal guiding principles, best expressed as human rights, is necessary to guide and coordinate social reform efforts, and "the insurgent architect has to be an advocate of such rights."[35]

The vaguely disquieting idea of a "long revolution" to be brought about piecemeal by specialist-rebels is a far cry from the cataclysmic global transformation commonly called for by Marxists in the 1960s. Since then the term *revolution* seems to have been de-politicized, not as often referring to replacement of constitutions, or even overthrowing the need for constitutions in a perfect world, as to the instruments of change: the information revolution, the scientific revolution, the technological revolution, and so on. Following meanings drawn out by Raymond Williams, it appears that the sense of *revolution* as bringing about an entirely different social order, once actively promoted by the socialist movement, has ceded considerable ground to "the sense of necessary innovation of a new order, supported by the increasingly positive sense of progress."[36] If there is any truth to the idea that a multi-dimensional worldwide transformation, often referred to as globalization, is presently occurring, that in particular the world is more closely integrated than ever before by technologies of travel and communication while global political and economic forces are combining in unprecedented ways, then why has the socialist idea of a global political and economic revolution lost its flavor? What makes it so difficult, even distasteful, for committed social reformers to consider programs of world liberation designed to bring about a cosmopolitan revolution, to at last build a borderless earthly city? Communism in all its permutations lost its appeal precisely at a time when imaginative communists could conceivably point to changes in world history that seemed to be ushering in an era of global economic convergence, separation of classes, and centralization of powers. The fragmentation of the Soviet empire, rather than simply signaling a western victory over communism, was the kind of event that imaginative neo-Marxists could use to reinvent and reinvigorate the idea of world revolution. Yet, with only a few exceptions, this did not happen. Instead, radical socialism has been pacified and in many cases infused with solid doses of liberalism.

Two of the possible reasons for this serve to highlight what I feel are some of the most important, and most frequently overlooked, features of global modernity. First, the idea of a world revolution led by an oppressed, disempowered, disenfranchised proletariat or "multitude" cannot accommodate the overwhelming emphasis on self-determination as a foundation for community integrity. For one thing, neo-Marxist socialism has consistently overestimated class and underestimated the legitimacy of the nation-state as the principal source identity and/or arbiter of identity conflicts within the state. Struggles for ethnic autonomy reinforce the (often tragically misguided) view that state borders and cultural boundaries should somehow coincide, and hold up membership in the "community of nations" as the pinnacle of collective recognition. Even the pursuit of distinct identities nested within nation-states is not a challenge to the legitimacy of states, but in some ways a confirmation of it. Appeals for recognition empower the would-be Recognizer. Although the contradiction between affirming cultural differences and implementing a politics of universalized individual rights is occasionally resolved in favor of distinct communities, there is still no evidence that the politics of identity are bringing the era of nation-states to an end.

Whether or not we agree that nation-states are withering away through the rise of transnational games and competing powers, it should be clear that in general *cultural* boundaries are being sharply defined, often together with invigorated territorial attachments. How are human differences to be accommodated in a new global society? If nationalism is an insidious, persistent form of "false consciousness" or an unenlightened attachment to the secondary powers of Empire, then what force or event could possibly make it disappear? How is the free-flowing multitude to be reconciled with existing and emergent ethnic identities? World integration, or at least the process of de-localization associated with it, has made the question "who are we?" *more* salient, more important for the expression of selfhood than it was for those who were once relatively unaffected by colonial or cultural domination. The pride of individuals is more than ever being resolved and expressed through the pride of peoples. Only a complete surrender to utopian fantasy could lead one to make so little of the power of identity, of the persistent attachments people hold to local cultures, traditions, communities, tribes, peoples, nations, languages, and lifestyles – the various attachments that in one form or another influence political aspirations and behavior everywhere in the world. Even if (as seems entirely unlikely) nation-states were to completely lose their power and legitimacy, could such persistent local identities ever be fully accommodated within a boundaryless paradise?

Second, enthusiastic visions of cosmopolitan socialism (à la Negri), inclined as they are to arbitrarily dismiss current regimes of democracy and human rights or to anticipate the emergence of a nebulous "powerful organization" as the catalyst for a boundaryless earthly city, have nothing to offer those with heightened expectations of accountability and democracy in global institutions. Democracy, loosely defined as, "a demand for the opportunity to make power in our adult lives always ultimately answerable to those over whom it is exercised" has become the overwhelmingly dominant standard for political authority.[37] If anything, demands for democratic accountability are widening in scope, no longer confined to governance within states. Rather, they are increasingly voiced in a realm occupied by "transnational advocacy networks" or "global social movements," emergent social forms that cumulatively make up a process referred to by Arjun Appadurai as "globalization from below" or "grassroots globalization."[38] Global social movements consisting of alliances and networks of non-governmental organizations (NGOs) have voiced opposition to the secretive, specialist-informed decision-making that has characterized the management of transnational commerce, particularly by the powerful troika of global institutions: the World Bank, the International Monetary Fund, and the World Trade Organization. At the same time, the complex variables that go into economic planning incline global organizations to dismiss or underestimate the force and significance of popular demands for democratic accountability. The demands for openness and accountability on the one hand, and the need for timely, effective management of international commerce and economic development on the other, appear to be in large measure mutually exclusive, resulting in what is sometimes called in diplomatic parlance a "dialogue of the deaf" between international NGOs and global economic institutions. Confederations of international NGOs, however, are a force to be reckoned with. Their ability to mass mobilize is sometimes astonishing, as in the 1992 Rio Earth Summit, which attracted over 20,000 participants from 9,000 environmental organizations based in 171 countries.[39] International NGOs or confederations of NGOs built around such interests as labor, environmental protection, the advancement of women, and the rights of indigenous peoples have indeed occasionally succeeded in pressuring multilateral economic organizations to tailor their global liberalizing agenda. Multilateral economic organizations are being forced to address the impacts of their policies, even if this openness sometimes takes on the quality of a safety valve for venting grievance that pre-empts any far-reaching restructuring of policies or styles of management.[40]

Notwithstanding the street-level visibility of the so-called antiglobalization movement, and in particular the minority within it that responds to calls to the barricades, the formidable influence of international NGOs is not revolutionary, but is largely directed toward piecemeal reforms in global governance – as in contesting the wording of new human rights instruments, checking the accuracy of environmental reports, or challenging particular uses of economic coercion to modify incompatible state policies. If we bear in mind that the labor movement and emancipation movements of the nineteenth century largely succeeded in tempering the worst abuses of early capitalism while contributing to the development of liberalism and social democracy, there is some hope that the recent exponential growth in numbers and influence of international NGOs can have a similar effect on global capitalism and its regulatory institutions.

So it is a gross misinterpretation of world events to attribute a decline in the ambitions and effectiveness of radical socialism exclusively or mainly to the rise of a powerful network of global commerce. The principal reasons for this relate back to the social forces that can be seen as resistant to "cultural globalization" and "free trade globalization," which I outlined in chapter three. In opposing currents of so-called cultural globalization, the world-liberating politics of cosmopolitan socialism have been hemmed in by persistent, boundary-erecting identity attachments; and in opposing free trade liberalism, neo-Marxism has been co-opted by the rise in influence of NGOs, in other words, by the multiplication of outlets for the expression of grievance, hope, compassion, personal ambition, and resistance to conformity.

Radical politics have therefore come to rely on sources of inspiration, often applied in uneasy combination, that lie far beyond Marx's critique of capitalism and promise of world revolution. Postmodernist fatalism and obscurantism encourage a conspiracy-centered approach to communities and organizations, aligning them with oppressive global forces while limiting emancipatory promise to a select community of insurgents. At the same time, transnational civil society has the potential to develop strategies of social reform and resistance that keep pace with changes in global governance and (though this is less certain) the global economy.

In a sense, the liberalization of radical politics is a practical response to the radicalization of liberal economics. The continuing influences of the ideals of democracy, human rights, scientific exploration, and above all the subjection of received ideas to dynamic criticism and reform, have now become possible sources of insurgency under circumstances in which economic and political forces with global reach are seen to be imposing a market-centered utopian vision that is not sufficiently responsive to democracy, human rights, and scientific insight.

Neo-Marxism is also central to a paradigm of liberation that seeks to counteract the far-reaching legacy of colonialism. In the next chapter I will consider postcolonialism as a style or system of thought that exhibits the same kind of approach to global culture that we have seen through much of this book: a universal model for the emancipation of self-defining communities or, seen another way, an ideal of local liberation that coalesces into aspirations toward a new humanity.

8

Paradigms of Postcolonial Liberation

Cultural Particularism and Universalism

The diverse cultural origins of the main figures in the postcolonial literature reveal an important trend toward intellectual diversity in American academic life, a trend characterized by one critic as "the end of the Cold War University."[1] Collectively, a coterie of British trained scholars from India probably has the highest profile among them, followed by a variety of others, no less intellectually prominent but fewer in numbers, from Africa, the Middle East, Latin America, and elsewhere. What this amounts to is that the once-unrepresented now have a powerful place in the production and exercise of ideas, with a largely vacant terrain of intellectual problems and possibilities at their disposal. This intellectual diversity has in general introduced a new vitality to the cultural study of politics, mostly by reformulating some of the European traditions' more rigid and outmoded ways of conceptualizing cultural encounter and colonial domination and by introducing into academic discourse the perspectives, as far as this is possible, of the marginal and dominated.

The various ways that postcolonial theory has depicted and confronted the multifaceted legacy of colonialism and described the ways, political and cultural, that new forms of imperialism insinuate themselves, make this a school of thought most likely to adopt a stand of counter-modernity resistant to what some might call the "hypermodernist" visions of financial globalization. But it has in the process become the most recent expression of identity-conscious cultural particularism, a return to the old idea, expressed with lasting influence by Gottfried Herder, that the spirit of a nation cannot be understood except on its own terms, that human nature is a pliant clay that takes on a miraculous variety of social forms, and that there is no possibility for absolute, immutable, perfect human happiness above the cultural reach of individual nations and communities.[2] Romanticism, for all the practical limitations of its way of ennobling the quest for perfect harmony, truth, justice, etc., had a profound impact on western thought and, indirectly, its course of history. Without the kind of counter-Enlightenment elevation of national language and identity set forth by Herder, for example, it is unlikely that European nationalism would have taken on the form that it did. And more than scant traces of Romantic idealism can be found in the revolutionary imaginings and efforts of the French Revolution. Romanticism pervaded both colonial empire building and the dismantling of imperialism through nation building. None of us can reasonably claim to be unaffected by it.

With its own set of historical and intellectual pedigrees, postcolonialism articulates several influential versions of the Romantic idea that each nation or people has an inscrutable, inviolable essence that expresses itself in opposition to the (specifically western) intellectual and political forces of human progress. This radical pluralism sometimes negates itself by superimposing a unified, globe-encompassing force of knowledge and social integration, without acknowledging the tendency for self-conscious relativism to possess its own universalizing, homogenizing inclinations. The universal project of diversity, as I will show, implies an impossible pair of conditions: a universalism that is formlessly liberating and a form of diversity that is free of identity constructs or cultural boundaries. The logical outcome of this is anarchic individualism, which postcolonialism avoids only by imposing double standards on its nemesis, the Occident.

Almost the entire corpus of postcolonial literature begins with the assumption that colonialism was a unique episode in human history, a catastrophic rupture, not just an extension of the age-old certainty that any society that acquires technological superiority will inevitably set out to dominate others. What principally made (or makes) colonialism not just any form of oppression, injustice, and occupation is the fact that it acquired an extraordinary and unprecedented global reach, fusing many societies with different historical and cultural traditions, forms of technology, and social organization into a single current of history and a single, externally controlled economic network.[3] Not only was colonialism in one form or another more or less geographically universal, it tainted everyone who had a part in it. To their credit, some of the earliest critics of colonialism (most of whom, probably not coincidentally, based their work on the particularly repressive French occupation of Algeria) described colonization as a pathological social condition, obviously one in which the colonized suffer the usurpations and brutality of occupation, but in which colonizers also suffered and were morally disfigured, even as they defended the colonial system in every conceivable way.[4] In the postcolonial literature, all the oppressed are alike in some ways, and even apologists of colonialism share somehow in an almost universal condition of ignorance and misery.

This sometimes led to a tension in postcolonial approaches to modernity between the new possibilities envisioned for humanity and the primary defense of cultural particularism – the values of community integrity, distinctiveness, warmth, and color. Overriding some of the approaches to colonial domination and liberation in the postcolonial literature, there is an assumption that because of the uniqueness of colonialism and its legacy, humanism now has possibilities never before imagined. The analog of master and servant and the descriptions of the places of ill fame created by colonial economies and relationships are not just for faraway settlements on the margins of empires but apply in some ways even to middle-class Europe and America. It has thus become possible to define and construct a new critical approach to cultural emancipation that has the world as its subject matter.

The Colonial Condition and its Aftermath

The main question of concern for those who first defined colonialism was how to get rid of it. Was change to be violent or peaceful? What kinds of relationships with colonial powers were to be maintained? If an independent nation-state was to be the political solution to independence, how was a diverse, newly independent state to establish and maintain a sense of nationhood? Whatever the answers to these questions, it was clear to most anti-colonial activists and freedom fighters that expelling the occupiers required various kinds of adaptive mimesis – acquiring the colonizers' military technology, setting political goals that corresponded with the structures of European imperial power, taking on nationalism as the form of identity most likely to politically succeed, defeating colonialism by taking away its civilizing mission, showing its regimes of governance to be hypocritically emasculated, completely lacking in the liberal principles of freedom, equality, and justice. The noble ideals of the colonizer were among the strongest weapons of decolonization. For if indeed, as many colonial schoolchildren were taught, all humans are equal in rights and dignity, what justification could be found for domination and exploitation by a foreign power? To those who experienced European domination, the logic of liberation was simple and infallible. If the colonizer tells us that belonging to the glorious imperial nation is the way to free ourselves from ignorance, superstition, and the tyranny of priests and chiefs, why not better this by liberating ourselves first from our European intruders?

This raised the question that has preoccupied virtually everyone who has ever been involved in a struggle against colonial domination: if colonialism was a unique event in human history that has destroyed all previously existing forms of governance, what new form of power are the colonized to be liberated into?

There have been several ways of imagining a colonial aftermath that dispenses fully with colonialism, of realizing complete autonomy from Europe, including its cultural, civilizing mission. Mohandas K. Gandhi, entering Indian politics in middle age after working as a lawyer in South Africa, settled on the idea of resisting British imperialism through a creative adaptation and reinvigoration of village life. He scornfully resented the adoption by Indians of English customs and "modern" technology. To him, the rise of *moha*, or attachment to superficial aspects of European life, was the root cause of India's colonial domination. "We brought the English, and we keep them," he declaimed, "Why do you forget that our adoption of their civilization makes their presence in India at all possible? Your hatred against them ought to be transferred to their civilisation."[5] The things that lay behind the terrible appeal of European civilization, Gandhi predicted, would also, ultimately, be the cause of its self-destruction. It would be brought down by its self-indulgent craving for luxury based upon individualistic competitiveness and by its imposition of poverty, inequality, and imperialist violence. The way to total freedom was not through violence – not only because violence violated the spiritual foundation of Gandhi's anti-modernism but also because it required yet further adoption of the colonial masters' technology and mentality – but through a popular revival of simple, decentralized village life, especially of the native industries that underpin village autonomy, and through a simultaneous refusal to recognize the national and civilizational values of Europe. To this end Gandhi proposed a utopian society of self-sufficient village communities. These were to be small patriarchies in which the ruler himself expressed the collective will through self-perfection and the resulting exemplary moral qualities. The organization of production was to be a perfect system of reciprocity based on the Hindu "varna" arrangements, but without the stigmas of caste, in which there would be no competition or status difference.[6] He thus arrived at a moral philosophy and alternative form of community that was consistently anti-modern, based on a non-canonical, monotheistic approach to Hinduism, while placing high value on folk traditions and village life.

At the opposite end of the anti-colonial spectrum was the revolutionary pursuit of a boundaryless global communism, or "tricontinentalism," an alternative to alignment with European nationalism in a postcolonial future to be realized through a kind of violent, messianic, global redemption.[7] This was the postcolonial future imagined, for example, by Frantz Fanon, the Algerian psychiatrist-turned-anti-colonial revolutionary.[8] For Fanon, colonial domination, like Marx's global capitalism, follows a universal logic resulting in identical patterns of domination and servitude. "On the level of underdeveloped humanity there is a kind of collective effort, a sort of common destiny."[9] The Algerian *fallah*, the Latin American peon, and the Indian coolie – all the world's day laborers and slave debtors are alike in the manner of their racial humiliation, their brutal physical exploitation, and the psychological mastery over them that convinces them of their inferiority and lulls them gently and unwittingly into passive compliance. But this very universality is cause for hope because it gives rise to the same pathways and opportunities for emancipation from colonial relationships everywhere. The armed struggle for national liberation is but the first step toward a glorious global future in which all vestiges of servitude and slavish imitation of colonial civilizations will at last be discarded. It is probably inevitable that the freshly discovered postcolonial identity should resolve itself into nationalism, but this is only a temporary expediency to be followed by a glorious unity of the liberated. Nationalism can serve temporarily to channel demands for social justice away from "primitive tribalism," toward a wider consciousness. Under conditions of national liberation, men and women will first experience working side by side in the factory, at school, and in the parliament; the inert districts will be stirred into action through "large-scale undertakings in the public interest"; and the consciousness of the young will be raised in the revolutionary "work of explanation."[10] But the revolutionary leadership must not delay in transforming nationalism into a new humanism, into a new political and social consciousness of all "underdeveloped peoples." Culture should no longer take on substance around the narrow-minded songs, poems or folklore of local communities or even around a wider negritude, but should be based on the struggles of peoples, and eventually the struggle of the masses, for liberation. The disappearance of the "colonial man" can only come about through the creation of a program shaped by revolutionary leaders, bringing about a wide unity of the oppressed that transcends nationalism. This is to be accomplished by taking up the dream that Europeans could never bring to a triumphant birth, and could never even pursue without descending into a monstrous "avalanche of murders": That never-achieved unity – the "whole man" – is a real possibility for the first time. Fanon was convinced that to bring this about, the overwhelming dominance of colonial powers must first be broken by revolutionary violence, by the kind of total resistance that shatters the intruders' military dominance, expels all forms of political mastery, and in the process restores the dignity and self-awareness of the once-colonized.

The contrasting paradigms of Gandhi and Fanon are two of the ways that a postcolonial condition was imagined from within fully developed colonial empires, those of the British in India and the French in Algeria. Between these poles (or perhaps far outside them) was the solution that looked no further than the devolution of colonial "possessions" into nation-states, a solution that was ultimately agreeable to both the European states anxious to divest themselves of what had become a political, military, and moral burden and to the mostly European-educated indigenous elite of the former colonies, that found in nationalism a new avenue to power that made use of their unique understanding of, and connections to, European governments. The post-colonial nation-state became the solution of choice, or at any rate the solution most readily put into effect.

But for those hankering after a distinct sense of liberation and separation from the European imperialism, the new nation-statism left a lingering sense of dissatisfaction, akin to being cheated of one's inheritance by a cardsharper. How can independent nation-statehood, along the lines of European nation-states but lacking power and international respectability, be reconciled with postcolonial identity? Is the nation-state – the entity most resembling the political structure and status of one's erstwhile colonial oppressor – all that can be hoped for as an expression of collective, autonomous selfhood? Disaffection with all forms of identity politics, with all forms of racial/ethnic/national rhetoric, grew out of a perception that postcolonial opportunists had somehow co-opted the possibilities of independence through unholy alliances and self-stereotyping. The challenge for those willing to resist this new condition of oppression was to create a politic of independence that stayed clear of intolerance and ethnic cleansing while maintaining enough cohesiveness to avoid being swallowed up by rebels, neighbors, or superpowers taking on the role of defenders of freedom. This called for an alternative, regenerative approach to independence, one that refused to make a pact with the postcolonial devil, and that refused above all to make political power reliant on boundary-enhancing hatreds.

Gandhi and Fanon might therefore more accurately be called *anticolonial* rather than postcolonial revolutionaries, even though they seriously grappled with the problem of what a truly liberated society would or should be like, or at least in vague outline what liberated peoples should proceed towards. What really defines the postcolonial literature, however, is that such calls for emancipation, situated historically and experientially within brutally repressive colonial situations, are largely peripheral. The *real* beginnings of postcolonialism are instead to be found in the struggles for identity and ideological emancipation in the period *after* the most visible power structures of colonialism have given way to national independence. Postcolonialism, true to its name, is situated in the aftermath of Fanon's revolutionary paradigm. Disillusioned with nationalism and chauvinistic ethnic particularism, postcolonialism engages in the struggle for a wider, more coherent form of independence and a more complete form of identity.

The Language of Imperialism

The basic premise of postcolonialism is that the essence of colonial domination is not just to be found in the whip and the gun – one does not even have to see the actual tools of repressive power for colonial relationships to be solidly in place – but is also, perhaps above all, in the thoughts and justifications that underpin colonial relationships. This means that colonialism has a power to last beyond the dismantling of empires. It also means that the need for resistance has a historical reach that extends well beyond the granting of national independence to former colonies. A consciousness-raising intelligentsia is therefore the new vanguard of postcolonial emancipation.

This approach was given considerable impetus by the work postcolonialists have called the founding text, source book, and "urtext" of postcolonialism, Edward Said's *Orientalism*, first published in 1978. One of the noteworthy features of all of Said's work, a legacy of books, essays, and opinion pieces that appeared with remarkable frequency and regularity until his death in 2003, is that it assiduously avoids engagement with the political entanglements and ambiguities of either anti-colonial resistance or the possibilities of the colonial aftermath. It is surprising, given the storminess with which his work has been received, that his attention was unwaveringly focused on the production of intellectual discourse and its place in consolidating colonial and imperial hegemony.

In *Orientalism*, Said provides compelling evidence of an intimate connection between the intellectual products of a "guild" of Orientalists (and this includes disciplines that might be called Africanist, Indianist, Americanist, and so on), a group of scholars with a specific history of complicity with imperial power.[11] Orientalist discourse was (and is), Said argues, strongly knitted together with the socio-economic and political institutions of imperialist domination. It acted together with an idea of Europe and Europeans as inherently superior to all non-European peoples and cultures. Ideas of the Orient reiterate and reinforce, directly and indirectly, the notion of European superiority over the backwardness of others. Orientalism was (and is) a form of domination that harbors little possibility of resistance, reinforced as it was by confidence in the authority of first-hand observation, the power of knowledge, and the limitless possibilities of science.

But the logic of Orientalist scholarship had less to do with uncovering new empirical realities than with expressing (in Said's most Freudian terminology) a "battery of desires, repressions, investments, and projections"[12] that find their way into scholarly institutions and products of scholarship, that cumulatively blur the already artificial boundary between pure and political knowledge. Political interests and realities inevitably insinuate themselves into the consciousness of the European observer. There is no escaping imperialism's consensual domination through the production of knowledge. Said makes this point in an important outline of his main argument:

> [I]f it is true that no production of knowledge in the human sciences can ever ignore or disclaim its author's involvement as a human subject in his own circumstances, then it must also be true that for a European or American studying the Orient there can be no disclaiming the main circumstances of *his* actuality: that he comes up against the Orient as a European or American first, as an individual second. And to be a European or American in such a situation is by no means an inert fact. It meant and means being aware, however dimly, that one belongs to a power with definite interests in the Orient, and more important, that one belongs to a part of the earth with a definite history of involvement in the Orient almost since the time of Homer.[13]

It is therefore almost impossible as a European or American cultural observer to escape entanglement in imperialist ambitions since one's political culture of origin defines one's perceptions, sometimes in almost imperceptible ways; and the imperialist project of domination, at least as far as Said is concerned, is the essence of European and American global politics.

The considerable erudition that Said amasses in support of the anti-Orientalist position, however, does not fully protect it against a simple counter argument. This argument does not deny the existence of a Euro-American scholarly tradition that objectifies, homogenizes, distorts, slanders, ridicules, and/or demonizes the Oriental other, but it sets out to show in addition the ways that this picture is significantly incomplete.

First, there is evidence from within the so-called Orientalist literature that does not fit the stereotypical picture of the imperialist stereotyper. This suggests that Said, along with many of his anti-Orientalist followers, have excluded a significant feature of European thought from the corpus of literature they draw upon. In other words, they have Occidentalized the so-called Orientalists. In so doing they have overlooked an element of subversion originating from within Euro-American scholarly traditions that can be found in the work of those colonial-era writers who demonstrated considerable understanding of the life, history, and culture of the "natives" and who even went so far as to object in the strongest possible terms to the conditions of colonialist and racial subjection they encountered. One example of this kind of sympathetic treatment of the colonized "Other" can be found in James Mooney's ethnographic and historical study of the Sioux Ghost Dance Religion of 1892, which characterized the so-called Indian uprising that ended in the Wounded Knee massacre as an enthusiastic, sincere call of spiritual distress in the midst of military defeat, forced settlement, and imposed hunger.[14] Another is the journal kept by the surrealist poet Michel Leiris during the Dakar–Djibouti expedition of 1931–33, published as *l'Afrique fantôme*, a work that transcends the genres of both travel literature and ethnography with an honest, at times satirical confrontation with the scientific mission of the expedition and the African colonial infrastructure that it relied upon.[15] And if we wanted to go further back, to the Enlightenment period that many postmodernists and postcolonialists consider the wellspring of western cultural imperialism, we could include in our anthology of non-Orientalizing Orientalism Wilhelm von Humboldt's observations of the Basques, the result of a linguistic and cultural "field" study that he undertook in the spring of 1801, in which he extolled the charm of the Basque villages, the strength of their character, the sophistication of their language, and the "complete democracy" of their representative system.[16] What is more, Humboldt's observations were in no way tied to the kind of condescending political philosophy that occasionally granted a pat on the back to those who show westernizing promise, but was connected to a political philosophy that considered the strict limitation of the legitimate functions of the state to be the only way to truly defend the integrity of distinct nations, and in particular the kinds of lifestyles pursued by farmers and craftsmen whose self-sufficiency cannot always hold back the leveling rationalism of the bureaucratic state.[17] This kind of western scholarship cannot by any stretch of the imagination be seen to fit into Said's picture of Orientalizing cultural hegemony. And presumably such examples could be multiplied to create a more complex view of the intellectual products of colonial occupation and imperialism.

But these examples could probably be dismissed as exceptions to the rule, not enough to make a case against the far greater mass of evidence that points to an inherent flaw in the western intellectual psyche – a pattern of thought that establishes a close connection in the West's struggle for supremacy between literary domination and colonial occupation – a connection, in other words, between ink and blood. In most cases it is possible to see strains of imperialism within even such apparently anti-imperialist voices – Said refers to these as "residual imperialist propensities"[18] – but it is enough to show that such dissidence is overwhelmed by a great cultural archive of intellectual and aesthetic investment in overseas dominion.[19]

By not giving due weight to the exceptions to his argument, by resorting to the device of "residual imperialism" to argue that even the most rigorous, best intentioned western scholars observing non-western societies inevitably fall into the trap of essentialism-in-the-service-of-imperialism, Said has fashioned a deeply troubling intellectual starting point to what has become the main current of postcolonial studies. This current, whether intentionally or not, largely precludes the possibility of empathetic understanding between cultures or civilizations. If the very acts of inter-civilizational study and narration inevitably wind up in an us/them dichotomy that serves the interests of imperialism, how, if at all, are people from politically conflicting cultures and civilizations to know one another and possibly be reconciled with each other? If postcolonialist anti-Orientalism is not to fall into a crippling double standard, it must admit to the equal pervasiveness of Occidentalism, to the unfair attribution to the West by non-Westerners of qualities it does not truly possess, to the same building up of politically interested, distorted, and misplaced perceptions of European and American culture that postcolonial theory attributes solely to the imperial Occident.[20]

This, to Said's credit, is an argument he was willing to make in his fifteen-year retrospective of the international response to *Orientalism*: "[A]ny attempt to force cultures and peoples into separate and distinct breeds or essences exposes not only the misrepresentations and falsifications that ensue, but also the way in which understanding is complicit with power to produce such things as the 'Orient' or the 'West.' "[21] But if such misrepresentation is endemic to all inter-cultural and inter-civilizational discourse, how, if at all, are we to understand one another?

The answer that Said provided relied on his own uncomfortable position between his Palestinian origins and western education, which he referred to as a state of diaspora – the position of being uncomfortably between two civilizations without being *of* either of them. The study of other cultures as a humanistic pursuit is only possible by not fully attaching oneself to a culture of one's own, by living and working in intellectual exile.[22] This is not to say that exile should be thought of as unreservedly beneficial. Rather, it inflicts suffering and loss; it implies a state of deep loneliness outside a communal habitation; and to overcome this solitude it pulls one in the direction of national pride and other exaggerated group assertions. At the same time, however, exile is a source of moderating detachment. It can free one from triumphant ideologies and thereby foster intellectual reserve, originality of vision, and moral courage.

But if this exile status supposedly provides one with a privileged vantage point from which to see the corrupted nature of the West, presumably this same lofty view can be used to understand, and even to critique, some significant cultural distortions and falsifications generated from within non-western civilizations or from within the guild of postcolonial theorists whose work produces its own essentialized entities such as "Europe," "America," and the "West." Many of Said's critics have called for just such a correction of what they perceive to be historically compensatory hypocrisy. It remains unclear how the interests of cultural understanding and reconciliation might be served by focusing exclusively and selectively on the intellectual production of cultural distortion, stereotyping, racism, and misunderstanding across any spectrum of culture or civilization. Such an intellectual orientation leads almost inevitably, though probably unintentionally, to mutually antipathetic elaborations of wounded pride and victimhood.

Said paid only lip service to such complexities. He adopted a postmodernist position concerning the saturation of meaning with power, but then applied it only here and there (mostly there), according to his own tastes and inclinations. A consistent application of the argument that cultures are hybrid and heterogenous, and that nailing them down into concrete entities is an exercise in power-serving, imperialist distortion, would lead naturally to a critique of all social categories, including imperialism itself, the Subaltern, the colonized, and even the idea of being diasporized – which implies, after all, a position between two stable cultural or civilizational entities; and how can one occupy a viable intellectual position between two civilizations that don't really exist, except perhaps as elaborations of imperialist consciousness? Said's main argument, through such selectiveness and overextension, develops into an odd kind of mellifluous paranoia.

The idea that there is a privileged vantage point from which to observe and criticize imperialism readily contributes, albeit indirectly, to a hardening of once-porous cultural boundaries. This is a characteristic of much of the literature that has followed from Said's early work. Postcolonial amnesia, explained as a result of imperialist distortions and erasures, calls for a renewed effort toward self-invention or self-discovery. The benefits of cultural diaspora, shifting boundaries, indeterminacy, and ambiguity usually fail to be understood by those who might identify themselves as the marginalized Subalterns identified by postcolonial theory. What they usually look for as an inspiration for resistance, and what they most readily select and assimilate from postcolonial discourse, are the simple ideas concerning the inherent antagonism between colonizer and colonized or between imperialism and those it displaces, or assertions of the need to make a new start by returning to the old, of independence and recovery, of avoiding at all costs the discomforts of hybridity and cultural miscegenation. Romanticism, ethnic excess, and other uncompromising assertions of closed collective values are clearly not unique to the West but generally arise in response to the uncertainty and humiliation of dispossession. It is much easier to therapeutically retrieve and reanimate the past than it is to reconcile oneself with those one holds responsible for one's misery.

Diversity as a Universal Project

The focus of attention in Postcolonialism has now shifted, apparently like almost everything even remotely involved in the production of ideas, to the problem of globalization. The Subaltern studies movement is today probably the leading source of postcolonialist reflection on "global designs." It began in the early 1980s among a small group of British-educated Indian scholars who sometimes referred to themselves as "the collective" and who worked within an intellectual milieu that still has the dubious distinction of being one of the few places where classical Marxism survives today.[23] From this starting point it set out on a course that was separate from Marxist orthodoxy, with an attempt to rework the concepts of class, state, and mode of production with a view to the specific context of colonial Indian history. Beyond this initial separation, it developed an approach to colonial and postcolonial subjection in which the study of "common people" has taken on a strong element of cultural particularism, expressed with an emphasis on the agency of the oppressed, marginalized, and culturally hybrid that rejects all grand designs of modernity (under the influence of postmodernism) and in which Marxism exists only in the form of a justification for radical social critique. The central problem of globalization is sometimes conceived by Subalternists as one in which "worldly culture" confronts those local ways of living that are simply called "culture," or in which "global designs" are in conflict with "local histories,"[24] or in which the village teaches us "to make the globe a world."[25] Postcolonialism now includes an approach that sees "diversity as a universal project" that will allow us "to imagine alternatives to universalism."[26]

There are several specific influences at work in the origins of the Subaltern studies movement that can be seen, in one way or another, to have created conditions favorable to this odd combination of culturalism and universalism. First, Mohandas K. Gandhi's anti-colonial, anti-modern resistance had a formative effect on the basic orientation of this movement, even though it has been largely unrecognized by postcolonial theorists themselves.[27] Despite Gandhi's gift for popular mobilization, he did not, after all, produce a sophisticated body of literature with which they could engage, and for this reason his influence on the work of Indian intellectuals is indirect, taking the form of a general infusion of ideas into Indian political culture. Gandhi's largely secularized, eclectic, tolerant version of Hinduism was not entirely out of keeping with the more uncompromising secularism of postcolonial theory, thus meeting, at the very least, a precondition for wider influence in neo-Marxist circles; but the actual source of Gandhi's influence was a radical challenge to prevailing ideas about anti-colonial ethics through an entirely new set of interrelated cultural, spiritual, and political values:[28] a sweeping rejection of modern industry and consumerist materialism, a commitment to non-violence as a strategy of resistance, an affirmation of the simple virtues of village life, and a somewhat unfashionable (especially in the context of the post World War II human rights movement) privileging of duties over rights.

The Gandhian flavor in Subalternism has been enhanced by Ashis Nandy's somewhat solitary route to postcolonialism, in which he first built upon Gandhi's counter-modernity with the argument that "colonialism is first of all a matter of consciousness and needs to be defined ultimately in the minds of men."[29] He expresses this idea more recently with an approach to the psychology of colonialism that emphasizes the constraints and passions that followed from British domination, or rather that continue to follow from derivative forms of post-colonial Indian nationalism (what he pugnaciously calls the "brown version of the white man's burden"), in which political and cultural elites have transplanted from the West a form of spiritless secularism that becomes every bit as strident and orthodoxy-ridden as religious zealotry – that in fact encourages such zealotry by marginalizing India's religion-as-faith traditions of tolerance. These "religious communities in traditional societies," Nandy informs us, "*have* known how to live with each other."[30] But they have been shunted aside by strident forms of modernity and have in response become silent and evasive. Hence they have been ineffectual in the face of intolerance and hatred, quietly making way for a quasi-religious secular modernity, "a new demonology, a tantra with a built-in code of violence."[31] A certain Gandhian influence comes through in Nandy's argument that the process of recovery and reclamation of these everyday traditions would provide an alternative theology of tolerance, one that is better suited to the state systems in South Asia than western models of secularism.

The work of the Italian neo-Marxist Antonio Gramsci was a more direct source of influence in the Subaltern studies movement. The term *subaltern*, after all, was Gramsci's substitution for the word "proletarian," a device used to conceal his Marxist musings from prison censors. One of his main sources of appeal among the Indian left in the 1980s was his study of the Italian peasantry as a source from which to rework Marxist class analysis, especially Marx's characterization of the Asiatic Mode of Production, which singled out India in particular as a stagnant, village-centered backwater beyond the reach of capitalist forces of production and hence an obstacle to the global conditions necessary for the final class struggle of the proletarian revolution. Gramsci's subalterns went beyond this class-centered formula. They were, to those left-leaning Indian intellectuals who had grown weary of orthodox Marxism, very much like the marginalized villagers of post-independence India, at least similar enough to provide a sense of recognition and, out of that recognition, a model for writing histories from "below" and developing a new agenda for the "politics of the people."

This change of historical perspective was given a concrete political justification in the aftermath of a Mao-inspired peasant insurgency in Naxalbari and Prime Minister Indira Gandhi's authoritarian response to such unrest during the "Emergency" years of 1975–77. These events were a catalyst that further inspired members of a disillusioned Indian left to explore the relationship between revolutionary theory and mass struggle in India. The early expressions of the approach to history that became known as Subaltern studies were therefore squarely situated in neo-Marxism. Their main divergence from Marxist orthodoxy was a readiness to consider India's peasantry as a social form worthy of counter-hegemony. The recognized founder of Subaltern studies, Ranajit Guha, spent much of his time in the early 1980s actively involved in Maoist student organizations, while developing an abiding interest in the apparently spontaneous makeup of the peasant rebel.[32] For Guha, class-oriented Marxism had failed to bring about a decisive victory over colonialism and, perhaps more importantly, had failed to create conditions for "the nation to come into its own." The time had come for the particular strengths and voices of the Indian peasantry to come out as a force of opposition against the hegemonic state, a view that he underscored with the slogan, "Let a hundred flowers blossom and we don't mind even the weeds."[33] Guha developed an uncomfortable starting point to the study of India's Subalterns, undeterred by the culturally leveling forces inherent in Marxism, or perhaps assuming them to be resolved by embracing Maoist peasant radicalism, while remaining deeply attached to peasant autonomy.

In the mid-1980s, after four editions of an annual *Subaltern Studies* volume (published by Oxford University Press in Delhi), the Indian Subaltern studies project faced internal dissention over the applicability of Marxist historical materialism to the postcolonialist effort to expose and contest Eurocentric systems of knowledge. The central question motivating the project's efforts had shifted.[34] Peasant revolutionary consciousness lost its preeminence to a broad critique of the Enlightenment, largely inspired by the combined influence of

Foucault, Derrida, and Said. Marxism, although residually significant as an inspiration for resistance, was itself now seen as part of the problem, part of a sweeping hegemony of western thought, the infusion of meaning with power, and at a certain level just another example of western historical determinism. The new challenge to be met in a "post-capitalist" world was to describe or create "desubalternizing knowledges,"[35] to build new possibilities for the liberation of meaning and the meaning of liberation beyond western concepts of knowledge and rationality.

From this point on, the Subaltern studies movement quite literally spilled over its borders. It inspired, directly or indirectly, a range of expressions of radical pluralism, in studies concentrating on particular nations, regions, or hemispheres, but always with a view to the idea of a wider pluralism, of nations without nationalism, civilizations without civilizing missions, and regions without regional hegemony.

Each regional study of postcolonial hegemony has voiced its own particular concerns and aspirations, but the general orientation of post-colonialism is nostalgia toward the local, toward those living within non-linear history and languages of oral indeterminacy. At the same time, it engages in broad criticism of the social and cultural forces that ignore, deny, and/or threaten such non-western epistemologies. A rationality of progress, aspiring toward universalism but in truth developing within a contingent and particular point of view, fails to recognize that all societies are complex, rich in vagaries, meanderings, and bifurcations, without necessarily dissolving or lacking a stable center. Fluctuations, volatility and indetermination are not necessarily equivalent to disorder, and the cultural representation of turmoil and instability should not necessarily be considered chaos.[36]

As subalternism engages with the issues and concepts surrounding globalization, the idea of the "Subaltern" is also being rethought, beginning with a new conception of the socio-political–cultural forces that produce them. According to Walter Mignolo, the ideas associated with global capitalism are the most recent manifestation of western blueprints for domination. Conquest, Christian evangelism, and Colonial domination were but a few of the forms of oppression that accompanied Occidentalist epistemological domination over the history, geography, language, and temporal space of Subalterns. The newest heritor of this legacy, neoliberalism, is, in keeping with the general pattern of western expansionism, "not just an economic and financial question but a new civilizing design."[37] But an alternative to it can be found in "border thinking," the liminal realm that situates the languages, conceptions, and collective memories of those marginalized by colonialism into the "imaginary of the modern world system."[38] "Border gnosis," Mignolo writes, "will help in imagining a world without rigid frontiers (national or civilizational) or a world in which civilizations will have to defend their unity and their purity."[39] Alternatives to modern western epistemology must come from outside the west. The rearticulation into "border gnoseologies" of such realms of understanding as Amerindian categories of thought, Afro-Caribbean experiences, and the "bilanguaging" of Latin America, are capable of fracturing the "European Mind," questioning the pursuits of a dominant intellectual and scientific culture, disrupting the projects of "business class intellectuals," and more broadly overturning the global projects of modernity.

Gayatri Spivak similarly finds a suspiciously close relationship between civil society – exemplified most clearly in her view by the international women's movement – and the global designs of capitalism. The civil structures advocated by internationally active feminists that are being shored up for gender justice have the effect of "providing alibis for the operation of the major and definitive transnational activity, the financialization of the globe, and thus the suppression of the possibility of decolonization."[40] Democracy is similarly subject to conspiratorial design, which in Spivak's counter-hegemonic language, takes the form of a "political restructuring entailed by the transformation of . . . state capitalisms and their colonies to tributary economies of rationalized global financialization . . . [carrying] an aura of the civilizing mission accompanying transformative projects from imperialism to development."[41] The futility and disadvantages of democracy are clearest for Spivak in her relationship with India's indigenous peoples, the so-called "scheduled tribes," marginalized oral societies surrounded and dominated by dominant Sanskritized literate cultures, whose lives she has entered as a "resident teacher-trainer." Among these people, there should be no effort to connect indigenous "democratic" structures to India's parliamentary democracy. This, she claims (without evidence, for this would amount to disciplinary anthropological reporting) would be both impractical and in violation of tribal consensus.[42]

It is now evident that for some of those engaged in the projects of postcolonial resistance, the newest source of civilizational hegemony has gained sharper focus: it begins with the Bretton Woods agencies and the World Trade Organization, in a "grand design to bring the world's rural poor under one rule of finance, one global capital . . . represented by the centreless centre of electronic finance capital."[43] And beyond this it includes – conspiratorially – those powerful nongovernmental organizations sometimes collectively known as "international civil society." In Spivak's view, this includes entities such as the international union movement (seen to serve managerial interests); and the women's movement, (seen to be engaged in a culturally coercive effort to bring the world's women under one rule of law and one civil society, as evidenced by the Platform of Action of the Fourth World Women's Conference in Beijing).[44] And notwithstanding his advocacy of "border thinking," Mignolo dismisses the world's tremendously diverse indigenous peoples' nongovernmental organizations (NGOs) by referring to them as "non-Amerindian organizations" run by "Creole intellectuals." So instead of seeking the reform of political relationships between indigenous communities and states and/or the participation of indigenous peoples in the international community, as are the general goals of the indigenous peoples' movement, Mignolo favors the kind of "symbolic restitution" that can be found in "pre-Colombian configurations" (how the elements of an oral pre-contact configuration can be brought to light without distortion by colonial perspectives or the modern politics of identity, we are not told) and, more hopefully, "a new space coming out of a double translation, a translation of Marxism into Amerindian cosmology and Amerindian into Marxist cosmology." The stress in both his pre-Columbian and Amerindian/Marxist configurations is on a realignment of meaning, accompanied by a naïve and possibly dangerous assumption that culture can be separated from politics, that cultural renewal inhabits a realm beyond considerations of nationalism, closed cultural boundaries, and the politics of identity.

Despite its great sympathy for the underdogs and the downtrodden of the world, however, Subalternism fails to address the specific crises faced by the world's most marginal peoples. This is largely because it is trapped in a paradox of representation. The oppressed can be ennobled as a universal category – Subalterns – because nobody from within the circle of Subalternists is able to say with any amount of specific certainty who on earth they are, what their grievances are, and in particular what they stand for politically. Their rejection of ethnographic reporting is much like trying to make a ghetto safer by knocking out the street lamps. On the one hand, Subalternists cannot themselves claim to be the protagonists or voices of the Subalterns (although the obvious validity of this point has not been a deterrent to somewhat surreal debates on Subaltern representation, mostly in the media of learned journals and conferences), and on the other hand they cannot or choose not to go further than this, to act as cultural brokers and intermediaries, to make instrumental use of the powers of knowledge and information to bring about constructive change. The prohibition on representing the Other is strictly enforced, mostly in favor of one-sided screeds against Occidental hegemony. Subalternists evince abhorrence toward almost any sort of outside-the-campus fact grubbing, while elevating an entirely loose, unconditional, and relativistic (except for its residues of Marxist universalism) approach to diversity as the only basis for supra-national cultural process.

Postcolonialism's advocacy of diversity without the rigorous practice of description brings it back full circle to an unresolved tension between universalism and particularism, expressed earlier in its Marxist critique of national historiography, which sought at the same time to raise the significance of autonomous villages. This time around, after uncovering new categories and geographies of oppression, the argument for the integrity of the "common people" has been universalized in the form of a widely embracing and expanding conception of the Subaltern, eventually working toward a globe-straddling conception of the oppressed. The disjunctures, discomforts, insecurity, and torments of Subalterns are somehow connected and cogent, brought together by a common neoliberal/neoimperialist design to create a world of receptive, culturally neutral consumers. There is a way of making the worlds of many oppressed people understandable as a single process. The task of the Subalternist is therefore to raise awareness of those all-encompassing, yet elusive sources of conspiracy that comprise the newest forms of global hegemony.

The most recent trend in postcolonialism thus gives the oppressed a name – Subalterns – that lacks definition and limit, except that it cannot apply to anyone who can be seen as a source of another definitionless term – hegemony. The purveyors of hegemonic meaning do not belong to the underclass of Subalterns. The world, in other words, consists of a vague, sinister dichotomy of oppressors and the oppressed. So, even though it may be impossible to both understand and report on other cultures, and immoral to even try, there is a basic, though disorderly, unity in the world. The vestiges of colonialism have combined with new forms of global capitalism to create a tricontinental or (if we include the migrant extensions of the oppressed into the West) global common denominator of domination. This sounds very much like an adaptation of the kind of Marxism that inspired Frantz Fanon's vision of a nation- and culture-transcending postcolonial utopia. And, although most postmodernists have forsworn the idea of world revolution, there is in postcolonialism a perception that an emerging form of hegemony is compatible with a global dimension to liberation.

The Grammar of Culture

The broad influence of postcolonialism in cultural studies was virtually guaranteed as soon as it took up its name. Who wants to be associated with colonialism, to advocate unashamedly in favor of new forms of imperialism, to take up the cause of repression? Within the broad parameters implied by rejecting colonial meaning and neo-colonial action, however, there is plenty of room for maneuver. Two postcolonial critiques of modernity can be differentiated by the way they tend to deal with questions of identity and cultural process. One, inspired by postmodern destabilization of social constructs (but not by its embrace of discursive incoherence or sweeping rejection of empirical investigation), tends more often to reject all rigid social boundaries in favor of relativistic flux and ambiguity. In another, exemplified by Subalternism, the source of domination tends to be more specific – there is an identifiable aggressor to which one is called upon to respond – and liberation, correspondingly, tends to draw upon or encourage identity attachments. The lines between the two critiques of modernity, like cultures themselves, tend to blur and miscegenate, but there are still recognizable differences between their most distinct expressions.

One of the significant features of what has been called *critical anthropology* is the development of a radically unstable approach to culture, which dismisses the culture concept's value as a category of "thing," as a noun that can be identified, described, compared with others, displayed in museums, presented at conferences, and decided upon in courts. This approach to culture shows strong indications of the influence of postmodernism, of a kind that arrives, perhaps unintentionally, at the instability of culture from the direction of negative relativism. By situating hegemony in meaning, it establishes a far-reaching connection between the entire gamut of a given society's beliefs and practices (that which is usually understood by "culture") and domination, control, and homogenization of differences.

Postmodernism, as we might recall from chapter 6, sets itself apart from all existing approaches to culture through dismissal of the ideas, first, that any civilization, form of society, institution, or idea can be a source of human progress and, second, that any form of methodological rigor, any systematic fact searching, can lead to a beneficial growth of knowledge. Instead, it privileges local identities and collective self-expression, keeping its attention firmly on hegemonic constructs, among which the static noun form of culture is squarely included. But the radical critique of culture and convention leaves postmodernism with a problem: if everything that is received must be dismantled, who, if anyone, receives the favor of convention, stability, and security? Even though there are some social entities small enough to swim through the grand-narrative net, they cannot escape the perception that their more limited social ideals, traditions, or (by extrapolation) "micro-narratives" are also related to legitimation of power and are the product of recent adaptive fabrications. Such ambiguities are fast on the way to being recognized as integral parts of the anthropological and historical points of view.

For Arjun Appadurai, a convincing exponent of this unstable *Weltanshauung*, cultures are not, or should not be, considered things-in-themselves. "Much of the problem with the noun form," he writes, "has to do with its implication that culture is some kind of object, thing, or substance, whether physical or metaphysical. This substantialization seems to bring culture back into the discursive space of race, the very idea it was originally designed to combat."[45] Culture should rather be looked at as adjectival, and researchers should describe its connection to "those differences that either express, or set the groundwork for, the mobilization of group identities."[46] On this view, culture (or more correctly, cultural process) embodies the essential aspects of boundary maintenance, identity politics, or the mobilization of groups in relationship to nation-states.[47]

Cultural self-definition is thus associated with social movements, with the self-conscious rearticulation of those aspects of ways of life that are most important, that answer the question "who are we?" If culture is to be used in noun form, therefore, it should reflect this quality of social production. This is accomplished with the suffix "ism." Culturalism, according to Appadurai's approach, represents a noun that is created by willing agents of reform. It is the product of ever-changing, creative self-identification. We can even, if we take the new grammar of culture to its logical conclusion, speak of "encultured" communities, whose identities have been clarified and in some cases politically mobilized in order to resist "acculturation" and state-imposed processes of assimilation.[48] Identity is, according to Appadurai's protégés Akhil Gupta and James Ferguson, "a mobile, often unstable relation of difference."[49] Cultures have lost their anchorages to specific places and "cultural territorializations" are "complex and contingent results of ongoing historical and political processes."[50]

Under the influence of postmodernist destabilization, the adjectival and verbal approach to the idea of culture has broadened out to apply to any self-identifying tribe, community, people, or nation. Cultures are now widely considered collective inventions, with varying degrees of self-conscious manipulation built into the attachments people have to "timeless" ways of life. An implication of this approach (though not, apparently, one that is recognized by Maffesoli, Lipovetsky, and probably many other postmodernists) is that when we consider a culture as a noun we are, willingly or unwillingly, buying into the political strategies and motivations that go along with it. Cultures may be entities, but not the friendly, warm, embracing, holdover-from-simpler-times kind of entity hoped for by cultural romantics. Cultures are "isms," the products of national awakening, created and defended by those who are erecting new political boundaries.

Other postcolonialists, particularly those who identify with the Subaltern studies movement, however, frequently (but usually unintentionally) run counter to the destabilized approach to culture, partly because of a prevalent urge to support the underdog and partly out of a corresponding inhibition from applying social criticism to the "weak."

Postcolonialism's insistence on the narrative inviolability of the oppressed specifically rejects observations, judgments, and criticism from those outside the womb of language and experience. By avoiding critical description of cultural process (outside the West) and by simultaneously promoting the existence of areas of life and consciousness that have never been acknowledged by the hegemonic Occident, they reinforce the tendency of all people to establish their own preferred cultures and identities as *things* that are opposable to the inferior cultures of ignorant or oppressive *others*. Even though Subalternist postcolonialism gives due weight to cultural ambiguities and impermanence, it at the same time creates intellectual conditions that encourage the resurgence of the noun form of culture. It reinforces the tendency for cultural process to be encultured. It tends to highlight us/them dichotomies through a conceptual refrain that positions self-defining, self-creating Subalterns in a position of subjection and opposition to western-influenced nationalism and global hegemony. It has thus become closely, though indirectly, involved in the process of collective rediscovery and small-scale nation building or "identity-building," by lending credence to claims of permanence and unity and by erecting barriers to representation, and above all to criticism, of Subalterns.

Postcolonialism's use of historical criticism, for better or worse, is a tool of cultural preservation that tries to slow down the most immediate forces of nation-statist and global assimilation by erecting a barrier between Subalterns and the supposedly hegemonic West, a barrier behind which new cultural boundaries can flourish. At the same time, however, it throws into relief the troublesome questions of identity and the need for recognition by dominant societies. Postcolonialism in some ways meets the need of marginalized people for an intellectual defense of their distinctiveness; above all it answers their call for academic empowerment. At the same time, however, it homogenizes societies even more by encouraging globally similar struggles for recognition. Cultural particularism is not entirely incompatible with the idea of global integration, including quasi-millenarian aspirations for a new world dispensation in which all peoples and communities can cohabit peacefully, beyond reach of all hegemonic interference.

9

Conclusion

A condition in which the separation of nations and peoples has diminished has made it more possible than ever to imagine a world in which nations and peoples no longer exist, or at least no longer matter. A cosmopolitan society is more than just imaginable – there are growing indications that it is emerging. No one, however much they may wish to, can isolate themselves to the point of living a simple existence, outside the reach of global institutions. The impacts of transnational extractive industries on subsistence economies may still be disputed in individual cases, but there is no denying the general fact that such activities as forestry, mining, construction of hydroelectric installations, and large-scale agriculture impose upon many communities a dramatic change in environmental sustainability that requires a shift from a subsistence autonomy to participation in the formal economy. Above this, the global economy has become just that, a network of production, exchange, and consumption that reaches everywhere, offering images of a good life that is usually far away, being enjoyed by someone else, sometimes taking forms that are unseemly or immoral by local ethical standards. In the Muslim world in particular the billboard now competes with the Book as the purveyor of truths to live by (or, according to some, of dangerous falsehoods to resist by every means possible), not to mention the cultural influence of television and the Internet.

More than ever before, those who see new opportunities and dangers inherent in global institutions want to see the world itself made better. It is not enough to aspire toward improving a corner of the world – a community, a neighborhood, or just oneself. A vogue is returning, after an absence during the late twentieth century, to imagine the possible and to-be-struggled-for along the lines of a world in which all people are united, but at the same time are liberated from imperialist structures and ways of thinking, making it possible for everyone to be alike principally in their ability to express themselves freely. Some of today's most important intellectual currents look to the concept of globalization as a way to communicate a message of world liberation.

But there is no secure prospect of reaching a compromise between the two most radical expressions of world culture: a totalizing individualism bent upon the assimilation and disintegration of traditional authority structures, or a form of utopian thought built upon irrationalism and obscurantism that commonly expresses its solutions to almost any conceivable problem in negative terms: a rejection of reason, an abandonment of the search for sources of knowledge, a distrust of that form of universal belief that is based on confidence in both what is known and the possibility of discovering what is unknown.

An obvious source of globalizing ideas and efforts comes from those who see universal institutions, policies, and values as the ultimate sources of human freedom and prosperity. Global finance is usually considered the starting point of culture-eroding universalism, but any conception of universal social good, even liberal democracy and human rights, applied without compromise, can have the same totalizing effect. No clear conceptualization of a world culture can be separated from a corresponding negation of distinct societies – societies that protect or aspire toward self-definition, self-actualization, and political self-determination. Those with the most ambitious agendas of global identity look for ways to make distinct societies inconsequential. They usually approach human difference with hostility, ambivalence, or pity, but only rarely with a spirit of accommodation.

The progressive integration of the world's nations, peoples, and cultures is bringing into global prominence an issue that has until now mostly occupied democratic states: how do liberal societies accommodate, assimilate, or dominate those illiberal societies that flout the principles of individual freedom and the dignity of the person? Just as the spirit of a nation can be captured by its approach to minorities, the essence of global ideals can be understood through their ways of counteracting the ambitions of those who are staunchly parochial, or universalist within a strictly limited space: an unbounded sense of the right to exist as a self-defining community. In the human rights movement in particular there is no consensus available on the kind of freedom, collective or individual, which merits our greatest attention and energy; but the major human rights agencies still act upon an approach to world culture in which global institutions are the purveyors of universal values.

So the battle lines of globalization are commonly conceived in a way that is not dissimilar from Seneca's understanding of world culture outlined in the epigram of this book: On the one hand, a vision that aspires to a vast, truly common state in which the bounds of our citizenship are measured by the path of the sun; and on the other, the community to which we have been assigned by the accident of birth.

But this is not the reality we live in today. It is not even close.

Besides the immediate, recognizable conceptions of world culture, we must add those that begin with rejection of universals, that aspire to tear down the edifices of global institutions, and that celebrate a possible future in which individuals or communities are fully liberated and self-actualizing. Such visions of liberation come around to world culture through a kind of globalization from below. In a typical paradox of world integration, the revolt against the forces of modernity often takes the form of internationalized particularism. There is an increasingly significant global dimension to the issues surrounding cultural preservation and collective self-determination. Even primordial cultures now rely upon global patterns of grievance and resistance. Universal concepts from the western tool kit of liberation have become a common heritage of humanity. To be resistant to assimilative forces all societies need philosophical, bureaucratic, and technological defenses. These defenses may answer the immediate call for legal and political empowerment, but over the long term they homogenize societies even further through globally similar struggles for recognition and self-determination. Both the ills and the remedies of modernity are rapidly becoming part of every cultural community. The cumulative effect of such global transformations has already been a reduction of possibilities for the expression of collective character.

It is sometimes supposed that if every distinct people must be left to determine its own way of life and above all its own criteria of belonging, if intercultural value judgments and censure are the only thing censurable, and if most of the world can still be united through common experiences of subjection and repression by hegemonic powers, then the barriers between distinct people will eventually begin to break down, illegitimate, censorious power will be overthrown, and people will be united more by bonds of brotherhood and sisterhood than those of distinct identities. This basic approach to human differences minimizes the significance of violence and distorted ambition among the marginalized. It assumes that the colors of culture can change but do not bleed. And out of this assumption easily comes the idea of a world made whole by those peoples that have thrown off imperialist constraints and are united with others in a common, self-actualizing humanity.

Many of the insidiously globalizing ideas expressed in the discontents of globalization can be traced to the influence of postmodernism and postcolonialism, in particular to the widely shared notion that, since the pursuit of truths valid for all of humanity at all times has shown itself to be so intimately connected with imperialism, our real source of hope lies in accepting the contingency of knowledge, the pervasiveness of hidden meaning, and the liberating possibilities inherent in relativist pluralism, tribalism, and the rise of "micrologies." Postmodernism is a thriving form of idealism based upon a postulate of counter-idealism and arriving, in its extreme form, at self-negating, apolitical anarchism. It rejects the tyranny of untrammeled capitalism but also expresses concern over the possibility of capitalism's success, the universalism of bourgeois life and values. Capitalism brings with it unarticulated demands of conformity, in postmodern terms, insidious forms of oppression and containment of the human spirit that can only be unearthed by a kind of painstaking archaeology of meaning, a method of "deconstruction" that exposes the artifacts of hegemony.

The way that Marxism has at times been blended with postmodernism demonstrates that even those who passionately oppose the most visible institutions and processes of global cultural integration are capable of arriving at their own version of world culture. The kinds of counter-hegemony that turn their backs on supranational organizations, law making, and lobbying often end up with their own forms of global thinking, forms that are far from the possibilities of institution building, democratic reform, investigative scrutiny, or public persuasion. The idea seems to be that global institutions are, *by their nature*, hegemonic, and that there is no way to oppose them other than to reject outright the idea of institution building, especially within and among nation-states and in global governance. A radically new foundation for the global order is to be found in the absence of order – hence, a borderless world: the Cosmopolis.

Postcolonialism overlaps with a corner of postmodernism's sweeping critique of modernity by rejecting the idea of culture-transcending knowledge. It therefore indirectly reinforces the notion that a people can only understand itself, within shared points of reference, defined principally by language, education, and collective values. It especially rejects criticism between cultures or civilizations, unless it is criticism of the weak toward the powerful, or of nearly anyone toward the West. Postcolonialism is a form of cosmopolitanism that, through its denial of universals and its elevation of marginality, Subaltern history, and diaspora, actually encourages redefinition of communities, and closure of cultural boundaries. Because it accepts the idea of the contingency of knowledge, postcolonialism disallows the project of working toward an understanding of cultural differences, collective grievances, and the conditions for peaceful coexistence. It indirectly encourages the awakening of a collective sense of self that combines victimization with the malleability of culture – a tried and true recipe for national, ethnic, or other minority insurgency. What brings distinct, marginalized communities together in postcolonialism is their common source of oppression, variously characterized as Anglo-American imperialism, Enlightenment rationalism, the West, and the Occident. While declaiming against all manner of hegemonic cultural reduction, many postcolonialists slip into a hypocritical cultural and philosophical reduction of what they perceive to be *the* source of *the world's* discontent.

The forceful idea – the most significant contribution of postmodernism and its offshoots – that colonization is a state of mind as much as a condition of subjection to overt tyranny was first very much a part of the delegitimation and disintegration of Europe's colonial projects. If it is true that an unprecedented, one-sided form of domination – exercised not only through force of arms but more insidiously through language and thought – was (and is) imposed on those who were previously accustomed only to regional tyrannies, hybridization with neighbors and local enemies, to the flux and reflux of cyclical forms of domination, then how were (and are) the victims of imperialism to conceive of liberation? How could they possibly free themselves from overwhelmingly dominant intruders who perceived themselves as liberators? Are we really to expect "ordinary" people to be happy occupying an identity space somewhere between conflicting civilizations, or to comfortably identify themselves as migrants, border occupants, or people in transition representing "hybrid" culture? Do those who are to participate in the universal project of diversity all similarly cherish the values of tolerance toward difference?

Postcolonialism's rejection of inter-cultural knowledge and representation prevents such questions from being seriously addressed. It elevates the global status of marginality and victimhood without providing a complete picture of how oppressed communities are formed or how they form themselves. By focusing on oppressive historiography, the equally oppressive glorification of the postcolonial nation, and other forms of hegemonic Occidental meaning, it overlooks the ways in which local identities can themselves take on qualities of strident nationalism motivated by wounded pride and defense of an all-embracing, artificially-bounded conformity. Postcolonialism, in other words, provides us with no understanding of micro-nationalism or the self-oppression of peoples. Its approach to diversity is premised upon unrealizable conditions for the legitimation of communities, global or local.

Under the complex circumstances of globalizing modernity a great impediment to the emergence of pluralist global democracy arises from the mere fact that many critically oriented intellectuals have given up on the possibility of effecting change in international institutions or of creating new institutions to meet the tremendous challenges of technological innovation, market expansion, and cultural integration. Postmodernism, the postmodernist-inspired neo-Marxism, and post-colonialism all advance skepticism toward public institutions and democratic processes precisely at a time when the most powerful global institutions are most in need of democratization. The global order clearly requires more – and better, more accountable – government, not less. But a common intellectual response to this need is to extend ideas about the powers of social conformity into the realm of politics, infusing all institutional life with the same taint of hegemony, depicting liberation through political participation as impossible – or worse, as complicitous with oppressive powers. Social critique has suffered a profound lapse into obscurantism, just at a moment when it needs more than ever to be instrumentally creative. In uncertain times, when new global powers are forming, many endowed with compassion and imagination are encouraging civic apathy; and the contests of world culture are being decided by the influence of passionate disengagement.

The achievement of a common denominator in human social attachments and loyalties would be impossible without the erosion of what are often seen to be socially closed, territorially circumscribed communities. Societies that try to reinterpret the past, to anchor social change to orthodoxy, to create clear, narrow pathways for their members – these societies are threatened by the unbounded individualism of global culture. Many of today's political contests center upon societies that are unwilling to surrender their land, control over their subsistence, their political self-determination, or their language and culture, to dominant societies or international ventures. The forms that this resistance takes, however, vary greatly; and the strategies that marginalized minorities choose for the reassertion of traditional values have important implications for the liberal ideals of freedom, especially the rights of individuals to both security and self-development.

Some of these individual-absorbing forms of life try to make use of global institutions in efforts to mitigate the destructive effects of state-sponsored monoculturalism and industrial degradation of their lands. Such peoples as the Samis pose fewer problems for nation-states through their reassertions of community boundaries because of their commitments to state institutions, peaceful internationalism, and the rule of law, even though they sometimes make nuisances of themselves (from the state point of view) with assertions of self-determination that come into conflict with constitutional uniformity, state supremacy in international organizations, and state-centered nationalist sentiment.

I have briefly considered the Wahhabi-inspired Islamic reformers in Mali as an example of more protective isolationism and exclusivism. The reformers willfully sundered relations with all those among their families, neighbors, and political representatives whom they saw as being – short of repentance and conformity-oriented atonement – beyond salvation. They looked for inspiration and guidance to the most conservative clerics from Islamic centers of learning, especially in Saudi Arabia, and in this sense can be seen as reaching beyond themselves and their surrounding milieu, beyond even the continent of Africa, to a wider civilization, to which the technology of travel and communication has given them easier access. In this sense, their quasi-medieval value orientation is incongruously very much a product of globalizing modernity. But they used the opportunities afforded by literacy, rapid communication, and (before their "house arrest") the possibility of rapid long-distance travel, to close themselves off as much as possible from the authority of state governance and, above all, from the "un-Islamic" political values and cultural influence of the West.

Such isolationism can be seen as an extreme kind of counter-modernity, a refusal to accept either marginalization or integration into a wider socio-political order. The reformers' choice of doctrine and way of putting it into effect reinforced some aspects of Songhay tradition, especially its core community values, the assurance (to the extent, in conditions of dwindling prosperity, that such an assurance could be made) of a life-spanning livelihood, the authority of elders, and the security of limited choice. It went beyond the Islamic requirements of salvation to the development of a community infrastructure and moral embrace that limited individual options and, in doing so, dissolved both individual differences and anxieties.

This so-called fundamentalist strategy for the reinforcement of basic community values, which can occur through any major religion, is at the furthest extreme from the quest for a universal culture, from the various ideals that I have discussed in this book of a shared human common denominator that transcends religious, linguistic, ethnic, and political allegiances. Whereas most expressions of universalism are usually open to some form of accommodation with particular cultural attachments, at least within certain limits, those who remain most firmly attached to tradition are more inclined to categorically reject any nod to relativism, any exercise in ecumenical tolerance, any notion that there may be more than one truth, different from one's own.

Imaginings of a perfect society therefore almost inevitably have difficulty with the problem posed by human differences. Pursuit of the ideal world order almost invariably comes up against non-compliant others (real, possible, and/or solely imaginary), those who stubbornly see their own way of life as an already perfect universe, the pinnacle of human possibility, at odds with those who surround them or with those who try to dominate them from afar. Those forms of illiberal traditionalism and nationalism that strive to submerge individuals with ideas and aspirations of the collective good do not normally arise spontaneously, but are rather germinated in conditions of opposition, assaults to pride and honor, and a sense of foreboding over the shrinking possibility of living an inherited existence. Such traditionalists stand in the way of those seeking some form of global unity. For the perfect world order to be realized along the lines of utopian cosmopolitanism, these recalcitrants must be vanquished or converted (or both, preferably in close succession). The ideal of peace and brotherhood must make concessions to conquest and domination, on a provisional and temporary basis of course, until all people are alike in their basic loyalty to the universal vision, whatever it may be. How else is the ideal society to come about? The mission inspired by a conception of universal social perfection must, if its model is to be realized in this world, in some way negate the influence of those distinct societies that reject human differences.

To some, this challenge might be seen as an invitation to new regimes of liberally inspired imperialism (though they almost certainly would not describe their efforts that way). The conflict between the values of individual liberty (including various neo-Marxist versions of the borderless world) and the equally compelling freedoms grounded in the self-determination of peoples has no obvious outcome. How can liberal freedoms be brought to those who, for example, cherish above all else the certainties of patriarchy, who place the duties of obedience within the community over the legitimacy of the state or of the international order, or who even see themselves engaged in a struggle against the ambiguities of cosmopolitan conciliation? Faced with this question there is at least one certainty: there is no morally uncompromising or logically consistent way to *impose* freedom. Whenever power is used to settle an argument, the vanquished can claim a victory.

Permissive cosmopolitanism suffers from quite another form of malaise. It imagines the good global society to consist of unrepressed "tribes," Subalterns, or "borderless communities" capable of transcending state boundaries, while loosely combining cultural self-definition with political self-determination. In its most extreme form it expresses the idea of collective freedom without the impositions of state boundaries or global governance. This cosmopolitan ideal assumes (usually implicitly) a kind of graduated relativism, in which societies are seen to be virtuous in inverse proportion to their power. Those on the margins of nation-states, those excluded and oppressed by the institutions of transnational capitalism and global governance, are tacitly seen to possess a form of honor and absolution from judgment that accrues only to the dispossessed. In response to the problems posed by terrorism, inter-ethnic violence, and repression of minorities-within-minorities, it provides only a sweeping faith in free societies to find their own equilibrium.

One of the most significant consequences of a rapidly globalizing modernity is the fact that the once isolated and powerless now have a more varied and effective armature of resistance. Those who are oppressed without being utterly destroyed are filling the ranks of transnational actors. Universalism is redefining particularism, and vice versa. The successfully articulated identity is increasingly one that combines local cultural (re)attachments with connections to some form of transnational civil society or network, be it, for example, through NGOs that openly and actively participate in human rights standard setting or through terrorist networks set upon the "purification" of sacred space through piecemeal acts of genocide. There is no inherent guarantee that the new possibilities of transnational activism will lead to peaceful and productive conditions of collective life.

Whatever form they take, dreams of a global Cosmopolis inevitably run up against (though usually without explicit acknowledgment) the cultural claims of closed societies. Pluralism still entails recognizing the rights of communities that reject pluralist values, or that adhere publicly to pluralism while putting into political practice something else altogether, often more closely resembling local despotism. So those globalization theorists who assert the emergence of a borderless, global cosmopolitan society have failed to take into account the durability of boundaries, both of nation-states and of minority communities, the persistence and extension to smaller political units of the nationalist principle of inclusion through exclusion, of strident local forms of religious nationalism, of consciousness of social homogeneity and collective myths of shared tradition and common destiny. Those on the other hand who adhere to a more politically active global liberalism are inevitably brought to the point of evangelizing, of somehow imposing freedom on societies that adhere to traditional constraints, often pursuing strategies of moral/political engagement that unintentionally lead to self-negating hypocrisy, inflammation of subject peoples' wounded pride, and counter-reactive reinforcement of their identity boundaries.

The persistence of such errors suggests that some of the major trends in globalization theory and the politics that follow from them are not entirely new but derive from a recurrent western legacy of utopian expectation. A major source of the ills of our globalizing world derives from the extension of such radical hope to a culturally leveling will to bring an imagined future into being.

Notes

CHAPTER 1

1   The latter term is the subject of a study by Helmut Willke, *Heterotopia: Studien zur Krisis der Ordnung moderner Gesellschaften* (Frankfurt am Main: Suhrkamp, 2003). For Willke, heterotopia refers principally to a generalized social condition that cultivates indifference toward cultural difference, together with a diminution in the social drive toward unity and order. My emphasis here is on the construction of such a sociological vision as a form of utopian hope.

2   The most influential source of this view is Francis Fukuyama's *The End of History and the Last Man* (New York: Avon, 1992).

3   On the decline of utopian ideas in the late twentieth century, see Isaiah Berlin's, "The Decline of Utopian Ideas in the West," in *The Crooked Timber of Humanity* (Princeton: Princeton University Press, 1990); Jürgen Habermas' "Die Krise des Wohlfahrtstaats und die Erschöpfung utopischer Energien" in *Die Neue Unübersichtlichkeit* (Frankfurt am Main: Suhrkamp, 1985); and Fredric Jameson's "The Politics of Utopia," (*New Left Review,* Vol. 25, Jan/Feb 2004:35–54).

4   Jürgen Habermas, "Die Krise des Wohlfahrtstaats."

5   One of the tasks to which Nazi ethnologists such as Wilhelm Mühlmann, R. Beck, and Gerhard Teich applied their intellectual gifts was the "de-ethnicizing" (*Umvolkung*) or assimilation of peoples whose territory (especially in Eastern Europe) the higher echelons of the political/military apparatus had ambitions of occupying. This was, it seems, approached not so much out of a misguided philanthropic spirit that sees a need to bring the light of a superior civilization to those living in darkness (more

characteristic of the British and U.S. missionary and boarding school programs among Native Americans), as from a pragmatic realization that
such peoples were capable of making themselves indigestible, of making
political nuisances of themselves, particularly under conditions of occupation. Their focus of study, well in advance of American, British, and
French anthropology or ethnology thus shifted to "inter-ethnic relations"
(*interethnischen Beziehungen*). See Ute Michel, "Neue ethnologische
Forschungsansätze im Nationalsozialismus? Aus der Biographie von
Wilhelm Emil Mühlmann (1904–1988)" in *Lebenslust und Fremdenfurcht:
Ethnologie im Dritten Reich*. Ed. Thomas Hauschild (Frankfurt: Suhrkamp,
1995).

CHAPTER 2

1 K'ang Yu-wei, *Ta T'ung Shu: The One World Philosophy*, translated with an
   Introduction and Notes by Laurence G. Thompson (London: George Allen
   and Unwin, 1958). Cited in Prasenjit Duara, *Rescuing History from the Nation*
   (Chicago: University of Chicago Press, 1995), p. 209.
2 Prasenjit Duara, *Rescuing History from the Nation*, p. 209.
3 In A. A. Long and D. N. Sedley, *The Hellenistic Philosophers: Volume 1,
   Translations of the Principal Sources with Philosophical Commentary*
   (Cambridge: Cambridge University Press, 1987), p. 133.
4 A. A. Long and D. N. Sedley take issue with the notion that Zeno's vision
   was internationalist, arguing that the fragments of his *Republic* provide no
   evidence that he envisaged a world state. This impression probably comes
   from Plutarch's advocacy of the unification "realized in practice" by
   Alexander the Great. Hence " 'citizen of the world' has less to do with the
   United Nations than with the rationality all humans share with their
   divine ruler." The "main contribution [of Stoic philosophy] to internationalism was their treatment of moral principles as laws of human
   nature, transcending all accidents of birth and local identities" (*The
   Hellenistic Philosophers*, p. 435.) But given the universality of moral principles and the quasi-religious nature of the ideal community, it seems to
   follow naturally that Zeno would have meant his republic to be inclusive
   of humanity, even if he did not address this question directly in what has
   survived of his teachings.
5 For a discussion of Zeno and the stoics in the context of utopian thought,
   see Isaiah Berlin's essay "The Decline of Utopian Ideals in the West" in
   The Crooked Timber of Humanity: Chapters in the History of Ideas (Princeton:
   Princeton University Press, 1990), p. 22 and Ernest Bloch, *The Principle of
   Hope* (Cambridge, MA: The MIT Press, 1995) vol. 2, pp. 492–93.

6 Ernst Bloch, *The Principle of Hope*, vol. 2, p. 492.
7 Marcus Aurelius, *Meditations*, translated by Maxwell Staniforth (New York: Penguin, 1964), p. 45.
8 Montaigne, "Of cannibals" in *The Complete Essays of Montaigne*, translated by Donald Frame (Stanford: Stanford University Press, 1958 [1578–80]), p. 153. The motif of an ideal society existing somewhere in newly discovered lands likely also had wide currency in Elizabethan England. Shakespeare reveals the influence of Montaigne's essay in *The Tempest*, where Gonzalo presents his idea of an ideal commonwealth (received skeptically by his listeners): "No use of metal, corn, or wine, or oil; no occupation, all men idle, all; And women too, but innocent and pure ..." (2.1.153–56).
9 As one resident of Bensalem explains to Bacon's anonymous fictional narrator, "about three thousand years ago, or somewhat more the navigation of the world . . . was greater than at this day." This is the simple device Bacon uses to establish a source for the Bensalemite's social organization and dedication to science. Francis Bacon, "New Atlantis" in *Three Early Modern Utopias*, edited by Susan Bruce (Oxford: Oxford University Press, 1999 [1627]), p. 162.
10 On the ambiguities of power in More's *Utopia*, see Susan Bruce's "Introduction" in *Three Early Modern Utopias* (Oxford: Oxford University Press, 1999), pp. xviii–xxvii.
11 See Isaiah Berlin, *Freedom and Its Betrayal: Six Enemies of Human Liberty* (Princeton: Princeton University Press, 2001) and Pierre Musso, *Saint-Simon et le Saint-Simonisme* (Paris: Presses Universitaires de France, 1999).
12 "We hold these truths to be self-evident, that all men are created equal, that they are endowed by their Creator with certain unalienable rights, that among these are life, liberty and the pursuit of happiness. That to secure these rights, governments are instituted among men, deriving their just powers from the consent of the governed. That whenever any form of government becomes destructive of those ends, it is the right of the people to alter or abolish it, and to institute new government." Paul Lauren, in *The Evolution of International Human Rights: Visions Seen*, offers this passage from the Declaration of Independence in a discussion of the antecedents or earliest expressions of the human rights movement. He also provides a useful outline of the influence of the French Revolution on the development of human rights, although he does not find room for a discussion of the important Jacobin excesses in bringing about their vision of a world constructed according to inherent rights.
13 Alain Pons, in his introduction to Condorcet's *Esquisse d'un tableau historique des progrès de l'esprit humain* (Paris: Flammarion, 1988), p. 33, points to a similar conception of perfectibility in Rousseau's *Discourse on*

the Origins of Inequality, in which the human capacity for improvement only serves to highlight a contrary tendency toward imbecility and regression.

14   [*Les hommes ne pourront s'éclairer sur la nature et le développement de leurs sentiments moraux, sur les principes de la morale, sur les motifs naturels d'y conformer leurs actions, sur leurs intérêts, soit comme individus, soit comme membres d'une société sans faire aussi dans la morale practique ses progrès non moins réels que ceux de la science même. L'intérêt mal entendu n'est il pas la cause la plus fréquente des actions contraires au bien général? La violence des passions, n'est-elle pas souvent l'effet d'habitudes auxquelles on ne s'abandonne que par un faux calcul, ou de l'ignorance des moyens de résister à leurs premiers mouvements, de les adoucir, d'en détourner, d'en diriger l'action.*] Condorcet, *Esquisse d'un tableau historique des progrès de l'esprit human; Fragment sur l'Atlantide* (Paris: Flammarion, 1988 [1795]), p. 285. My translation.

15   [*la réunion générale des savants du globe dans une république universelle des sciences.*] Condorcet, *Esquisse*, 1988 [1795], p. 303. My translation.

16   [*une raison forte et pure aura dicté les lois et combiné les institutions.*] Condorcet, *Esquisse*, 1988 [1795], p. 301. My translation.

17   Condorcet "Dedicatory Epistle to the Negro Slaves." In *The French Revolution and Human Rights: A Brief Documentary History*, edited and translated by Lynn Hunt. (Boston: Bedford/St. Martin's, 1996 [1781]).

18   See Lynn Hunt (ed.) *The French Revolution and Human Rights*, p. 10. "*Sodomie*" was the term normally to designate homosexuality in eighteenth-century France, an indication in itself of the stigma associated with it.

19   Cited in Hunt, *The French Revolution and Human Rights*, p. 78.

20   Richard Tuck, *Natural Rights Theories: Their Origin and Development* (Cambridge: Cambridge University Press, 1979), p. 68.

21   Hans Maier, *Wie universal sind die Menschenrechte?* (Freiberg: Verlag Herder, 1997), p. 58.

22   Jacques Maritain, *Man and the State* (Washington, D.C.: The Catholic University of America Press, 1951), pp. 91–92.

23   Jacques Maritain, *The Rights of Man and Natural Law*, translated by Doris Anson (New York: Charles Scribner's Sons, 1943), p. 63.

24   Maritain, *The Rights of Man and Natural Law*, p. 55.

25   Maritain, *The Rights of Man and Natural Law*, p. 24.

26   Maritain, *Man and the State*, p. 79.

27   Useful discussions of Christian elements in the development of human rights can be found in: Wolfgang Vögele, "Christliche Elemente in der Begründung von Menschenrechten und Menschenwürde im Kontext der Entstehung der Vereinten Nationen." In *Ethik der Menschenrechte: Zum Streit um de Universalität einer Idee*, edited by Hans-Richard Reuter (Tübingen:

Mohr Siebeck, 1999); and Hans Maier, *Wie universal sind die Menschenrechte?* (Freiburg: Verlag Herder, 1997).

28 Cited in Glendon, *A World Made New*, p. 75.

29 See Wm. Theodore de Bary, *Asian Values and Human Rights: A Confucian Communitarian Perspective* (Cambridge, MA: Harvard University Press, 1998) and Wm. Theodore de Bary and Tu Weiming (eds.), *Confucianism and Human Rights* (New York: Columbia University Press, 1998).

30 Cited in Vögele, "Christliche Elemente in der Begründung von Menschenrechten," p. 123.

31 Cited in Vögele, "Christliche Elemente in der Begründung von Menschenrechten," p. 124.

32 With the publication of an American edition of *Social Statics* in 1864, Spencer took the opportunity to disclaim some of its views, mostly in the form of qualifications, while leaving the leading principles intact; and in 1892, some 42 years after its first appearance, Spencer issued a new edition in which he discarded his discussions of the Perfect State, leaving a cautious book that had lost much of its initial appeal. It was the original 1850 edition, however, that had a significant impact on nineteenth-century thought; it is also this edition that has since been reprinted and has continued to represent Spencer's evolutionist vision. Spencer invested his hopes for the future in his youthful work (written at the age of 30), and it was through his salvationist approach to history that he acquired the supporters (and detractors) who were to make him famous.

33 Ricardo's democratic political philosophy is discussed by Murray Milgate and Shannon Stimson in *Ricardian Politics* (Princeton: Princeton University Press, 1991). Milgate and Stimson argue that Ricardo closely connected democracy and economic growth, arguing against Edmund Burke's model of the heroic legislator, one whose visionary schemes could not be understood by an infantile public. In his opposition to such views, Ricardo undertook a vigorous defense of a form of liberal democracy in which "the people themselves, through the means of their representatives, should have a preponderating voice" (cited p. 24). The great emphasis placed on Ricardo's brilliant economic formulations overshadows his concern with reforms of the House of Commons, informed by a deep knowledge of political theory.

34 Herbert Spencer, *Political Writings* (Cambridge: Cambridge University Press, 1994 [1884]) p. 75.

35 Herbert Spencer, *Social Statics* (New York: Robert Schalkenbach Foundation, 1995 [1850]), p. 389.

36 Spencer, *Social Statics*, p. 391.

37 Spencer, *Social Statics*, p. 369.

38 Spencer, *Social Statics*, p. 368.

39   Spencer, *Social Statics*, p. 267.
40   Karl Marx and Friedrich Engels, *The Communist Manifesto* (New York: New American Library, [1848] 1998), pp. 54–55.
41   Karl Marx and Friedrich Engels, "Address to the Communist League," in *The Marx-Engels Reader*, edited by Robert C. Tucker (New York: W.W. Norton, 1978), p. 504.
42   Karl Marx, *The 18th Brumaire of Louis Bonaparte* (New York: International Publishers, [1852] 1963), p. 124.
43   Cited in Edward Said, *Orientalism* (New York: Vintage Books, 1994 [1978]), p. 154.

CHAPTER 3

1   Anthony Giddens, *Runaway World: How Globalization is Reshaping our Lives* (New York: Routledge, 2000).
2   The cumulative impact of this era of exploration is effectively described by Stefan Zweig in *Triumph and Tragik des Erasmus von Rotterdam* (Frankfurt am Main: Fischer, 2002 [1938]), pp. 24–25.
3   A long historical view of some of the historical connections that result in social integration is provided by Charles Tilly in *World History* (New York: Harcourt, Brace & Company, 2003). The division between "globalization skeptics" and "hyperglobalizers" is discussed in the introduction to David Held, Anthony McGrew, David Goldblatt, and Jonathan Perraton, *Global Transformations: Politics, Economics, and Culture* (Stanford: Stanford University Press, 1999). A systematic and persuasive historical approach to globalization is presented by Jürgen Osterhammel and Niels Petersson in *Geschichte der Globalisierung: Dimensionen, Prozesse, Epochen* (Munich: C.H. Beck, 2003).
4   Anthony Giddens provides an important, early formulation of this idea in his discussion of *disembedding*, which he defines as "the 'lifting out' of social relations from local contexts of interaction and their restructuring across indefinite spans of time-space" in *The Consequences of Modernity* (Stanford: Stanford University Press, 1990), p. 21. John Tomlinson, in *Globalization and Culture* (Chicago: University of Chicago Press, 1999), p. 107, prefers the term *deterritorialization* to describe the way that the "stretching of social relations affects the character of the localities that we typically inhabit."
5   See, for example, Nestor García Canclini's *Hybrid Cultures: Strategies for Entering and Leaving Modernity*, translated by Christopher Chiappari and Silvia López (Minneapolis: University of Minnesota Press, 1995).
6   Tomlinson, *Globalization and Culture*, p. 138.

7 See Tomlinson, *Globalization and Culture*, pp. 141–149 for a useful summary of the concept of cultural hybridization. Walter D. Mignolo, in *Local Histories/Global Designs* (Princeton: Princeton University Press, 2000) takes such a counter-hegemonic approach to hybridity through the concept of "border thinking."

8 Jean-Loup Amselle, in *Mestizo Logics: Anthropology of Identity in Africa and Elsewhere* (Stanford: Stanford University Press, 1998) approaches "mestizo logics" from an ethnographic starting point, as a vital feature of relationships between the colonizer and the colonized and between the ethnographer and his or her subject. In the postcolonial context, Amselle argues, the "accumulation of administrative or academic writings was appropriated by local actors" (159) in a process of ethnological feedback that combined exaggerated, privileged observations with local identities, sometimes resulting in a "bizarre conjunction of nineteenth-century European racial theory with the history of a local population" (p. 160). Amselle argues more strongly that globalization is merely the most recent form of *métissage* among the *déjà-métissées* in *Branchements: Anthropologie de l'universalité des cultures* (Paris: Flammarion, 2001), ch. 1.

9 Homi Bhabha, *The Location of Culture* (London: Routledge, 1994), pp. 1–2.

10 See Stener Ekern's discussion of human rights and development in Guatemala "Development Aid to Indigenous Peoples," 1998.

11 Donnelly, *Universal Human Rights in Theory and Practice*, p. 121.

12 An example of consensus politics acting as a check on the abuses of state government can be found in the 2001 Berber-led insurrection in Algeria. See Ignacio Ramonet, "Kabylie" in *Le Monde Diplomatique*. July 2001, p. 1. The doctrine of *ijmā'* is rejected by the Hanbali judicial school, as practiced by the Saudi Arabian Wahhabiyya and most other radical Muslim reformers, a fact that highlights their common tendency toward difference-effacing authoritarianism. I provide an example of such a reformist community in sub-Saharan Africa (see below, pp. 59–66).

13 Donnelly, *Universal Human Rights in Theory and Practice*, p. 121.

14 Weber argued that political legitimacy based on bureaucracy and law (he sometimes used the terms interchangeably) is inherently incompatible with earlier social forms reliant on tradition and charisma to motivate people to action; and it progressively destroys them. Combinations of these "ideal types" (or analytical constructs) can occur; tradition can survive in various forms in modern societies; charisma can periodically inspire people to enthusiastic collective action; but over the long haul the regularity, reliability, and rational power of bureaucracy will everywhere win out over other forms of legitimacy. Instrumental rationality (*zweckrationalität*) is superior to other sources of social energy and is therefore surpassing and replacing the outdated machinery that relies on them. This

was not, for Weber, an unmixed blessing; in important ways it was not a blessing at all. The process made societies more powerful – and the use of great power is almost always morally ambiguous; at the same time it left unfulfilled the human search for meaning and purpose in life, limited the range of social possibilities, imposed a gray uniformity on every human society and hence on the human spirit. Disillusionment (*Entzauberung*) – which for Weber did not mean disappointment as much as it implied a breaking of a spell, a loss of "magic" (*Zauberei*) or trust in spiritual forces to explain and justify the human place in the cosmos – is an outcome of modernity's success.

Weber's vision was not commanding in the evocative way some descriptions of totalitarianism have been. Nor does it conjure the same sympathy as the concrete ethnographic accounts of societies in transition, the suffering and disillusionment of those whose lives are altered by the forces he describes. One of the great merits of Weber's model of convergence, however, is that it does not assume the changeover to be already complete. The stage may be set, but there is much that remains to happen. The most important processes of transition are not necessarily easy to see, not always publicly noteworthy. The mechanisms of legal integration, as Weber himself clearly understood, are much subtler than armed conquest.

15 The example of the indigenous peoples' movement, first drawn together in the late 1970s by analogous networking strategies, identities, and hopes of liberation, comes to mind first. This movement, which I discuss further in chapter 4, involves a strategy for the protection and restoration of the lands and traditions of the world's "first peoples" in which networks are established, identities formed, and lobbying occurs under the global rubric "indigenous peoples" – a term first coined in international law. See Ronald Niezen, *The Origins of Indigenism: Human Rights and the Politics of Identity* (Los Angeles: University of California Press, 2003).

16 United Nations Development Programme, *Human Development Report 2001: Making New Technologies Work for Human Development* (Oxford: Oxford University Press, 2001), p. 50.

17 Paddy Chayefsky, screenplay for "Network" (Burbank, CA: Time Warner Entertainment, 1976).

18 Pierre Bourdieu, *Acts of Resistance: Against the Tyranny of the Market* (New York: The New Press, 1998), p. 35.

19 David Harvey, *Spaces of Hope* (Los Angeles: University of California Press, 2000), p. 13.

20 Michael Hardt and Antonio Negri, "What the Protesters in Genoa Want." (*The New York Times*, July 20, 2001).

21 George Soros, *The Crisis of Global Capitalism: Open Society Endangered* (New York: Public Affairs, 1998); and *George Soros on Globalization* (New York: Public Affairs, 2002).

22 Joseph Stiglitz, *Globalization and Its Discontents* (New York: Norton, 2002), p. 227.

23 The German term is *Raubtierkapitalismus*. Helmut Schmidt, *Globalisierung: Politische, ökonomische und kulturelle Herausforderungen* (Stuttgart: Deutsche Verlags-Anstalt, 1998), p. 30

24 Jagdish Bhagwati, "Coping with Antiglobalization: A Trilogy of Discontents." *Foreign Affairs* (January/February, 2002:2–7) p. 7.

25 Jagdish Bhagwati, *Free Trade Today* (Princeton: Princeton University Press, 2002), p. 79.

26 Douglas Irwin discusses many of these limitations of the ILO in *Free Trade Under Fire* (Princeton: Princeton University Press, 2002), pp. 216–17. The U.S. disengages itself from ILO conventions ostensibly because their language may conflict with national policy and/or state legislation. Convention number 111 on the abolishment of discrimination on the basis of sex and race has not been ratified, for example, because of its potential to conflict with affirmative action. In developing countries, government and corporate indifference to ILO conventions is related to widespread reliance on child labor and the difficulties inherent in implementing international standards without touching off worker displacements, wider poverty, and possibly even the collapse of entire industries. Like Bhagwati, Irwin does not appear to be at all concerned by the absence of any international authority capable of controlling corporate labor practices, and agrees with the recusement of the WTO from the issue: "The effort to push labor standards onto the WTO's lap would undermine the ILO as well as burden the WTO with something it is not well equipped to handle" (p. 219).

27 See Susan George, "L'ordre libéral et ses basses oeuvres" (*Le Monde Diplomatique*, August 2001, pp. 1, 5 and 6), p. 6. An English version, translated by Barbara Wilson, is available under the title "Democracy at the barricades" (*Le Monde Diplomatique* [English] August 2001, pp. 1, 8 and 9). According to George, the proceedings of this meeting were posted on the Internet by Bruce Silverglade, who attended as a representative of the Center for Science in the Public Interest.

28 Bhagwati, *Free Trade Today*, p. 72.

29 An essentially similar argument was made in 1852 by the German philologist Wilhelm von Humboldt in his Enlightenment-inspired foray into political thought, *The Limits of State Action*. Humboldt was critical of all limitations of individual self-development, whether imposed by states or by the conditions of wage labor. Human diversity, choice, and energies dwindle with the imposition of external control, and self-development is thwarted by the capitalist demand for mechanical exactness. Humboldt's essay, however, was composed many years before it appeared, and hence was not written in response to Spencer's opposing view of

political individualism expressed in *Social Statics*, which appeared the previous year.

30   In *Free Trade Today*, Bhagwati touches on this problem only in passing, with reference to the film industry: "[T]he desire to preserve one's cinema is better addressed by subsidies to the local production of movies rather than by restrictions on the showing of foreign films" (Jagdish Bhagwati, *Free Trade Today*, pp. 81–82). But he has nothing to offer those who fervently wish their identities and cultural attachments to be minimally impacted by industry or consumerism. It is not always possible to subsidize a non-consumerist art form, ceremonial practice, or way of life without hastening the impact of consumerism. The very reliance on subsidies may imply a web of relationships and values that are at odds with the practices for which protection is sought.

31   In the context of Eastern Europe's post-1989 transitions, for example, those societies that were most impoverished by the leap across the communist/global market chasm usually failed to take the expected next step toward democracy. Where such societies have been "stripped of their traditional sources of energy and spontaneity," Neal Ascherson observes, "it has been difficult to construct durable political movements which are not built round either 'the nation' or the personality of one ambitious individual." Neal Ascherson, "1989 in Eastern Europe," in *Democracy: The Unfinished Journey 508 BC to AD 1993*, edited by John Dunn (Oxford: Oxford University Press, 1992), p. 235. Ascherson points out that in post-1989 Eastern Europe the IMF and, to a lesser extent, private banks were able to impose policies tailored to meet the demands of recession and debt rather than pursue a more hands-on Marshall Plan style restructuring. They precluded "Third Way" experiments in social ownership or worker's self-management that may have been preferred by some governments of the post-communist transition period.

CHAPTER 4

1   A detailed example of changes to social hierarchy and family patterns under the impact of French colonization is provided in Jean-Pierre Olivier de Sardan's *Les Sociétés Songhay-Zarma* (Paris: Karthala, 1984). The most comprehensive study of the impacts of modernity on family relationships worldwide remains William J. Goode's *World Revolution and Family Patterns* (New York and London: Free Press and Collier-Macmillan, 1963).

2   I have published further material on the Jama'a Ansar al-Sunna in a number of articles, notably: Ronald Niezen, "The 'Community of Helpers of the Sunna': Islamic Reform among the Songhay of Gao (Mali)," *Africa*.

60(3):399–424, 1990; Ronald Niezen, "Hot Literacy in Cold Societies: A Comparative Study of the Sacred Value of Writing," *Comparative Studies in Society and History*. 33(2):225–254, 1991; and Ronald Niezen and Barbro Bankson, "Women of the Jama'a Ansar al-Sunna: Female Participation in a West African Islamic Reform Movement," *The Canadian Journal of African Studies*. 29(3):403–428, 1995.

3 Enid Schildkrout provides a picture of the convoluted politics of these migrant communities in *People of the Zongo* (Cambridge: Cambridge University Press, 1978).

4 J. Spencer Trimingham remains a central authority on the history and practice of Islam in West Africa. See especially *Islam in West Africa* (Oxford: Oxford University Press, 1959). Jean Rouch, in *La religion et la magie Songhay* (Paris: Presses Universitaires de France, 1960) provides a detailed account of the kind of practices rejected by the reformers. An ethnography with a focus on Songhay ceremonies of spirit possession, as practiced in Niger but with similarities to those of the Gao region is offered by Paul Stoller's *Fusion of the Worlds: An Ethnography of Possession Among the Songhay of Niger* (Chicago: University of Chicago Press, 1997).

5 The earliest Saudi influence on the practice of Islam in Mali is discussed in Jean-Louis Triaud, "Abd al-Rahman l'Africain (1908–1957), pionnier et précurseur du wahhabisme au Mali," in *Radicalismes islamiques*, vol. 2, edited by Olivier Carré and Paul Dumont (Paris: Harmattan, 1986).

6 Muhammad Ibn Sulaiman, *Mubādī al-Islām* (Medina: Light Printing and Binding Establishment, 1976).

7 The events that took me from the sub-Saharan region to the meeting rooms of the Palais des Nations in Geneva were both abrupt and years in the making. In 1987 I was hired as a consultant by the Cree Board of Health and Social Services of James Bay, despite my qualifications as an Africanist and my lack of experience in the north. The CBHSSJB was then a relatively new regionally autonomous aboriginal administration in northern Quebec. My task was to conduct a survey of the needs and activities of its eight community offices scattered throughout the James Bay region of northern Quebec. This was my first experience with native communities that had been displaced or otherwise disrupted by the construction of large dams. As I toured the northern communities, I was surprised by the prevalence of family violence, addictions, and suicide, which many Crees justly attributed to the shock and sorrow of a forest-based way of life suddenly brought into conflict with the ambitions of modernity. It also introduced me to the multigenerational impact of state-sponsored policies of assimilation, directed toward indigenous people with especially disastrous consequences through compulsory education in residential schools, total institutions dedicated to uprooting the supposed

backwardness and barbarism of native life to be replaced with the combined virtues of Christianity and civilization.

Over the space of about a decade I was to build on this experience with further research visits to the communities of northern Quebec, an extension of my work into several Cree communities in northern Ontario, and a stay of two years, from 1998 to 2000, in Cross Lake, Manitoba. My working relationship with the Crees of northern Canada also took the form of attendance at several United Nations meetings in Geneva on the rights of indigenous peoples. I attended several of such meetings as an observer delegate of the Grand Council of the Crees, one of seventeen indigenous nongovernmental organizations worldwide with consultative status at the U.N.'s Economic and Social Council.

8   A detailed study of the legal foundations of the rights of indigenous peoples is provided by James Anaya's *Indigenous Peoples in International Law* (Oxford: Oxford University Press, 1996).

9   The Geneva Declaration on the Health and Survival of Indigenous Peoples (unpublished document, Indigenous & Tribal Peoples Center, http://www.itpcentre.org/legislation/english/who99.htm, 1999), p. 2. Unaccountably, I was unable to locate this document on the World Health Organization's main website.

10   Geneva Declaration, p. 1.

11   Geneva Declaration, p. 3.

12   Geneva Declaration, p. 3.

13   Gro Harlem Brundtland, "International Consultation on the Health of Indigenous Peoples, Geneva, 23 November 1999" (World Health Organization. Unpublished document. http://www.who.int/director-general/speeches/1999/english/19991123_indigenous_people.html. 1999), p. 1.

14   I discuss the origins and uses of the term "indigenous peoples" more fully in chapter 1 of *The Origins of Indigenism: Human Rights and the Politics of Identity* (Los Angeles: University of California Press, 2003).

15   Paul Brown, "Seeking room for the reindeer to roam." *Guardian Weekly.* November 23–29, 2000, p. 24.

16   These cases are *I. Länsman et al. v. Finland.* 1994. U.N. doc. CCPR/C/52/D/511/1992 and *O. Sara et al. v. Finland.* 1994. U.N. doc. CCPR/C/50/D/431/1990. Besides these complaints involving the intrusions of extractive industries into herding territories, a complaint was also brought against the government of Sweden (*Ivan Kitok v. Sweden.* 1988. U.N. doc. CCPR/C/33/D/197/1985) involving the alleged victim's loss of membership in his natal Sami Village and his subsequent loss, through the ruling against him of the highest administrative court of Sweden, of his immemorial rights as a Sami minority. The Human Rights Committee

concluded that the official denial of membership in the Sami community did not make the Swedish government responsible for a denial of the alleged victim's political and cultural rights, above all because it did not prevent him from pursuing herding and fishing. In this case the complaint was seemingly as much directed toward the arbitrariness of the Sami village in determination of membership, which, as the Human Rights Committee observed, acted much like the "closed shop" rule of a trade union. Only State parties, however, are officially responsible for observing human rights treaties. The jurisprudence of the Human Rights Committee is available over the Internet at: http://www.unhchr.ch/tbs/doc.nsf.

17 Kristian Myntti, "The Nordic Sami Parliaments," in *Operationalizing the Right of Indigenous Peoples to Self-Determination*, edited by Pekka Aikio and Martin Scheinin (Åbo, Finland: Institute for Human Rights, Åbo Akademi University, 2000), pp. 210–11.

18 The concept and ambitions of *Aanischaaukamikw* are explained on the website, www.creeculture.ca/e/institute/what.html. Accessed August 7, 2003.

19 SameNet/Sápmi Online, http://www.sapmi.net/topp.htm. Accessed October 17, 2002. I am grateful to Kristian Myntti for bringing this website and some of its significant features to my attention.

20 The Sámi Intranet does not have a mechanism for on-line voting, probably because of the limited number of subscribers and the ongoing influence of village-based, consensus-oriented, face-to-face political values.

CHAPTER 5

1 Jean-François Lyotard, *The Postmodern Explained* (Minneapolis: University of Minnesota Press, 1992), p. 78.

2 Michael Ignatieff, *The Rights Revolution* (Toronto: House of Anansi Press, 2000), p. 2.

3 See Ronald Dworkin, "Terror and the Attack on Civil Liberties," *The New York Review of Books*. 1 (17):37–41, 2003.

4 See Paul Gordon Lauren, *The Evolution of International Human Rights: Visions Seen* (Philadelphia: University of Pennsylvania Press, 1998), ch. 2, for a discussion of the involvement of early nongovernmental organizations in establishing the legitimacy and universal orientation of human rights.

5 I am more concerned here with some of the implications of this feature in western societies rather than the much wider problem of explaining it.

6 Mary Ann Glendon, *A World Made New: Eleanor Roosevelt and the Universal Declaration of Human Rights* (New York: Random House, 2001), p. 236.

7   Plato's *Republic* is probably the most influential source in western thought of the ideas that desire leads us astray, that reason is the only reliable source for interpreting perceptions and guiding behavior, and that an ideal society can be constructed in accordance with its dictates. Injustice is for Plato a revolt against reason, a source of psychosocial turmoil that pits one part of the soul against the whole. And, in accordance with the balance to be found in individuals, the just society, through reason, order, leadership of the wise, and the readiness of followers to act upon their duty, is the surest path toward the most perfect expression of the human spirit. See Charles Taylor, *Sources of the Self* (Cambridge, MA: Harvard University Press, 1989), ch. 6 and pp. 536–37 ff. for an informative discussion of Plato's influence on the western sense of self.

8   See Abdullahi Ahmed An-Naćim (ed.), *Human Rights in Cross-Cultural Perspectives: A Quest for Consensus* (Philadelphia: University of Pennsylvania Press, 1992).

9   David Stoll, "To Whom Should We Listen? Human Rights Activism in Two Guatemalan Land Disputes." In *Human Rights, Culture and Context: Anthropological Perspectives,* edited by Richard A. Wilson (London: Pluto Press, 1997).

10   Cited in Glendon, *A World Made New,* p. 222.

11   Richard A. Wilson, "Human Rights, Culture and Context: An Introduction." In *Human Rights, Culture and Context: Anthropological Perspectives,* edited by Richard A. Wilson (London: Pluto Press, 1997), p. 2.

12   Government of Zimbabwe, "Statement Delivered by the Hon. P. A. Chinamasa, M.P. Minister of Justice, Legal and Parliamentary Affairs and Head of the Zimbabwe Delegation to the World Conference Against Racism, Racial Discrimination, Xenophobia and Related Intolerances." Durban, South Africa, September 3, 2001.

13   This point is forcefully argued by Jack Donnelly in *Universal Human Rights in Theory and Practice*: "Even if we allow the existence of collective human rights of peoples, societies, and families, we must draw the line at states, which are artificial legal and territorial entities. And we must draw the line here because of the very real threat that the so-called human rights of states will be set against the human rights of individual citizens, transforming human rights from an instrument of human liberation into a new and particularly cruel cloak for repression and domination" (Ithaca: Cornell University Press, 1989), p. 146.

14   Lauren, *The Evolution of International Human Rights,* 1998, p. 101.

15   Hannah Arendt, *The Origins of Totalitarianism* (San Diego: Harcourt, 1968) p. 297.

16 Will Kymlicka, in *Multicultural Citizenship: A Liberal Theory of Minority Rights* (Oxford: Oxford University Press, 1995) is one of the few advocates of liberalism to acknowledge the problems posed by illiberal minorities while advocating gradual reform: "[L]iberal reformers inside the culture should seek to promote their liberal principles, through reason or example, and liberals outside should lend their support to any efforts the group makes to liberalize their culture. Since the most enduring forms of liberalization are those that result from internal reform, the primary focus for liberals outside the group should be to provide this sort of support" (p. 168). This argument is usefully restated in Will Kymlicka and Raphael Cohen-Almagor's, "Ethnocultural minorities in liberal democracies," in *Pluralism: The Philosophy and Politics of Diversity*, edited by Maria Baghramian and Attracta Ingram (New York: Routledge, 2000): "The question of identifying a defensible liberal theory of minority rights is separate from that of imposing that liberal theory. Internal restrictions may be inconsistent with liberal principles, but it does not yet follow that liberals should impose their views on minorities which do not accept some or all of these liberal principles" (p. 242).

17 See Ernest Gellner, *Conditions of Liberty: Civil Society and its Rivals* (London: Penguin, 1994), p. 8.

CHAPTER 6

1 Jean-François Lyotard, *The Postmodern Explained*, translation edited by Julian Pefanis and Morgan Thomas, translated by Don Barry, Bernadette Maher, Julian Pefanis, Virginia Spate, and Morgan Thomas (Minneapolis: University of Minnesota Press, 1993) p. 18.

2 Lyotard, *The Postmodern Explained*, p. 19.

3 Lyotard, *The Postmodern Explained*, p. 21.

4 See Yves Boisvert, *Le monde postmoderne: Analyse du discours sur la postmodernité* (Paris: L'Harmattan, 1996) pp. 30–35. An excellent introduction to postmodernism in architecture is provided by Diane Ghirardo in *Architecture after Modernism* (London: Thames and Hudson Ltd, 1996).

5 Lyotard, *The Postmodern Explained*, p. 12.

6 For a more comprehensive definition and critique of relativism, see the first addendum to Karl Popper's *The Open Society and Its Enemies*, Vol. 2 (Princeton: Princeton University Press, 1966).

7 The most definitive elaboration of this view can be found in Jean-François Lyotard, *La condition postmoderne: Rapport sur le savoir* (Paris: Les Éditions de Minuit, 1979), ch. 7.

8   Karl Popper, in *The Open Society and Its Enemies*, p. 377, outlines this aspect of relativism, although without, of course, applying it to postmodernism, which had not yet developed at the time it was written. The latter task (somewhat in the Popperian tradition) is taken up by Ernest Gellner in *Postmodernism, Reason and Religion* (New York: Routledge, 1992). Again, the most direct exposition of postmodernism's relativist skepticism can be found in Jean-François Lyotard's *La condition postmoderne*.

9   As Isaiah Berlin once described it, "if the home for which they are seeking, if the harmony, the perfection about which they talk could be granted to them, they would reject it. It is in principle, by definition, something to which an approach can be made but which cannot be seized, because that is the nature of reality." Isaiah Berlin, *The Roots of Romanticism* (Princeton: Princeton University Press, 1999), p. 106.

10 Lyotard, *The Postmodern Explained*, p. 15.

11 Jacques Derrida is probably the most influential exponent of postmodernism's concern with the hegemony of meaning. With the simultaneous appearance in 1967 of *L'écriture et la différence* (*Writing and Difference*, translated by Alan Bass [Chicago: University of Chicago Press, 1978]) and *De la grammatologie* (*Of Grammatology*, translated by Gayatri Spivak [Baltimore: Johns Hopkins University Press, 1997]), he succeeded in establishing a method of "deconstruction," a kind of free-floating examination of philosophical concepts in order to expose those qualities that are hidden, repressed, or tellingly absent.

12 Gilles Lipovetsky, in *L'ère du vide: Essais sur l'individualisme contemporain* (Paris: Éditions Gallimard, 1993), makes this playful element of postmodernism explicit. The term "postmodern" came into use, he says, "not without an ironic wink" [*non sans clin d'oeil ironique.*] (p. 315).

13 Michel Maffesoli, *The Time of the Tribes: The Decline of Individualism in Mass Society*, translated by Don Smith (London: Sage, 1996), p. 7. The third French edition, *Le temps des tribus: Le déclin de l'individualisme dans les sociétés postmodernes* (Paris: La Table Ronde, 2000) contains some new material that does not appear in the English translation.

14 A succinct comparison between the Frankfurt School and postmodernism can be found in Martin Jay's 1996 preface to *The Dialectical Imagination* (Berkeley and Los Angeles: University of California Press, 1996), pp. xvi–xix.

15 C. Wright Mills, *The Sociological Imagination* (Oxford: Oxford University Press, 1959) pp. 166–167.

16 Gianni Vattimo, *La fine della modernità: Nichilismo ed ermeneutica nella cultura post-moderna.* (Rome: Garzanti Editore, 1985).

17 Gilles Lipovetsky, *L'ère du vide: Essais sur l'individualisme contemporain* (Paris: Éditions Gallimard, 1993).

18 [*le kaleidoscope de l'individu post-moderne est plus que jamais à l'ordre du jour.*]
Gilles Lipovetsky, *L'ère du vide*, p. 315. My translation.

19 Michel Maffesoli, *Le temps des tribus: Le déclin de l'individualisme dans les sociétés postmodernes* (Paris: La Table Ronde, 2000). Translated by Don Smith as *The Time of the Tribes: The Decline of Individualism in Mass Society* (London: Sage, 1996).

20 Maffesoli, *The Time of the Tribes*, p. 117.

21 There is a small step between this celebration of subcultural currents of "tribalism" and full blown cultural nostalgia directed toward actual tribal societies, past and present. Aboriginal peoples, for those preservationists who adopt this position, are living representatives of environmental wisdom; at the very least they have the potential to put into practice a form of subsistence and a form of life based upon intimacy with and respect for the natural world. Paleolithic knowledge, or what we can today understand of it, stands as an alternative to the project of modernity, industrial exploitation, destruction, and "improvement" of entire forest ecosystems. Such preservationism includes the perspective of a self-avowed "Paleolithic counterrevolutionary," who sees the strongest possible contrast between the environmental sagacity and gentleness of pre-agricultural society and modern industrial society's self-destructive hubris, a taming of all things wild and free, and a uniform lifestyle of social intensity in the subjection of nature for the projects of industry and civilization. "The modern project, which has long promised the total humanization of the earth's surface, is paradoxically destined to fail through its own success," writes Max Oelschaeger in *The Idea of Wilderness: From Prehistory to the Age of Ecology* (New Haven: Yale University Press, 1991) p. 8.

22 [*aucun rapport avec ce qui est vécu.*] Michel Maffesoli, *Le temps des tribus: Le déclin de l'individualisme dans les sociétés postmodernes* (3rd edition. Paris: La Table Ronde), p. v. My translation. This citation is from the preface to third French edition, not included in the English translation.

23 Jean-François Lyotard, to his credit, points to this trap as an inherent aspect of the critique of modernity: As grand narratives lose their credibility, he suggests, "one is then tempted to give credence to a grand narrative of the decline of the grand narratives." This, he says, will not do because "as we know, the grand narrative of decadence was already in place at the beginning of Western thought, in Hesiod and Plato. It follows the narrative of emancipation like a shadow," *The Postmodern Explained*, p. 29. But acknowledging this difficulty does little to dispel it. We are still left with the question, what is one to do about it? Lyotard's solution, though vague, seems to rely simply on an extra effort to avoid possible sources of futurist contamination. What this really implies, however, is

the creation of a grand narrative built upon the avoidance of grand narrative of the decline of grand narrative. There is no way to avoid this regress if one begins with a universalist approach to the rejection of universalism.

24 This point is consistent with a significant remark by Ernest Gellner: "[in postmodernism,] liberty makes its reappearance in the form of a logically permissive and pluralist obscurity." *Postmodernism, Reason and Religion* (New York: Routledge, 1992) p. 30.

25 This was again an idea that C. Wright Mills expressed well in advance of contemporary postmodernism when he argued that, "much power today is successfully employed without the sanction of reason or the conscience of the obedient" and that the effects of what has been called "democratic totalitarianism" have not been counteracted by effective intellectual/public engagement (*The Sociological Imagination*, p. 41).

26 Lyotard, *The Postmodern Explained*, p. 50.

27 For an outline of this aspect of capitalism, see John Dunn's conclusion to *Democracy: The Unfinished Journey 508 BC to AD 1993* (Oxford: Oxford University Press, 1992) p. 263.

28 Boisvert, *Le monde postmoderne*, p. 18.

29 Lipovetsky writes: "It is only in this broad democratic and individualistic continuity that the originality of the postmodern moment takes shape." [*C'est seulement dans cette large continuité démocratique et individualiste que se dessine l'originalité du moment postmoderne.*] *L'ère du vide*, p. 165. My translation.

30 Maffesoli, *The Time of the Tribes*, p. 117.

31 Boisvert, *Le monde postmoderne*, pp. 138–139. This reference especially attracted my attention because since 1987 the Crees of different communities in northern Quebec, Ontario, and Manitoba have periodically hosted me as a researcher.

CHAPTER 7

1 Francis Fukuyama, *The End of History and the Last Man* (New York: The Free Press, 1992).

2 John Dunn (ed.), *Democracy: The Unfinished Journey* (Oxford: Oxford University Press, 1992) pp. 252–253.

3 Octavio Paz, *El laberinto de la soledad y otras obras* (New York: Penguin Books, 1997), p. 21.

4 Jean-Paul Sartre, *Sartre on Cuba* (New York: Ballantine Books, Inc., 1961), p. 86. As I first skimmed through this passage, I originally read the word "same" as "sane," and, in fact, a substitution along these lines would make

Sartre's view more understandable. An existentialist hero would fit Sartre's definition of sanity and enlightened leadership, while a "same" man could just as easily turn out to be a megalomaniacal despot.

5   See, for example, Hannah Arendt, *The Origins of Totalitarianism* (New York: Harcourt, Inc., 1968) for an early (first published in 1949) and immensely detailed appraisal of various forms of total state, which should have, but apparently did not, tempered Sartre's enthusiastic search for the existentialist hero.

6   [*Vi al comunismo como un regimen burocrático, petrificado en castas, y vi a los bolcheviques, que habían decretado, bajo pena de muerte, la »comunión obligatoria«, caer uno tras otro en esas ceremonias públicas de expiación que fueron las purgas de Stalin.*] Paz, *El laberinto de la soledad*, p. 22. My translation.

7   [*J'accomplis sans Cœur les tâches practiques-critiques qu'exigeaient la situation et l'honneur.*] Jean-François Lyotard, *Dérive à partir de Marx et Freud* (Paris: Éditions Galilée, 1994) p. 10. My translation.

8   Jacques Derrida, *Specters of Marx: The State of the Debt, the Work of Mourning, and the New International* (New York: Routledge, 1994), pp. 53–54.

9   Jacques Derrida, *Specters of Marx*, p. 85.

10 Jacques Derrida, *Specters of Marx*, p. 59.

11 David Harvey, *Spaces of Hope* (Los Angeles: University of California Press, 2000) p. 195. In this sentence Harvey proposes the revival of utopianism in the form of a rhetorical question. I have taken the liberty of presenting it as a statement since the context makes it clear that he does not want utopianism to "die an unmourned death."

12 Karl Popper, *The Open Society and Its Enemies: Volume II, The High Tide of Prophecy: Hegel, Marx, and the Aftermath* (Princeton: Princeton University Press, 1966) p. 95.

13 A chronology of events surrounding Negri's various criminal prosecutions can be found on the web page, "Amnesty for Toni Negri," http://lists.village.virginia.edu/~forks/TNChronology.htm, visited March 16, 2002.

14 Michael Hardt and Antonio Negri, *Empire* (Cambridge, MA: Harvard University Press, 2000), p. 9

15 Hardt and Negri, *Empire*, p. 10.

16 Hardt and Negri, *Empire*, p. 36.

17 Hardt and Negri, *Empire*, p. 37.

18 Michael Hardt and Antonio Negri, "What the Protesters in Genoa Want." (*New York Times*, July 20, 2001).

19 Georg Lukács, *History and Class Consciousness: Studies in Marxist Dialectics*, translated by Rodney Livingstone (Cambridge, MA: The MIT Press, 1971) pp. 27–28.

20   Karl Marx and Friedrich Engels, *The Communist Manifesto* (New York: New American Library, [1848] 1998), p. 55. See above, pp. 49–50.

21   Hardt and Negri, *Empire*, p. 364.

22   Hardt and Negri, *Empire*, p. xv.

23   Antonio Negri, *Time for Revolution* (New York and London: Continuum, 2003), p. 260.

24   Hardt and Negri, *Empire*, p. 393.

25   Hardt and Negri, *Empire*, p. 411.

26   Hardt and Negri, *Empire*, p. 397.

27   Hardt and Negri, *Empire*, p. 413.

28   [*Ein neuer kosmopolitischer Realismus liegt in der Luft!*] Ulrich Beck, *Macht und Gegenmacht im globalen Zeitalter: Neue weltpolitische Ökonomie* (Frankfurt am Main: Suhrkamp, 2002), p. 14. My translation.

29   Ulrich Beck, *The Brave New World of Work*, translated by Patrick Camiller (Cambridge, England and Malden, MA: Polity and Blackwell, 2000), p. 33. Beck pursues a virtually identical line of argument in *What is Globalization?* translated by Patrick Camiller (Cambridge, England and Malden, MA: Polity and Blackwell, 2000) and in *Macht und Gegenmacht im globalen Zeitalter* (Frankfurt am Main: Suhrkamp, 2002).

30   Beck, *World Risk Society*, p. 152.

31   Beck, *World Risk Society*, p. 152.

32   Beck, *What is Globalization?* p. 109.

33   David Harvey, *Spaces of Hope* (Los Angeles: University of California Press, 2000), p. 238.

34   Harvey, *Spaces of Hope*, p. 240.

35   Harvey, *Spaces of Hope*, p. 252.

36   Raymond Williams, *Keywords: A Vocabulary of Culture and Society*, revised edition (Oxford: Oxford University Press, 1976), p. 273.

37   John Dunn, *Democracy: The Unfinished Journey 508 BC to AD 1993* (Oxford: Oxford University Press, 1992), p. 264.

38   Arjun Appadurai, "Grassroots Globalization and the Research Imagination," (*Public Culture*, 2000. 12(1):1–19). Appadurai stresses an emancipatory politics of globalization that relies upon reconfiguring the place of the imagination in social life, above all by internationally reformatting the geography of "research areas" and paying greater attention to flux and process, by conducting research in ways that would empower grassroots activists in international forums. I agree with this, with one major proviso. My sense is that to be truly empowering such research would do well to move beyond postmodernist concerns with meaning and the imagination and instead look critically at the new avenues of authority and uses of coercion to be found among both institutions of global governance and emergent transnational advocacy networks. One

cannot empower a critical realm of social life by elevating it beyond criticism.

39 C. A. Meyer, cited in Robert O'Brien, Anne Marie Goetz, Jan Aart Scholte, and Marc Williams, *Contesting Global Governance: Multilateral Economic Institutions and Global Social Movements* (Cambridge: Cambridge University Press, 2000), p. 114.

40 O'Brien, Goetz, Scholte, and Williams, *Contesting Global Governance*, pp. 5–6.

CHAPTER 8

1 I came across this expression in José Saldívar's back-cover review of Walter Mignolo's *Local Histories/Global Designs* (Princeton: Princeton University Press, 2000), though it very likely has a much wider circulation as a catch phrase.

2 See Gottfried Herder, *Ideen zur Phlosophie der Geschichte der Menschheit* (Frankfurt am Main: Deutcher Klassiker Verlag, 1989 [1791]), especially book 15. Despite his growing recognition as a counterpoint to Enlightenment rationalism, there are only a few scattered English translations of his work. A useful introduction to a wide range of his ideas can be found in *Philosophical Writings*, translated and edited by Michael Forster (Cambridge: Cambridge University Press, 2002). The secondary literature is dominated by the work of Isaiah Berlin especially, *Three Critics of the Enlightenment: Vico, Hamann, Herder* (Princeton: Princeton University Press, 2000).

3 Robert Young, concentrating largely on the points of view emerging from liberation movements, argues for world-historical uniqueness as the starting point of postcolonial, or as he prefers, "tricontinental," literature. *Postcolonialism: An Historical Introduction* (Oxford: Blackwell, 2001), p. 5.

4 Albert Memmi, *The Colonizer and the Colonized* (Boston: Beacon Press, 1967).

5 Cited in Leela Gandhi, *Postcolonial Theory: A Critical Introduction* (New York: Columbia University Press, 1998), p. 19.

6 Prasenjit Duara, *Rescuing History from the Nation: Questioning Narratives of Modern China* (Chicago: University of Chicago Press, 1995), pp. 214–215. Duara goes on to provide an interesting comparison of Gandhi's anti-modernism with the visions of Mencius and Mao.

7 Robert Young (*Postcolonialism*, p. 5) adopts the term "tricontinental," in preference to the problematic "Third World" and the "bland homogenization of 'the South'," pointing to a historically specific justification:

"the tricontinental marks an identification with the great Havana Tricontinental of 1966, which initiated the first global alliance of the peoples of three continents against imperialism."

8   Juxtapositions of the anti-colonial strategies and postcolonial possibilities imagined by Gandhi and Fanon are provided by Leela Gandhi in *Postcolonial Theory* and G. Prakash, ed. in *After Colonialism: Imperial Histories and Postcolonial Displacements* (Princeton: Princeton University Press, 1995).

9   Fanon, *The Wretched of the Earth* (New York: Grove Press, 1963), p. 203.

10 Fanon, *The Wretched of the Earth*, pp. 201–202.

11 Edward Said, *Orientalism* (New York: Vintage, 1994), p. 341.

12 Said, *Orientalism*, p. 8.

13 Said, *Orientalism*, p. 11.

14 Mooney, James, *The Ghost Dance Religion and the Sioux Outbreak of 1890* (Lincoln: University of Nebraska Press, 1991 [1896]).

15 Michel Leiris, *L'Afrique fantôme* (Paris: Éditions Gallimard, 1934).

16 Wilhelm von Humboldt, "Die Vasken, oder Bemerkungen auf einer Reise durch Biscaya und das französische Basquenland im Frühling des Jahrs 1801," in *Werke*, vol. 2, edited by Andreas Flitner and Klaus Giel (Stuttgart: J. G. Cotta'sche Buchhandlung, 1969), especially p. 466.

17 See Wilhelm von Humboldt's *The Limits of State Action*, edited by J. W. Burrow (Indianapolis: Liberty Fund, 1993 [1854]). See also Robert Leroux's immensely detailed study of Humboldt's early intellectual development, *Guillaume de Humboldt: La formation de sa pensée jusq'en 1794* [Paris: Les Belles Lettres, 1932], p. 334.)

18 Edward Said, *Culture and Imperialism* (New York: Vintage, 1994), p. xx.

19 Said, *Culture and Imperialism*, p. xxi.

20 David Cannadine, in his recent book *Ornamentalism* (Oxford: Oxford University Press, 2001), offers an elegant historical rebuttal to Said "and his Orientalist followers" along these lines, by describing how the British Empire was concerned as much or more with the "construction of affinities" as it was with the creation of inferior "Others." "The British Empire was about the familiar and domestic, as well as the different and the exotic" Cannadine argues, "indeed, it was in large part about the domestication of the exotic" (p. xix). In a sense, however, Cannadine's approach is very much like Said's, in that he demonstrates the way that a dominant paradigm of cultural perception (Said's) has simplified and distorted an essential cultural reality, in this case the way that the British imagined their empire hierarchically, more in terms of class and status than race or "otherness." He presents, in other words, an anti-Occidentalist critique of anti-Orientalism that ultimately reinforces the postcolonialist emphasis on the incommensurability of distinct cultures.

21 Said, *Orientalism*, p. 347.

22 See especially the title essay in Edward Said's *Reflections on Exile and other Essays* (Cambridge, MA: Harvard University Press, 2000). Roughly a year before his death, Said momentarily left aside his near-impossible prerequisites for the study of other cultures in an acerbic review of Bernard Lewis's *What Went Wrong?* Said argued with considerable righteous anger that Lewis was taking advantage of Americans' sense of insecurity by promoting sweeping partial truths about Arab civilization: "Instead of making it possible for people to educate themselves in how complex and intertwined all cultures and religions really are, available public discourse is polluted with reductive clichés that Lewis bandies about without a trace of skepticism or rigor. The worst part of this method is that it systematically dehumanizes peoples and turns them into a collection of abstract slogans for the purposes of aggressive mobilization and bellicosity." Said went on to say more hopefully that "the study of other cultures is a humanistic, not a strategic or security pursuit" ("Impossible Histories: Why the Many Islams Cannot be Simplified," [*Harper's*, July, 2002], p. 73). Perhaps in response to such flawed generalizations as those made by Lewis, Said recognized more fully and consistently the importance of a rigorous, humanistic body of western scholarship about other cultures and, had he lived longer, may even have abandoned his earlier assumption that hegemony lurks in every Orientalist corner.

23 Young, *Postcolonialism*, p. 355.

24 Walter Mignolo *Local Histories/Global Designs* (Princeton: Princeton University Press, 2000), p. 40.

25 Gayatri Spivak, *A Critique of Postcolonial Reason: Toward a History of the Vanishing Present* (Cambridge, MA: Harvard University Press, 1999), p. 391.

26 Mignolo, *Local Histories/Global Designs*, p. 310.

27 Notable exceptions are Leela Gandhi's *Postcolonial Theory* and Robert Young's *Postcolonialism* (especially pp. 337–338).

28 Young, *Postcolonialism*, p. 338.

29 Cited in Robert Young, *Postcolonialsim*, p. 340. Young presents Ashis Nandy's *Intimate Enemy: Loss and Recovery of Self under Colonialism* (Delhi: Oxford University Press, 1983) as his most influential elaboration of Gandhian counter-modernity.

30 Ashis Nandy, *Time Warps: Silent and Evasive Pasts in Indian Politics and Religion* (New Brunswick, NJ: Rutgers University Press, 2002), p. 79.

31 Nandy, *Time Warps*, p. 75.

32 Vinayak Chaturvedi (ed.), *Mapping Subaltern Studies and the Postcolonial* (London: Verso, 2000), p. x. Chaturvedi provides a useful, succinct outline of the origins of Subaltern Studies in the introduction to this edited volume.

33 Ranajit Guha, "On Some Aspects of the Historiography of Colonial India," in *Mapping Subaltern Studies and the Postcolonial,* edited by Vinayak Chaturvedi (London: Verso, 2000), p. 6.

34 Chaturvedi, "Introduction" in *Mapping Subaltern Studies and the Postcolonial,* p. xi.

35 Mignolo, *Local Histories/Global Designs,* p. 7.

36 In Achille Mbembe's study of political imagination in Africa, *De la Postcolonie: Essai sur l'imagination politique dans l'Afrique contemporaine* (Paris: Karthala, 2000, pp. 20–21), for example, a central concern is with stereotypes that emphasize the continent's failures and disasters. Western representations of Africa's Politics and economics have failed to go beyond research into the causes of deficiency. The postcolonial subject is seen only as embroiled in war, self-destruction, genocide, raging pestilence, destitution, and famine. Applied knowledge using rational calculation as a foundation for normative judgment – judgments that are beyond history, beyond linguistic competence, and beyond any form of local understanding – is a new form of impatient, ignorant colonial subjection.

37 Mignolo, *Local Histories/Global Designs,* p. 279.

38 Mignolo, *Local Histories/Global Designs,* p. 23.

39 Mignolo, *Local Histories/Global Designs,* p. 310.

40 Spivak, *A Critique of Postcolonial Reason,* p. 399.

41 Gayatri Spivak, "The New Subaltern: A Silent Interview," in *Mapping Subaltern Studies and the Postcolonial,* edited by Vinayak Chaturvedi (London: Verso, 2000), p. 332.

42 Spivak, "The New Subaltern," p. 336. In response to the powerful new forces of hegemony and the consequences of globalization, Spivak calls for a global socialist strategy of resistance that takes up cultural particularism, that rejects the idea of the U.S. melting pot, and that joins "the globe-girdling Social Movements in the South through the entry point of their own countries of origin" (*A Critique of Postcolonial Reason,* p. 402). Resistance can be led by an alliance of those whom she vaguely describes as "globe-trotting postcolonials, ready for entanglements in new global complicities" (*A Critique of Postcolonial Reason,* p. 363). One way to resist global imperialism is through migrant activism situated in the old nation, organized through an equally global network of socialist activism.

43 Spivak, "The New Subaltern," p. 328.

44 Spivak, "The New Subaltern," p. 328.

45 Arjun Appadurai, *Modernity at Large: Cultural Dimensions of Globalization* (Minneapolis: University of Minnesota Press, 1996), p. 12.

46 Appadurai, *Modernity at Large,* p. 13.

47 An earlier seminal work on self-conscious cultural innovation and political mobilization edited by Eric Hobsbawm and Terrence Ranger, *The*

Invention of Tradition, discusses the use of symbols and ceremonies by colonial powers to create histories and traditions where none had previously existed. Culture, in this set of examples, is a near miraculous ideological raw material used to shore up regimes on the brink of illegitimacy. Eric Hobsbawm and Terrence Ranger (eds.), *The Invention of Tradition* (New York: Columbia University Press, 1983).

48 For James Clifford, the inexplicit nature of the concept of culture was revealed by the ambiguities and intellectual dissonance of a 1976 trial in which the pivotal issue was to determine whether or not the group calling itself the Mashpee Tribe should in fact be accorded recognition as a tribe by the U.S. government (as a preliminary step in settling land claims). "The culture concept," Clifford concludes, "accommodates internal diversity and an 'organic' division of roles but not sharp contradictions, mutations, or emergences . . . It sees tribal 'traditionalists' and 'moderns' as representing aspects of a linear development, one looking back, the other forward. It cannot see them as contending or alternating futures." *The Predicament of Culture* (Cambridge MA: Harvard University Press, 1988), p. 338.

49 Akhil Gupta and James Ferguson (eds.), *Culture Power Place: Explorations in Critical Anthropology* (Durham and London: Duke University Press, 1997), p. 13.

50 Gupta and Ferguson, *Culture Power Place*, p. 4.

References

Amselle, Jean-Loup, 1998 Mestizo Logics: Anthropology of Identity in Africa and Elsewhere. Claudia Royal, trans. Stanford: Stanford University Press.

——2001 Branchements: Anthropologie de l'universalité des cultures. Paris: Flammarion.

Anaya, S. James, 1996 Indigenous Peoples in International Law. Oxford: Oxford University Press.

An-Na'im, Abdullahi Ahmed, ed., 1992 Human Rights in Cross-Cultural Perspective: A Quest for Consensus. Philadelphia: University of Pennsylvania Press.

Appadurai, Arjun, 1996 Modernity at Large: Cultural Dimensions of Globalization. Minneapolis: University of Minnesota Press.

——2000 Grassroots Globalization and the Research Imagination. Public Culture. 12(1):1–19.

Arendt, Hannah, 1968 The Origins of Totalitarianism. New York: Harcourt.

Ascherson, Neal, 1992 1989 in Eastern Europe: Constitutional Representative Democracy as a "Return to Normality"? *In* Democracy: The Unfinished Journey 508 BC to AD 1993. John Dunn ed. Oxford: Oxford University Press.

Aurelius, Marcus, 1964 [*c.*180] Meditations. Maxwell Staniforth, trans. New York: Penguin.

Bacon, Francis, 1996 [1627] New Atlantis. *In* Three Early Modern Utopias. Susan Bruce ed. Oxford: Oxford University Press.

Beck, Ulrich, 1999 World Risk Society. Cambridge, England and Malden, MA: Polity and Blackwell.

——2000a The Brave New World of Work. Patrick Camiller, trans. Cambridge, England and Malden, MA: Polity and Blackwell.

——2000b What is Globalization? Patrick Camiller, trans. Cambridge, England and Malden, MA: Polity and Blackwell.

——2002 Macht und Gegenmacht im globalen Zeitalter: Neue weltpolitische Ökonomie. Frankfurt am Main: Suhrkamp.

Berlin, Isaiah, 1990 The Crooked Timber of Humanity: Chapters in the History of Ideas. Princeton: Princeton University Press.

——1999 The Roots of Romanticism. Princeton: Princeton University Press.

——2000 Three Critics of the Enlightenment: Vico, Hamann, Herder. Princeton: Princeton University Press.

——2001 Freedom and Its Betrayal: Six Enemies of Human Liberty. Princeton: Princeton University Press.

Bhabha, Homi, 1994 The Location of Culture. London: Routledge.

Bhagwati, Jagdish, 2002a Coping with Antiglobalization: A Trilogy of Discontents. Foreign Affairs. January/February:2–7.

——2002b Free Trade Today. Princeton: Princeton University Press.

Bloch, Ernst, 1995 The Principle of Hope. 3 vols. Neville Plaice, Stephen Plaice, and Paul Knight, trans. Cambridge, MA: The MIT Press.

Boisvert, Yves, 1996 Le monde postmoderne: Analyse du discours sur la post-modernité. Paris: L'Harmattan.

Bourdieu, Pierre, 1998 Acts of Resistance: Against the Tyranny of the Market. Richard Nice, trans. New York: The New Press.

Brown, Paul, 2000 Seeking room for the reindeer to roam. Guardian Weekly. November 23–29:24.

Bruce, Susan, 1999 Introduction. Three Early Modern Utopias: Utopia, New Atlantis, The Isle of Pines. Oxford: Oxford University Press.

Brundtland, Gro Harlem, 1999 International Consultation on the Health of Indigenous Peoples, Geneva, November 23, 1999. World Health Organization. Unpublished document. http://www.who.int/director-general/speeches/1999/english/19991123_indigenous_people.html.

Canclini, Nestor García, 1995 Hybrid Cultures: Strategies for Entering and Leaving Modernity. Christopher Chiappari and Silvia López, trans. Minneapolis: University of Minnesota Press.

Cannadine, David, 2001 Ornamentalism: How the British Saw Their Empire. Oxford: Oxford University Press.

Chaturvedi, Vinayak, ed., 2000 Mapping Subaltern Studies and the Postcolonial. London: Verso.

Chayefsky, Paddy, 1976 Network. Burbank, CA: Time Warner Entertainment. Screenplay.

Clifford, James, 1988 The Predicament of Culture. Cambridge MA: Harvard University Press.

Condorcet, 1988 [1795] Esquisse d'un tableau historique des progrès de l'esprit humain; Fragment sur l'Atlantide. Paris: Flammarion.

——1996 [1781] Dedicatory Epistle to the Negro Slaves. *In* The French Revolution and Human Rights: A Brief Documentary History. Lynn Hunt, ed. and trans. Boston: Bedford/St. Martin's.

de Bary, Wm. Theodore, 1998 Asian Values and Human Rights: A Confucian Communitarian Perspective. Cambridge, MA: Harvard University Press.

de Bary, Wm. Theodore and Tu Weiming, eds., 1998 Confucianism and Human Rights. New York: Columbia University Press.

Derrida, Jacques, 1978 Writing and Difference. Alan Bass, trans. Chicago: University of Chicago Press.

——1994 Specters of Marx: The State of the Debt, the Work of Mourning, and the New International. Peggy Kamuf, trans. New York: Routledge.

——1997 Of Grammatology, corrected edition. Gayatri Spivak, trans. Baltimore: John's Hopkins University Press.

Donnelly, Jack, 1989 Universal Human Rights in Theory and Practice. Ithaca: Cornell University Press.

Duara, Prasenjit, 1995 Rescuing History from the Nation: Questioning Narratives of Modern China. Chicago: University of Chicago Press.

Dunn, John, ed., 1992 Democracy: The Unfinished Journey 508 BC to AD 1993. Oxford: Oxford University Press.

Dworkin, Ronald, 2003 Terror and the Attack on Civil Liberties. The New York Review of Books. 1(17):37–41.

Ekern, Stener, 1998 Development Aid to Indigenous Peoples is an Exercise in Crossing Boundaries. *In* Human Rights in Developing Countries: Yearbook 1997. Hugo Stokke, Astri Suhrke, Arne Tostensen and Øystein Rygg Haanæs eds. The Hague: Kluwer Law International and Oslo: Nordic Human Rights Publications.

Fanon, Frantz, 1963 The Wretched of the Earth. New York: Grove.

Fukuyama, Francis, 1992 The End of History and the Last Man. New York: The Free Press.

Gandhi, Leela, 1998 Postcolonial Theory: A Critical Introduction. New York: Columbia University Press.

García Canclini, Nestor, 1995 Hybrid Cultures: Strategies for Entering and Leaving Modernity. Christopher Chiappari and Silvia López, trans. Minneapolis: University of Minnesota Press.

Gellner, Ernest, 1992 Postmodernism, Reason and Religion. New York: Routledge.

——1994 Conditions of Liberty: Civil Society and its Rivals. London: Penguin.

Geneva Declaration on the Health and Survival of Indigenous Peoples, 1999 Unpublished document. Indigenous & Tribal Peoples Centre. http://www.itpcentre.org/legislation/english/who99.htm.

George, Susan, 2001 L'ordre libéral et ses basses oeuvres. Le Monde Diplomatique. August, pp. 1, 5 and 6.

Ghirardo, Diane, 1996 Architecture after Modernism. London: Thames and Hudson.

Giddens, Anthony, 1990 The Consequences of Modernity. Stanford: Stanford University Press.

——2000 Runaway World: How Globalization is Reshaping our Lives. New York: Routledge.

Glendon, Mary Ann, 2001 A World Made New: Eleanor Roosevelt and the Universal Declaration of Human Rights. New York: Random House.

Goode, William J., 1963 World Revolution and Family Patterns. New York and London: Free Press and Collier-Macmillan.

Guha, Ranjit, 2000 On Some Aspects of the Historiography of Colonial India. *In* Mapping Subaltern Studies and the Postcolonial. Vinayak Chaturvedi ed. London: Verso.

Gupta, Akhil and James Ferguson, eds., 1997 Culture Power Place: Explorations in Critical Anthropology. Durham and London: Duke University Press.

Habermas, Jürgen, 1985 Die Neue Unübersichtlichkeit. Frankfurt am Main: Suhrkamp.

Hardt, Michael and Antonio Negri, 2000 Empire. Cambridge MA: Harvard University Press.

——2001 What the Protesters in Genoa Want. New York Times. July 20.

Harvey, David, 2000 Spaces of Hope. Los Angeles: University of California Press.

Held, David, Anthony McGrew, David Goldblatt, and Jonathan Perraton, 1999 Global Transformations: Politics, Economics and Culture. Stanford: Stanford University Press.

Herder, Johann Gottfried, 1989 [1791] Ideen zur Philosophie der Geschichte der Menschheit. Frankfurt am Main: Deutscher Klassiker Verlag.

——2002 Philosophical Writings. Michael Forster, trans and ed. Cambridge: Cambridge University Press.

Hobsbawm, Eric and Terrence Ranger, eds., 1983 The Invention of Tradition. New York: Columbia University Press.

Humboldt, Wilhelm von, 1969 Werke. 5 vols. Andreas Flitner and Klaus Giel eds. Stuttgart: J. G. Cotta'sche Buchhandlung.

——1993 [1854] The Limits of State Action. J. W. Burrow ed. Indianapolis: Liberty Fund.

Hunt, Lynn, ed. and trans, 1996 The French Revolution and Human Rights: A Brief Documentary History. Boston: Bedford/St. Martin's.

Ibn Sulaiman, Muhammad, 1976 Mubādī al-Islām. Medina: Light Printing and Binding Establishment.

Ignatieff, Michael, 2000 The Rights Revolution. Toronto: House of Anansi.

Irwin, Douglas, 2002 Free Trade Under Fire. Princeton: Princeton University Press.

Jameson, Fredric, 2004 The Politics of Utopia. New Left Review. 24:35–54.

Jay, Martin, 1996 The Dialectical Imagination: A History of the Frankfurt School and the Institute of Social Research, 1923–1950. Berkeley and Los Angeles: University of California Press.

K'ang Yu-wei, 1958 Ta T'ung Shu: The One World Philosophy. Laurence Thompson, trans with an Introduction and Notes. London: George Allen and Unwin.

Kymlicka, Will, 1995 Multicultural Citizenship: A Liberal Theory of Minority Rights. Oxford: Oxford University Press.

Kymlicka, Will and Raphael Cohen-Almagor, 2000 Ethnocultural minorities in liberal democracies. In Pluralism: The Philosophy and Politics of Diversity. Maria Baghramian and Attracta Ingram eds. New York: Routledge.

Lauren, Paul Gordon, 1998 The Evolution of International Human Rights: Visions Seen. Philadelphia: University of Pennsylvania Press.

Leiris, Michel, 1934 L'Afrique fantôme. Paris: Éditions Gallimard.

Leroux, Robert, 1932 Guillaume de Humboldt: La formation de sa pensée jusqu'en 1794. Paris: Les Belles Lettres.

Lewis, Bernard, 2002 What Went Wrong? Western Impact and Middle Eastern Response. Oxford: Oxford University Press.

Lipovetsky, Gilles, 1993 L'ère du vide: Essais sur l'individualisme contemporain. Paris: Éditions Gallimard.

Long, A. A. and D. N. Sedley, 1987 The Hellenistic Philosophers: Vol. 1, Translations of the Principal Sources, with Philosophical Commentary. Cambridge: Cambridge University Press.

Lukács, Georg, 1971 History and Class Consciousness: Studies in Marxist Dialectics. Rodney Livingstone, trans. Cambridge, MA: The MIT Press.

Lyotard, Jean-François, 1979 La Condition Postmoderne: Rapport sur le Savoir. Paris: Les Éditions de Minuit.

—— 1992 The Postmodern Explained. Julian Pefanis and Morgan Thomas eds. Don Barry, Bernadette Maher, Julian Perfanis, Virginia Spate, and Morgan Thomas, trans. Minneapolis: University of Minnesota Press.

—— 1994 Dérive à partir de Marx et Freud. Paris: Éditions Galilée.

Maffesoli, Michel, 2000 Le temps des tribus: Le déclin de l'individualisme dans les sociétés postmodernes. 3rd edition. Paris: La Table Ronde. Translated by Don Smith as The Time of the Tribes: The Decline of Individualism in Mass Society. London: Sage, 1996.

Maier, Hans, 1997 Wie universal sind die Menschenrechte? Freiburg: Verlag Herder.

Maritain, Jacques, 1943 The Rights of Man and Natural Law. Doris Anson, trans. New York: Charles Scribner's Sons.

——1951 Man and the State. Washington, D.C.: The Catholic University of America Press.

Marx, Karl, 1963 [1852] The 18th Brumaire of Louis Bonaparte. New York: International Publishers.

Marx, Karl and Friedrich Engels, 1978 The Marx-Engels Reader. Robert. C. Tucker ed. New York: W. W. Norton.

——1998 [1848] The Communist Manifesto. New York: New American Library.

Mbembe, Achille, 2000 De la Postcolonie: Essai sur l'imagination politique dans l'Afrique contemporaine. Paris: Karthala.

Memmi, Albert, 1967 The Colonizer and the Colonized. Boston: Beacon.

Michel, Ute, 1995 Neue ethnologische Forschungsansätze im Nationalsozialismus? Aus der Biographie von Wilhelm Emil Mühlmann (1904–1988). *In* Lebenslust und Fremdenfurcht: Ethnologie im Dritten Reich. Thomas Hauschild ed. Frankfurt: Suhrkamp.

Mignolo, Walter, 2000 Local Histories/Global Designs: Coloniality, Subaltern Knowledges, and Border Thinking. Princeton: Princeton University Press.

Milgate, Murray and Shannon Stimson, 1991 Ricardian Politics. Princeton: Princeton University Press.

Mills, C. Wright, 1959 The Sociological Imagination. Oxford: Oxford University Press.

Montaigne, 1958 [1578–80] Of Cannibalism. *In* The Complete Essays of Montaigne. Donald Frame, trans. Stanford: Stanford University Press.

Mooney, James, 1991 [1896] The Ghost Dance Religion and the Sioux Outbreak of 1890. Lincoln: University of Nebraska Press.

Moses, Ted, 2000 The Right of Self-Determination and Its Significance to the Survival of Indigenous Peoples. *In* Operationalizing the Right of Indigenous Peoples to Self-Determination. Pekka Aikio and Martin Scheinin eds. Åbo/Turku: Institute for Human Rights, Åbo Akademi University.

Musso, Pierre, 1999 Saint-Simon et le Saint-Simonisme. Paris: Presses Universitaires de France.

Myntti, Kristian, 2000 The Nordic Sami Parliaments. *In* Operationalizing the Right of Indigenous Peoples to Self-Determination. Pekka Aikio and Martin Scheinin eds. Turku/Åbo, Finland: Institute for Human Rights, Åbo Akademi University.

Nandy, Ashis, 1983 Intimate Enemy: Loss and Recovery of Self under Colonialism. Delhi: Oxford University Press.

——2002 Time Warps: Silent and Evasive Pasts in Indian Politics and Religion. New Brunswick, NJ: Rutgers University Press.

Negri, Antonio, 2003 Time for Revolution. Matteo Mandarini, trans. London: Continuum.

Niezen, Ronald, 1990 The "Community of Helpers of the Sunna"; Islamic Reform among the Songhay of Gao (Mali). Africa. 60(3):399–424.

——1991 Hot Literacy in Cold Societies: A Comparative Study of the Sacred Value of Writing. Comparative Studies in Society and History. 33(2):225–254.

——2003 The Origins of Indigenism: Human Rights and the Politics of Identity. Los Angeles: University of California Press.

Niezen, Ronald and Barbro Bankson, 1995 Women of the Jama'a Ansar al-Sunna: Female Participation in a West African Islamic Reform Movement. The Canadian Journal of African Studies. 29(3):403–428.

O'Brien, Robert, Anne Marie Goetz, Jan Aart Scholte, and Marc Williams, 2000 Contesting Global Governance: Multilateral Economic Organizations and Global Social Movements. Cambridge: Cambridge University Press.

Oelschlaeger, Max, 1991 The Idea of Wilderness: From Prehistory to the Age of Ecology. New Haven: Yale University Press.

Olivier de Sardan, Jean-Pierre, 1984 Les Sociétés Songhay-Zarma. Paris: Karthala.

Osterhammel, Jürgen and Niels Petersson, 2003 Geschichte der Globalisierung: Dimensionen, Prozesse, Epochen. Munich: C.H. Beck, 2003.

Paz, Octavio, 1997 El laberinto de la soledad y otras obras. New York: Penguin.

Pons, Alain, 1988 Introduction. *In* Condorcet, Esquisse d'un tableau historique des progrès de l'esprit humain. Paris: Flammarion.

Popper, Karl, 1966 The Open Society and Its Enemies: Vol II, The High Tide of Prophecy: Hegel, Marx, and the Aftermath. Princeton: Princeton University Press.

Prakash, G., ed., 1995 After Colonialism: Imperial Histories and Postcolonial Displacements. Princeton: Princeton University Press.

Ramonet, Ignacio, 2001 Kabylie. Le Monde Diplomatique. July 2001, p. 1.

Rouch, Jean, 1960 La religion et la magie Songhay. Paris: Presses Universitaires de France.

Said, Edward, 1994 [1978] Orientalism. New York: Vintage Books.

——1994 Culture and Imperialism. New York: Vintage Books.

——2000 Reflections on Exile and Other Essays. Cambridge, MA: Harvard University Press.

——2002 Impossible Histories: Why the Many Islams Cannot be Simplified. Harper's. July:69–74.

Sartre, Jean-Paul, 1961 Sartre on Cuba. New York: Ballantine.

Schildkrout, Enid, 1978 People of the Zongo. Cambridge: Cambridge University Press.

Schmidt, Helmut, 1998 Globalisierung: Politische, ökonomische und kulturelle Herausforderungen. Stuttgart: Deutche Verlags-Anstalt.

Seneca, 1932 Moral Essays. John W. Basore, trans. Cambridge, MA: Harvard University Press.

Soros, George, 1998 The Crisis of Global Capitalism: Open Society Endangered. New York: Public Affairs.

——2002 George Soros on Globalization. New York: Public Affairs.

Spencer, Herbert, 1994 [1884] Political Writings. John Offer ed. Cambridge: Cambridge University Press.

——1995 [1850] Social Statics: The Conditions Essential to Human Happiness Specified, and the First of them Developed. New York: Robert Schalkenbach Foundation.

Spivak, Gayatri, 1999 A Critique of Postcolonial Reason: Toward a History of the Vanishing Present. Cambridge, MA: Harvard University Press.

——2000 The New Subaltern: A Silent Interview. *In* Mapping Subaltern Studies and the Postcolonial. Vinayak Chaturvedi ed. London: Verso.

Stiglitz, Joseph, 2002 Globalization and Its Discontents. New York: Norton.

Stoll, David, 1997 To Whom Should We Listen? Human Rights Activism in Two Guatemalan Land Disputes. *In* Human Rights, Culture and Context: Anthropological Perspectives. Richard A. Wilson ed. London: Pluto.

Stoller, Paul, 1997 Fusion of the Worlds: An Ethnography of Possession Among the Songhay of Niger. Chicago: University of Chicago Press.

Taylor, Charles, 1989 Sources of the Self. Cambridge, MA: Harvard University Press.

Tilly, Charles. 2003 World History. New York: Harcourt, Brace & Company.

Tomlinson, John, 1999 Globalization and Culture. Chicago: University of Chicago Press.

Triaud, Jean-Louis, 1986 Abd al-Rahman l'Africain (1908–1957), pionnier et précurseur du wahhabisme au Mali. *In* Radicalismes islamiques, vol 2. Olivier Carré and Paul Dumont eds. Paris: Harmattan.

Trimingham. J. Spencer, 1959 Islam in West Africa. Oxford: Oxford University Press.

Tuck, Richard, 1979 Natural Rights Theories: Their Origin and Development. Cambridge: Cambridge University Press.

Tucker, Robert C., ed., 1978 The Marx-Engels Reader. 2nd edition. New York: Norton.

United Nations Development Programme, 2001 Human Development Report 2001: Making New Technologies Work for Human Development. Oxford: Oxford University Press.

Vattimo, Gianni, 1985 La fine della modernità: Nichilismo ed ermeneutica nella cultura post-moderna. Rome: Garzanti Editore.

Vögele, Wolfgang, 1999 Christliche Elemente in der Begründung von Menschenrechten und Menschenwürde im Kontext der Entstehung der Vereinten Nationen. *In* Ethik der Menschenrechte: Zum Streit um die Universalität einer Idee. Hans-Richard Reuter ed. Tübingen: Mohr Siebeck.

Williams, Raymond, 1976 Keywords: A Vocabulary of Culture and Society. Revised edition. Oxford: Oxford University Press.

Willke, Helmut, 2003 Heterotopia: Studien zur Krisis der Ordnung moderner Gesellschaften. Frankfurt am Main: Suhrkamp.

Wilson, Richard A., 1997 Human Rights, Culture and Context: An Introduction. *In* Human Rights, Culture and Context: Anthropological Perspectives. Richard A. Wilson ed. London: Pluto Press.

Young, Robert, 2001 Postcolonialism: An Historical Introduction. Oxford: Blackwell.

Zimbabwe, 2001 Statement Delivered by the Hon. P. A Chinamasa, M.P. Minister of Justice, Legal and Parliamentary Affairs and Head of the Zimbabwe Delegation to the World Conference Against Racism, Racial Discrimination, Xenophobia and Related Intolerances. Durban, South Africa, September 3.

Zweig, Stefan, 2002 [1938] Triumph and Tragik des Erasmus von Rotterdam. Frankfurt am Main: Fischer.

Index